POSITIVE ENERGY

"Dr. Judith Orloff has written a brilliant, intriguing, and extremely practical book on how to embrace the energies of life in order to create wellness, wisdom, and abundance. Judith is the type of physician we all wish we had. She has broken through conventional thinking about health. I consider her to be a true visionary."

CAROLINE MYSS, PH.D.,
author of *Sacred Contracts* and *Anatomy of the Spirit*

OTHER BOOKS BY JUDITH ORLOFF, M.D.

Dr. Judith Orloff's Guide to Intuitive Healing
Second Sight

POSITIVE ENERGY

10
EXTRAORDINARY
PRESCRIPTIONS
FOR TRANSFORMING
FATIGUE, STRESS,
AND FEAR
INTO VIBRANCE,
STRENGTH,
AND LOVE

Judith Orloff, M.D.

HARMONY BOOKS · NEW YORK

GRATEFUL ACKNOWLEDGMENT IS MADE TO THE FOLLOWING FOR PERMISSION TO REPRINT PREVIOUSLY PUBLISHED MATERIAL:

COLEMAN BARKS: Excerpts from Rumi translations. Copyright © Coleman Barks. Reprinted by permission of the author.

BEACON PRESS: Excerpt from "When Death Comes" from *New and Selected Poems of Mary Oliver*. Copyright © 1992 by Mary Oliver. Reprinted by permission of Beacon Press, Boston.

GROVE/ATLANTIC, INC. AND MARY OLIVER: Excerpt from "Shadows" from *Dream Work* by Mary Oliver. Copyright © 1986 by Mary Oliver. Reprinted by Grove/Atlantic, Inc., and the author.

HOUSE OF ANANSI PRESS: Excerpt from "He Sits Down on the Floor of a School for the Retarded" from *Alden Nowlan: Selected Poems*. Copyright © 1967 by Irwin Publishing Inc. Reprinted by permission of House of Anansi Press, Toronto.

PERSEUS BOOKS GROUP: Excerpt from "Rhapsody" from *The Leaf and the Cloud* by Mary Oliver. Reprinted by permission of the Perseus Books Group.

TIMES BOOKS: Excerpt from *Dr. Judith Orloff's Guide to Intuitive Healing* by Judith Orloff, M.D. Copyright © 2000 by Judith Orloff, M.D. Reprinted by permission of Times Books, a division of Random House, Inc.

Copyright © 2004 by Judith Orloff, M.D.

Published by Harmony Books, New York, New York. Member of the Crown Publishing Group, a division of Random House, Inc.
www.crownpublishing.com

HARMONY BOOKS is a registered trademark and the Harmony Books colophon is a trademark of Random House, Inc.

Printed in the United States of America

DESIGN BY ELINA D. NUDELMAN

Library of Congress Cataloging-in-Publication Data

Orloff, Judith.
  Positive energy : 10 extraordinary prescriptions for transforming fatigue, stress, and fear into vibrance, strength, and love / Judith Orloff.—1st ed.
    (Hardcover)
    1. Vital force—Therapeutic use. 2. Energy—Therapeutic use. 3. Mental healing. I. Title.
    RZ999.O753 2004
    615.8'51—dc22   2003023727

ISBN 0-609-61010-4

10 9 8 7 6 5 4 3 2 1

First Edition

FOR BERENICE GLASS,
MY BEST FRIEND

ACKNOWLEDGMENTS

I'm grateful to the many people who've sustained me in my writing: Richard Pine, literary agent, ferocious believer in my work and steadfast ally. Betsy Rapoport, beloved editor, whose caring, humor, and intelligence always inspire. Shaye Areheart, publisher, woman of spirit, and champion of this project. Thomas Farber and Susan Golant, who helped me structure and shape this book. Coleman Barks, sweet lover of language, intuition, and truth. Stephan Schwartz, friend and mentor, intrepid explorer of consciousness. I'm also grateful to Tina Constable, Penny Simon, and Katherine Beitman at Harmony Books, and to Heidi Krupp, for disseminating my work to the world.

I offer special thanks to the entertainers and notable figures who've given interviews for this book: Jamie Lee Curtis, John Densmore, Eve Ensler, Wavy Gravy, Amy Gross, Quincy Jones, Naomi Judd, Goldie Hawn, Larry King, Norman Lear, Kenny Loggins, Shirley MacLaine, Rosa Parks, Cheryl Tiegs, and Iyanla Vanzant.

In addition, my appreciation for life stories, suggestions, and soul support to: my two(!) psychotherapists, Richard Metzner and Regina Pally. Also: Hafsat Abiola, Lori Andiman, Barbara Baird, Michael Beckwith, Laurie Sue Brockway, Ann Buck, Janus Cercone, Paula Cizmar, Laura Crouse, Jennifer Cook, Molly Malone Cook, Elizabeth Cox, Larry Dossey, Dan Duncan, Linda Garbett, Weili Gu,

Catherine Ingram, Tom Justin, Jonathan Kirsch, Michael Manheim, Mary Morrissey, Caroline Myss, Mary Oliver, Dean Ornish, Dean Orloff, Phyllis Paul, Charlotte Reznick, Sharon Salzberg, Lisa Schneiderman, Madeleine Schwab, Hayden Schwartz, Mark Seltzer, Danny Sheehan, Don Singer, Christina Snyder, Leong Tan, Suzanne Taylor, Roy Tuckman, Cynthia Watson, Mary Williams, Beth Zacher, Zuleikha. Finally, gone but not at all forgotten, my parents Maxine Ostrum-Orloff and Theodore Orloff, still guiding me, now from the Other Side.

Finally, I am indebted to my patients and workshop participants from whom I continue to learn so much. Please note I've changed their names and identifying characteristics to protect their privacy.

CONTENTS

IX

part two

CREATING POSITIVE RELATIONSHIPS AND COMBATING ENERGY VAMPIRES

When it's over, I want to say: all my life

I was a bride married to amazement.

I was the bridegroom, taking the world into my arms . . .

I don't want to end up simply having visited this world.

—MARY OLIVER

POSITIVE ENERGY

INTRODUCTION TO THE POSITIVE ENERGY PROGRAM AND ENERGY PSYCHIATRY: CLAIMING YOUR ENERGETIC POWER

ARE YOUR FOREVER IN A RUSH, staving off exhaustion? Are you desperately overcommitted, afraid to say "no"? Do you have fang marks from being bled dry by energy vampires? Does the onslaught of violence in the news leave you drained?

A hidden energy crisis threatens our world. Our high-tech, volatile society thrusts many of us into chronic physical, emotional, and spiritual depletion. Bombarded by information overload, burned out by enslavement to beepers, e-mail, faxes, and phones, we sink into technodespair. Meanwhile, geopolitical realities grind us down. We're confronted with hostile forces on a global scale. No surprise: our energy suffers. Most alarming, we've learned to tolerate tired, joyless states as normal. We must shift this socially condoned pattern of madness, no matter what external threats are looming. Using extraordinary solutions to liberate energy, I'll show you how to alleviate tensions that can do you in and how to design a life that nurtures and supports you.

In this book I want to introduce you to Energy Psychiatry, a term I've coined to describe a new kind of psychotherapy I practice that addresses the subtle energetic underpinnings of health and behavior. It's a subspecialty of Energy Medicine, which views our bodies and spirits as manifestations of subtle energies, what indigenous cross-cultural healing traditions revere as life force—a concept that's missing in mainstream health care. This is a travesty: there's no way to fully grasp who we humans are without it. Energy Psychiatry mixes traditional medicine with an explanation of how we can maximize our life force in everyday ways. It distills a broad body of knowledge about subtle energy and specifically applies it to psychiatry, an increasingly prescription-dependent field that could use a little reinvention. All the healing arts can benefit from my approach too.

As a board-certified psychiatrist and Assistant Clinical Professor at the University of California, Los Angeles (UCLA), with twenty years in practice, I now believe that the most profound transformations can take place only on an energetic level. I've met a slew of people who've spent lots of time and money in intellectually oriented therapies hoping that rational insights alone can bring the joy they seek. It's true—the mind will set you on the path, and the depth of emotional healing can be phenomenal. However, as much as I encourage and work with both traditional and complementary therapies, my approach coordinates them with a conscious rebuilding of subtle energies—learning to wield the raw power of your life force itself.

My style as a psychiatrist has never been to play it safe just to satisfy some status quo. To offer my patients all that's in me, I've pushed the envelope of what a physician can be. Along with my conventional training, I'm also an intuitive, descended from a long line of intuitives—my grandmother, mother, and aunts, including Aunt Bertha, the Tarot-toting undertaker. In Energy Psychiatry, I integrate nonlinear messages from images, knowings, and interpretations of energy fields to help my patients—a potent alchemy that strengthens my practice of medicine. (I've described my struggle to blend intuition with the academic world of science in my books *Dr. Judith Orloff's Guide to Intuitive Healing* and *Second Sight*.) What I do isn't just a job. It's my life's passion. I consider sessions with patients sacred time. For fifty minutes, each one becomes my world; my attention is total. I listen to what they say, and what they don't say. It's exhilarating to track my patients with both intellect and intuition, to function as a finely tuned instrument, a medium offering surprise prescriptions to what often seems unsolvable.

The problem is, we physicians aren't taught the full story about energy in medical school. I've always been incorrigibly curious, with a rebellious streak, and I have no qualms rejecting what doesn't ring true. (Like my female predecessors, I shot out of the womb stubborn and strong!) No wonder that as a medical student the conventional dull take on energy never jibed for me. Professors, who looked bored themselves, taught us that energy was like gasoline: we fuel up with a healthy diet, sleep, and exercise, then set out to face the world. (Even these basics were mentioned only as a tag-on to the "hard core" sciences.) Our energy level is gauged by how much we accomplish. When our tanks are low, we just refuel. As deeply grateful as I am for my medical education—I consider it Mystery school training—I've come to realize that this traditional model of energy is stuck in the Dark Ages. It grasps energy only in its crudest form. To plug into a far vaster source, we must also draw on the dormant, subtler energies that lie beneath. In most people, they remain only potential.

We need to retool the medical school curriculum to teach people how to sense and access the full range of their energy reserves. It's not enough to teach someone how to eat healthfully if you don't also teach them how to select foods that offer them specific energetic boosts. What good does it do to tell someone to get more sleep if you haven't shown them how to relax? This is why traditional advice about energy doesn't work. It's not your fault if you follow doctor's orders and still feel drained. You just need a more complete prescription. I'll give it to you here.

This book is a call to activism, an imperative to claim your vitality using the methods of Energy Psychiatry I'll share. It's dedicated to people under stress who may have low energy or only so much to give. You'll find it pivotal if you're a workaholic, if you have a job that devours every last minute, or if you're a parent balancing family and career. You'll sigh with relief, suddenly finding answers to "psycho-somatic" symptoms such as chronic fatigue, fibromyalgia, depression, and anxiety. The book is also for those inundated by the upheaval of our times, struggling to keep themselves together. You'll learn ways to protect yourself from people who drain your energy, and also how to counter feelings of helplessness or doom about societal tumult. Further, you'll benefit if you feel good but want to feel better. All of us can soar with higher energy.

We live in a world of violence, selfishness, an erratic economy, and scary diseases—as well as a world of love, miracles, and healing. All this affects our energy, while our own energy affects people around us. We are part of great swirling invisible energy fields, positive and negative, that shape personal and planetary health. I'll teach you the formula for expanding energy, how to build the positive and turn negativity around—a requisite for peace of mind and survival. In the words of Helen Keller, "To keep our faces toward change and behave like free spirits in the presence of fate is strength undefeatable." This book is your guide to this unseen realm. It will give you a new mastery of your energy so you'll understand where it goes and how to recoup it.

We all know that energy comes from diet, sleep, and exercise. But we're also influenced by an extensive network of energy fields undetectable to our five senses. Think of gravity, the force of attraction to the earth's center, which holds us to the ground. Or magnetic fields: you remember those metal filings mysteriously drawn toward the magnet in grammar school science class. Similarly, there's an energy field or "vibe" emanating from everything we encounter, from food to friends to current events. Our response to these vibes is manifested in our energy level. What we usually think of in physical, emotional, and sexual terms, using words like "My heart's racing," "I'm afraid," or "I'm aroused," are different expressions of subtle energy. If you're a particularly sensitive person who frequently feels drained or exhausted, this information can make the difference between an exuberant life and one you're constantly recovering from.

This book gives you tools from Energy Psychiatry to access this unseen realm. Energy isn't some vague phenomenon. I'll show you how to break it down and make it work for you. To begin, envision energy as conveying two qualities—either positive or negative. You must become acquainted with each to take charge of your health and moods.

You'll learn how to harness the power of positive energy—loving and nurturing forces from within, such as compassion, courage, forgiveness, and faith. (Being the best people we're capable of being brings wholeness to a broken world.) Or from without: supportive friends, creative work, the ability to laugh, or vibrant sexuality. Positive energy comes from an honoring of the Earth and all its creatures, a deep capacity for tolerance, as well as the passion to achieve a peaceful civilization. These are as central to our sustenance as food or oxygen.

You'll hone skills to combat and reverse negative energy, which enfeebles us, causing dis-ease. Negative energy keeps us small, unhealthy; it alienates us from our best selves. We may generate it with our own fear, self-loathing, rage, or shame—an emotional terrorism we inflict on ourselves without realizing the toll. Unless we're committed to identifying and healing such negative forces, they will enervate us. Worse, they'll inevitably get acted out in social and political spheres, wreaking destruction. The stakes keep getting higher. We, as a nation, have no choice but to deal with negative energies: international terrorism ("a virus in the human community," says a Navy friend who coordinated Special Ops in Afghanistan), racism, global pollution, and denigration of women. Or take our daily lives. Toxic people, traffic, sexual harassment in the workplace, and technodespair are as insidious as second-hand smoke.

We must each pinpoint what zaps us, large and minute; the causes may differ. For example, in *O Magazine,* Oprah Winfrey said, "Television has its own energy field—it's sending energy, but it's also taking energy. So I read." Similarly, you need to pinpoint and eliminate influences that diminish you. Or if you can't avoid them, discover how to both protect yourself and transmute them. For every luminous moment, there's always some outer or inner force ready to bring us down. When you embrace the positive and say "no" to the negative, high energy and optimism become a choice.

I understand how brutally difficult honoring your energy can be without a conscious strategy. For years I'd vacillate between intense weeks of speaking tours from Manhattan to Montana to bouts of exhaustion at home. I know too well what it's like to drag home zombie-like after a long day and collapse on my bed, leaden. Exhausted, I couldn't decline "irresistible" opportunities, so I'd accept them all and pay the price. However, the minute I'd recover, I was off and running again. Another drastic energy swing. Here was my quandary: I trusted my intuition, was personally and professionally committed to living by it. But in recent years, I was forced to admit my blind spot. Successful as I was at helping others trust their intuition and lead high-energy lives, I stubbornly disregarded dire warnings about my own energy crisis. Even though I knew better, it was a terrible battle to honor my body's rhythms. Finally, my fatigue was so profound I had to change. My commitment to writing this book is testament that I'm no longer willing to do violence to my capacity for passion.

My path has always been to live what I teach. I'm not the type who sails through life. I trudge. I fall. I pick myself up. I keep going. With each challenge I become wiser, freer, more in love with the precious days we've been given. Maybe you're like me: When I had energy, I assumed I'd always have it. But when it bottomed out, and then I regained it, I felt utterly reborn. Utterly grateful at having been spared. Whether your crisis is mini or, like mine, brings you to your knees, this program will teach you how to treat energy as a sacrament. You're going to experience how mind-blowing it feels to run

6

on full capacity—how this involves being as well as doing. Your energy is more mystical, more sexy, more ecstatic than you've ever imagined.

While Westerners may consider subtle energy esoteric or New Age, it's been central to many healing traditions for millennia. I liken our society's response to the proverbial elephant in the living room; it's right in front of us, but we can't see it. In Chinese medicine, subtle energy is called *chi* or *qi*. It's *mana* to Hawaiian kahunas, *prana* to Indian Yogic practitioners and in Ayurveda, *ni* to Native Americans, *num* to African shamans, biofields to American scientists, and morphic fields to a growing renegade breed of international physicists and biologists. Australian aborigines believe that people attuned to subtle energy can heal and telepathically communicate. For me, there's something deeply amiss in a culture that utterly lacks a power word for the multifaceted energy so many belief systems presume we are.

Belatedly, Western science is catching on. We've all seen Einstein's famous formula $e = mc^2$: energy and mass are interchangeable. Only now are scientists beginning to extrapolate his universal law of physics to our personal health. Energy Psychiatry recognizes the importance of balancing our bodies (mass) and spirit to prevent disease. Though the structure of subtle energy isn't yet fully defined, increased photon emissions and electromagnetic readings have been recorded around practitioners who generate it. Most revolutionary, though, is Cambridge University physicist Stephen Hawking's "brane theory." It proposes that the world we experience is perched on a thin membrane separating us from other vast energetic realms. The irony is, our limited perception stops us from seeing these realms which exist right under our three-dimensional noses!

Also delighting me, the National Institutes of Health are funding reams of new research on energy therapies—from how yoga can help insomnia to how *qigong* can serve as an adjunct to cancer treatment. Therapeutic touch (hands-on healing) has already been shown to accelerate wound healing and immune response and to relieve pain.

At New York's Columbia Presbyterian Hospital, energy healers have even been utilized during open-heart surgeries. Still more cutting-edge, though, is distant healing, the scientifically documented ability to positively effect enzymes, plants, and humans by sending subtle energy from afar. Energy healing recently hit the headlines when both *Time* magazine and the *Western Journal of Medicine* reported a landmark study showing that it could reduce debilitating symptoms in advanced AIDS patients. All this indicates we're at the forefront of discovery in the field of human energetics. I'm enormously excited both by what's already been found, and by all that seems imminently forthcoming.

My approach in Energy Psychiatry will immediately help you engage and master your energy. (Energy Psychiatry differs from the field of energy psychology, which also honors the subtle realm but has chiropractic origins; it emphasizes acupressure techniques and muscle testing.) My focus is heavily experiential, not "in the head." I don't just sit there detached in a white lab coat and say "Uh-huh, uh-huh." I don't ask my patients (or you) to take my word that subtle energy exists. It's mandatory to feel it. I really work my patients!

To begin, I teach patients to sense the energy that penetrates and surrounds the body in a capsule-like field. I help them experience the midline energy centers called *chakras*. This isn't just the territory of mystics; it's for gloriously ordinary people too. In this learning process, I'm a guide for my patients. When they say, "I can't do it," or "I don't feel anything," I don't let them stop there. For instance, I hold my palm close to theirs, but not touching. Then I walk them through what energy passing between the palms feels like. I explain that we can't analyze our way to such insight. To detect energy's gradations, I train my patients to hone their intuition. A potent inner wisdom not mediated by the rational mind, intuition allows us to sense beyond the physical. The payoff is practical. For example, knowing if someone's vibes feel good or not is critical to making smart choices.

Our culture's worship of the intellect has caused our intuition to atrophy. I reverse the trend, weaving intuition into every aspect of Energy Psychiatry: I read my patients and counsel them how to tune in too. I've long since concluded that it's ethically irresponsible to sit on some pedestal of authority and read people without also mentoring them to develop their own intuition. Hogwash that it's only for some gifted few. With practice, everyone can be taught to do it. I love to watch my patients' elated faces the first time they intuitively sense energy—a rite of passage as memorable as the first kiss. What an electric awakening! (My first time, the energy was numinous, like heaven. I felt I'd found what I'd always been looking for.) Once patients get a taste of this, I help them to delineate what's positive and to combat negativity, including unlodging traumas in their subtle fields that cause chronic drain. Many of us are at a loss without such basic living skills.

Frequently, patients come to me skeptical or confused about subtle energy. I can't blame them. It's hard to make sense of this area. As I reviewed the literature, the language intimidated me. It was either obscured by Western scientific jargon, psychobabble, or Chinese medical terms. In the spirit of essayist John Ruskin's words, "The greatest thing a soul ever does . . . is to *see* something and tell what it *saw* in a plain way," my job is to be a translator. I give all patients, new or experienced, a simple way to frame energy on a human level. I avoid buzzwords that trigger resistance. For instance, I prefer using the phrase "subtle energy" instead of "chi" or "aura." For some, chakras sound woo-woo, but when I explain them as energy centers, people are more able to embrace the idea.

It's not my aim to cater to the converted. I want all my patients to be at ease with subtle energy. The more linear-minded appreciate hearing about its history and science. I ground chakras in Western medical research, currently in a very early stage: how light frequencies are measured from them that match colors that sensitives have reported for centuries; how chakras are theorized to be the basis of nervous and immune function. Also, I stress that ancient traditions, including Egyptian, Hebrew, Chinese, Greek, and Native American, describe the equivalent of the Yogic chakras. As civilizations fell, great libraries were burned, destroying volumes filled with esoteric wisdom about energy that were considered subversive, dangerous. (Suppression of any kind makes my blood curdle, but book burning has always seemed particularly diabolical.) Still, truths so potent can never die. The beauty of putting energy work to use is that we're reconstructing lost wisdom in modern times.

Other patients come to me already familiar with subtle energy. Even so, they find Energy Psychiatry different, compelling because of its hands-on application in psychotherapy and self-empowerment. Though they've been introduced to "qi" in yoga classes, martial arts, or acupuncture, they've never practiced a daily energy program unifying spirit, emotions, and the body. I've always felt claustrophobic with the narrow psychological boundaries of traditional therapy. In Energy Psychiatry sessions, I first enlarge it by teaching intuition and the sensing of energy fields. Then I help patients take a microscope to their patterns of relating energetically to all aspects of life— responses to people, thunderstorms, places, food, noise, movies, smells, light. I train them to notice the constant interplay with their environment: what brings peace or agitation. Then I teach them how to create healthy coping mechanisms and alter dysfunctional ones.

As an Energy Psychiatrist, I don't minimize my patients' perceptions. From personal experience, I appreciate how exquisitely— sometimes painfully—sensitive to energy we can be. One extremely shy artist patient had a nose like a hound dog; she was perennially beset by noxious odors. To defend against them, she used inordinate amounts of energy to wall herself off. Worse, she felt ashamed of her sensitivity. As we worked together, she learned that though it was harrowing to speak up, she had to request that friends not wear perfume around her, and ask her boyfriend to get his teeth regularly cleaned. With such changes by sympathetic others, she could begin to let her guard down; her energy increased.

Because our medical system doesn't acknowledge how subtle energy affects health, I've seen many patients suffer. For years, they run from doctor to doctor with no relief. Energy provides a missing piece that can lead to miraculous breakthroughs. I've helped agora-phobics (who panic in crowds) overwhelmed by energy fields in con-gested malls get off Valium by using shielding techniques. I've treated compulsive overeaters, who've put on hundreds of pounds to buffer themselves from the energy of others, lose weight when given tools to stop being a sponge. I've provided tortured "crazy hypochon-driacs" with centering exercises to stop absorbing other people's symptoms. When we cannot name how we react energetically—par-ticularly to global atrocities that can demolish highly receptive people—crucial components of our behavior are ignored and left untreated.

We each have our own energetic styles. Some serve us, others don't. As my patients do, you'll become aware of ways you instinc-tively process vibes. For instance, intellectuals tend to constrict energy, whereas intuitive empaths give too much away. My goal for patients and for you is to find a comfortable way of navigating life that balances vulnerability with emotional security.

Like me, you may be an intuitive empath: a person who's so sen-sitive that you often unknowingly absorb energy from others and are drained by it. To cope, we escape into solitude to ward off over-load. In Energy Psychiatry, I help patients appreciate that intuitive empathy can aggravate disorders such as chronic fatigue syndrome, sexual shutdown, and obesity. Empaths are so uncannily attuned that we feel what's going on inside other people emotionally and physically, making it hard to distinguish whether it's us or them. We get struck down, and don't know what hit us. As a child, I'd arrive at packed shopping malls feeling fine and leave exhausted, depressed, or with some new ache or pain. Dismayed, I'd tell my physician mother, who loved to shop. She'd respond, "Sweetheart, you're just overly sensitive." My mother doted on me, wasn't intending to be unkind. She (and my father, also a physician) just didn't realize crowded places heighten an empath's experience of energy and can overwhelm.

My own healing path required reconciling intuitions such as empathy with medical science. Knowledge is power. If you've ever been accused of being "overly sensitive," an appreciation of the mechanics of empathy will enlighten you, transforming a burden to an asset. Empathy can eat at you until you learn to work with it. Now that I have tools to center myself and not take on the world's woes, empathy has become a gift. When I'm both grounded and responsive, it intensifies my sense of aliveness, compassion for others, and balance to withstand our sobering times. I want to share these specific, everyday tools with you.

I've devised the Positive Energy Program, based on my practice of Energy Psychiatry, because I know how life-saving it has been for me and my patients to maximize our energetic power. My emphasis is on action and technique, and it is passionately practical: improving your life, your health, your relationships. If previous wellness plans have failed, despite diligence and the best intentions, you may have picked ones that were counterintuitive to your body's needs. I've watched intelligent, aware patients battle horrible constipation while on a high-protein regimen for weight loss. Their bodies scream for a balanced diet, yet they persist until they get sick and have to quit. Other patients hire trainers who push their bodies so hard they suffer severe injuries. One actress, obsessed with being thin for roles, ignored her body's signals until a torn knee ligament put her out of commission for months. I understand the desire to lose weight and be fit. But we don't have to martyr our bodies.

This program helps you find a method you're in harmony with. It's based on compassion; hurting yourself in any way becomes abhorrent. Using intuition to sense what feels right isn't about slacking off. It means trading a culturally acceptable masochism for a wellness approach that makes inner sense. Doing so prevents burnout and fosters enduring success.

The Positive Energy Program is based on ten prescriptions, one per chapter. They are:

THE FIRST PRESCRIPTION: Awaken Intuition and Rejuvenate Yourself

THE SECOND PRESCRIPTION: Find a Nurturing Spiritual Path

THE THIRD PRESCRIPTION: Design an Energy-Aware Approach to Diet, Exercise, and Health

THE FOURTH PRESCRIPTION: Generate Positive Emotional Energy to Counter Negativity

THE FIFTH PRESCRIPTION: Develop a Heart-Centered Sexuality

THE SIXTH PRESCRIPTION: Open Yourself to the Flow of Creativity and Inspiration

THE SEVENTH PRESCRIPTION: Celebrate the Sacredness of Laughter, Pampering, and the Replenishment of Retreat

THE EIGHTH PRESCRIPTION: Attract Positive People and Situations

THE NINTH PRESCRIPTION: Protect Yourself from Energy Vampires

THE TENTH PRESCRIPTION: Create Abundance

Following each chapter I've included an interview I've had the privilege of doing with heroes of mine, public figures from Quincy Jones to Rosa Parks, who illustrate how they use a particular prescription to increase energy in their lives. I hope these interviews inspire you as much as they have inspired me.

The program has two sections. Part One, "Building Your Energy," presents prescriptions one through seven. It offers simple vitality-boosting strategies to follow, from how to overcome weight gain that's energetically based to how to connect with your intuition and inspiration. The secret to kindling energy is to get beyond the cerebral. You'll do this by practicing exercises I give patients. For instance, to revive sensuality after a long day, a federal judge jumps into a jasmine-scented tub filled with rose petals. (Water is a purifier.) Or to shake off negative vibes from back-to-back pitch meetings in his office, a film executive burns sage. You'll also learn pleasurable options to unwind. Most of us are pleasure-deprived. Subtle energy quick fixes are a remedy. When introducing skills that require more effort, I'll start slowly, make each task achievable.

Part Two, "Creating Positive Relationships and Combating Energy Vampires," presents prescriptions eight through ten. It zeros in on energy as the missing piece in the puzzle of human relationships. Here I'll give strategies to help you identify the energy flow between yourself and others. You'll learn how to evaluate who gives you energy, who saps it, and how to generate the positive energy that will attract nurturing people and situations. I'll teach you to recognize the energy vampires that can suck you dry, and how to protect yourself. You can use this knowledge to gain a new openness in the world and to create more loving connections. Finally, this section explores abundance and generosity from an energy perspective. You'll understand the difference between codependent giving, which leaves us spent, and giving from the heart, which summons up positive energy and creates intimate ties with others.

The purpose of this program is to be of service to you—to make your life easier. I suggest focusing on a prescription a week, completing the program in ten weeks. (However, if a specific energy topic calls to you—start there.) Then, you can keep deepening the themes. I assure you this isn't just hard work or "another thing to do." Tapping into subtle energies feels divine! The exercises, including a "Treat Yourself" section at each prescription's end, will be compatible with your schedule and lifestyle.

Energy Psychiatry and the Positive Energy Program begin with the individual, but the goals aren't simply personal. Beyond self-regeneration you'll gain a profound feeling of collective communion. There is an energetic bond between everyone on earth. *This life-changing realization is missing in our world.* Once it becomes real, very real, our sense of separateness dissolves; discriminations of class, race, and gender are obliterated. Until we recognize each other as brother and sister, it is still night. To achieve planetary peace, the illusion of Us versus Them must transform into the wholeness of We: one global union honoring commonalties, united by mutual respect.

I'd love for you to use this program to fashion a passionate, self-styled life and worldview. The changes I suggest won't force you to revamp your old life, merely change your focus. I've seen everyone from stressed-out moms to hard-charging executives benefit. Let my prescriptions be champions of inspiration, the antidote to conformity and complacency. Gaining more energy won't only allow you to be ultraproductive at work, excel at time management, or run a marathon in record time. It also means you'll be able to breathe in the sweetness of night-blooming jasmine, marvel at the sight of storms converging in the twilight sky, or giggle unpredictably at the silliest things. It will allow you to commit yourself, personally and politically, to avoiding a life tyrannized by fear—rather guiding your actions by the heart and intuition.

Positive Energy is about slowing down time to match your natural rhythms to be fully present for your life. What has this done for me? Colors are brighter, the scent of the sea more pungent, my lover more mine. And I more his. Our stay on Earth is far too short. If you're like me, you won't stand for missing a single moment. Recovering your energy means recovering your most impassioned self—a revolutionary process that subverts all people and situations seeking to keep you small. My deepest wish is that you join me in this practice and quest.

part one

BUILDING YOUR ENERGY

1

THE FIRST PRESCRIPTION:
AWAKEN INTUITION AND
REJUVENATE YOURSELF

LET ME TELL YOU A SECRET that will change your life. It's about energy, creativity, the rhythms of existence—how their compelling interconnection gives birth to an inner voice so sophisticated it'll teach you to harness the positive and dispel negativity. Intuition brings magic to traditional wellness approaches, but also opens you to the intriguing realm of energy fields—vibes that radiate from people, places, plants, the night sky. Think of the contagious electric buzz of Tokyo or Rome; the mellow, cool groove of Coltrane's sax; or the orgasmic surge of applause at Yankee Stadium when the home team wins. Each day you'll encounter a wonderfully diverse but often unacknowledged range of energies. In this prescription you'll see how intuition registers them and sharpens your sensitivity to your life force's fire, showing ways to metabolize and protect it. By awakening your intuition, you can access your full energy. This is the true secret of secrets: I won't be satisfied with anything less and hope you won't either.

As a specialist in Energy Psychiatry, and personally, I worship my high-octane intuitions: I owe the blessing of becoming a physician to one. However, at twenty, when an unwavering inner voice told me I was going to medical school, it was the last thing I thought I wanted. Yes, I was the only child of two physician parents with twenty-five physicians in my family, from cancer researchers to gynecologists, a lineage I seemed ordained to join. But I'd never liked science, would get bored around my parents' doctor friends. At the time I was a hippie living in an old converted brick Laundromat with my muralist boyfriend in Venice Beach. I worked in the May Company's towel department. Still, as my intuition sank in, it gave me tremendous energy. So, dubiously, I enrolled in one course in a junior college just to see. One course became two, became . . . fourteen years of medical training—a trek that would've pushed Indiana Jones to the edge. But my intuition had staying power, provided all the oomph needed to propel me to my calling.

Similarly blessed, my patient Laura literally owes her life to an intuition about energy. A math teacher with moxie, at forty-five she began experiencing a terrible pounding in her ear, diagnosed by a top neurologist as a routine recurring migraine. Despite his reassurance, she kept feeling "an energy like a train roaring through my body screaming something was wrong." As I heard the dire immediacy of this intuitive warning, I convulsed with chills. I was very afraid for Laura; she had to act. At my urging, Laura sought a second opinion.

I'm all for protesting when something doesn't feel right. It's foolish, even reckless to ignore such energy signals. An angiogram was ordered; dangerous blockages in her cerebral arteries were found. This new doctor told her: "The good news is you didn't have a stroke or die. The bad news is you have fibromuscular dysplasia. You'll need surgery to keep your arteries from collapsing." Arteries collapsing? Of course, Laura was terrified, but also relieved to have a possible solution. Then, the medical machine kicked into high gear. Laura's emergency brain surgery both cured her symptoms and saved her life. For a year, her angiograms have been fine. Now, Laura listens to her intuition like a fiend. She and her doctor agree: doubting it would have proven lethal.

In my Energy Psychiatry practice I advocate a "take no prisoners" style of intuition. This gut-centered voice is committed to your happiness, health, and survival. With practice, you can learn to tune into it. I want you to start listening. Really listening. I guarantee: your positive energy will grow. Why? You'll be operating from a spot inside that's juicy, core-felt, authentic—not from an impulse to conform or disown your strength. You won't be seduced by what may look good but betrays your gut. Intuition is a truth detector. When you deviate even a nanofraction from your inner voice, your energy will wane, whether a subtle seepage or radical bottoming out. The more ferociously faithful you are to this truth, the more energized you'll be.

Intuition offers a direct line to your life force and also, as I experience it, to a divine intelligence. It's the language of energy. You need to speak it to thrive, though our techno-crazed society doesn't recognize this essential fact. At best it equates intuition with a woman's trait (try telling that to Native American male shamans!). At worst, it's considered a magic trick or fluff. No surprise there's an epidemic of worn-down, confused people out there.

Our energy issues are solvable, but we can't afford to remain deaf to intuition's messages. Its expertise is energy; its job is to know every nuance of what makes you tick. A master at reading vibes, intuition is constantly tallying: what gives you positive energy, what dissipates it. Your intuition evaluates who you meet, where you go, your job, your family, current events—all crucial data this program will show you how to interpret and apply.

As an Energy Psychiatrist, I train patients and workshop participants to tune into vibes, a skill you'll learn. I've watched thousands of people do it. Consider Gloria, who's driven a sixteen-wheeler for thirty years: "I can sense the bad vibes of someone's road rage and maneuver around the aggravation." Or Janet, a homicide detective: "By shielding my energy, I'm not emotionally destroyed by gruesome crimes." My friend serving in an elite naval team in Afghanistan told me, "An effective point man catfooting behind enemy lines has to use 'Spidy Sense,' like Spider-Man does. It means reading energy, attending to internal alarms beyond the five senses." Whatever your field, you'll benefit from intuiting energy too. Get ready to put the Positive Energy Program's First Prescription into action.

GET IN SYNC WITH YOUR LIFE

Think of yourself as a spy whose mission is to detect how much in tune you really are with your life—the big picture and the details. Unlike more cerebral methods, intuition offers you the edge of having X-ray vision into all energy matters. Whether revealing the hard truth about toxic relationships, your exhaustion level, or a thankless job, intuition is always trying to communicate, though you may not hear. It resides in a quiet place obscured by the chatter of everyday thoughts. I will take you there.

Prepare to raise your antennae. You're constantly having intuitions about energy, but may not realize it. Suddenly, bam! A gut feeling, goose bumps, or a flash affirm what fuels or depletes you. Intuitions can be positive. For instance, you'll feel a burst of aliveness, clarity, or tension lifting about a new project. Or negative—your skin crawls or you wilt at the prospect of a sleazy business deal. In the Positive Energy Program, you'll get in the habit of intuitively tracking your energy response. (Mine soars around full moons, puppies, and during uninterrupted days of writing alone, but shrinks at the thought of black-tie events, greasy food, and fast talkers.) As I do and teach my patients, you'll identify information that zings and feels right. By noticing your energy's fluctuations, you'll get a jump on where you're off-center—in relationships, health, and career—so you can change.

Intuition also involves picking up vibes. People and situations can give off welcoming positive energy that invigorates, or oppressive negative energy that repels. Our colloquial language reflects these intuitions. One patient affectionately calls his gangly, six-foot-five brother a "tall drink of water"; another says, "My boss shoots daggers with his eyes." Sensing vibes provides instinctual gauges of your comfort level.

22

Techniques for Sensing Positive and Negative Energy

In the mid-eighties when I'd just begun to expand my traditional psychiatric practice to include intuition and energy, I did plenty of experimenting. My good buddy for the first few years of this exploration was Michael Crichton, filmmaker, author, and Harvard M.D. A towering six foot nine, Michael has a wicked mix of intellect and humor with a cynical edge. For me, he was the perfect companion to investigate a dimension of health I'd never heard of in medical school: our body's subtle energy system.

My world has never been the same; this was my initiation into Energy Psychiatry. I want to share with you our discoveries, and what I've been learning since. Being able to sense and direct our life force gets positive energy going: we exude it, attract it, and can read it in others. Our subtle system is the engine that drives well-being. Acupuncture activates energy by placing tiny needles in meridian points in the body. So does exchanging good vibes with people. First, I'll teach you what energy feels like, a sublime experience that intuition conveys. You may perceive it as colors, light, or positive and negative vibes. This program makes real for you what Energy Psychiatry is based on: that our bodies and spirits are microsystems of energy, and that health is about balance, which intuition helps us achieve.

Friends can be the best coconspirators in charting the unknown. Michael and I set out to experience energy, a real adventure given our "rational" medical backgrounds. We were the blind leading the blind, but so curious. Here's what we did, an exercise you'll try later: I'd lie on my back on the floor as Michael placed his palm about two feet from my head. Slowly he'd edge closer until he described feeling "a distinct contour of warmth" inches above me—the halo depicted in sacred art. We all have halos, not just angels. Michael used the same sensing technique to outline my energy field from head to toe. Starting a few feet away, he'd move his palm nearer until he definitely felt warmth, tingling, quivering or pressure, marking an invisible energy border inches to a foot from my body. Then we'd switch places, and I'd practice with him. Michael describes this process in his autobiography, *Travels:* "I was terrifically excited like a kid with a new toy, a new discovery I didn't think about, I just kept doing it. I could feel this warm contour just as distinctly as you can feel hot bath water when you put your hand into it."

As part of the First Prescription, I'd like you to try sensing energy too. This is important because the energy that people exude can profoundly influence your health and mood. Once you know how to read it, you'll better determine who nurtures or saps you. Practice with a friend: be playful. See how his or her energy feels.

MAKE CHANGES NOW

EXPERIENCE ENERGY THROUGH

BODY SCANNING AT HOME

Sit beside your friend as she lies on her back on the floor or a bed. Together, take a few deep, calming breaths. Once relaxed, observe your friend's eyes, hair, clothes, then look further. Picture a capsule of light surrounding her body, what Carlos Castaneda calls "a luminous egg." This is the energy you're going to intuitively sense.

Start by cupping your hand a few feet over her head. Then slowly come closer. With the palm as your sensing device, notice a point at which you hit a subtle border of heat, coolness, pressure, a hum or vibration—the outer rim of her energy field. Raise your hand, then lower it against the rim until you're sure. It's all about feel. You also may see colors. Similarly, continue to map the subtle energy around her entire body, without touching the skin.

When you're finished, it's your friend's turn. Then compare notes.

What a hoot to realize we are more than our physical selves! Each of us radiates a palpable energy. In practical terms: Have you ever sat next to someone at a luncheon and were drawn to her immediately? It wasn't so much what she said or did, but how refreshing she felt to be around. Or how about that coworker who seemed congenial, but you always left a conversation feeling run down? We are medicine for each other, sometimes good, sometimes bad. An exchange occurs whenever you interact with someone.

Certain people give off positive energy, others negative. It's the quality of someone's being, a measure of the love with which they've led their lives. It also reflects the inner work they've done, their efforts to heal anger, hatred, or self-loathing, which poison us like toxic fumes. Energetically these linger, precluding joy from shining through. It's important to grasp, however, that once you undertake the process of healing, it changes the quality of even the negativity that remains. Don't be too hard on yourself—we're all works in progress.

SIGNS OF POSITIVE ENERGY IN PEOPLE

- They exude an inviting sense of heart, compassion, and support.
- You intuitively feel safe, relaxed, wanting to get closer.
- They emanate a peaceful glow.
- You feel better around them. Your energy and optimism increase.

SIGNS OF NEGATIVE ENERGY IN PEOPLE

- You experience a sense of being demeaned, constricted, or attacked.
- You intuitively feel unsafe, tense, or on guard.
- You sense prickly, off-putting vibes. You can't wait to get away from them.
- Your energy starts to fizzle. You may feel beleaguered or ill.

Beginning to differentiate these energies, I was able to name something I'd always intuited: why as a child, within seconds of meeting someone, I knew whether or not I liked them. This knowing wasn't about looks or how nice a person seemed. Rather, I could sense invisible tendrils reaching out to me from a person that transmitted information about them. It would happen before we exchanged a word. The confusing part for us is that people aren't always as they appear. Sensing energy reveals a fuller picture. I don't care how intelligent or attractive someone is on paper, if he zaps your energy, he isn't for you. True chemistry is more than intellectual compatibility. Beyond surfaces, you must be intuitively at ease.

MAKE CHANGES NOW

EXPERIENCE ENERGY THROUGH

BODY SCANNING IN THE WORLD

You can practice sensing positive and negative energy everywhere. Have fun. See what you find. The secret is to stand within two feet of someone—whether a coworker or shopper in the mall—and notice how he or she feels. Ask yourself: Am I attracted? Repelled? Unsettled or at ease? Honestly assess: Do I feel more robust or worn out?

Establish a baseline for each person. You'll quickly know who nurtures you. If a loved one is in an arduous phase, try to cut him some slack. But also pinpoint those who consistently drag you down. Then, with a more realistic understanding, you can take better care of yourself.

I'm a big fan of being proactive in generating positive energy. The First Prescription's formula for success: Do whatever makes your inner light brighter. In other words, try to treat yourself and everyone else with love. It's a constant process of tuning in: finding people who support your spirit, trusting your gut-centered decisions to guide you. Then you won't end up in a relationship that looks right but feels wrong. Or miss the chance to meet a loving man or woman because he or she doesn't fit some preconception. When you're with trying people, aim for the high road; find common ground rather than inflame negativity (more to come in Chapter 4). The care with which you approach life is intuitively evident in your energy field. We can feel each other's love: that's the great attraction. Spread openheartedness around. Stay true to your intuition. Your positive energy will blossom.

INTUITIVE EMPATHY: HOW TO STAY OPEN AND NOT ABSORB NEGATIVITY

In Energy Psychiatry, my patients use intuition to understand their energetic health, and also to scrutinize their reactions to positive and negative vibes. So much happens to us that remains subliminal—the smile of a coworker; witnessing a devastating three-car pile-up while driving to work; the sight of children skating on Christmas Eve in Rockefeller Plaza—all pass through our consciousness so fast we may miss how each registers. Intuition is a master at bringing our attention to interactions, large and subtle, that modulate our energy.

For many patients and myself, staying receptive to positive energy has been the easy part. This openness I adore lets me live with more gratitude—for intimates, but also for Rick, my wisecracking Bronx-born plumber, and Khalsa, the white-turbaned mail carrier who, rain or shine, delivers packages to my door. The energetic quality of all our connections matter. Every moment seems wildly extravagant. Sipping morning coffee or gazing at the galaxies above, appreciation of positive energy instills wonder in the days we so casually inhabit.

For me, negative energy has taken more getting used to. An intuitive empath as a child, I was so attuned to people's feelings, positive and negative, that I unknowingly absorbed them. Normally, when you have empathy, your heart goes out to someone in distress. When you're an intuitive empath, you take on their tribulations. If a friend was upset or physically hurting, in a flash her discomfort would lodge in my body. As I've explained, crowded places intensified my empathy. Whereas shopping malls are havens for some, for me they were war zones: I was bombarded by the swarms of people, but couldn't explain why. An angst-sucking sponge, I coped by shutting down. A teenager in the sixties, I numbed myself for a few years by taking drugs. Finally a wise therapist referred me to a UCLA lab that studied intuition, where I could meet other empaths. What a relief not to feel so out of control or alone. With their support, I developed ways to handle my empathy, to see it as a potent type of intuition, an asset.

To take charge of your energetic health, you must know if you're an intuitive empath. Ordinary stress is a bear to deal with, but compounded with the angst of our times, it can be treacherous. Like it or not, empaths process all stress in their bodies, are more prone to take in a personal or global trauma's energetic residue. Vulnerable to negativity, whether miniscule or horrendous, many empaths have chronically low energy, a common complaint that baffles traditional physicians. The symptoms of intuitive overload include depression, psychosomatic complaints, and overeating. Negative energy arises from people, especially energy vampires (discussed in Part Two), places, and situations. Densely populated areas can be negative hot spots. My friend, a magazine editor in Manhattan, can barely inch from train station to office without feeling assaulted by the mobs. Let me be clear: life doesn't have to be like this. Despite the indisputable negative energy around you, you can learn ways not to assimilate it. I regularly give workshops to hundreds of people who are courageously healing wrenching emotions from self-hatred to rage, and I rarely absorb any of it. I want to teach you the life-saving skills I depend on daily.

To determine if you're an intuitive empath, take the following quiz. First, identify the signs. If you answer "yes" to one of these questions, it's likely you're being enervated by empathy. Responding "yes" to every question suggests that empathy is compromising your energy.

QUIZ: AM I AN INTUITIVE EMPATH?

Ask yourself:

- Have I been labeled as overly sensitive?
- If a friend is distraught or in physical pain, do I start feeling it too?
- Am I drained in crowds, going out of my way to avoid them?
- Do I get anxious in packed elevators, airplanes, or subways?
- Am I hypersensitive to noise, scents, or excessive talking?
- When I see gruesome newscasts, does my energy plummet?
- Do I get burned out by groups, require lots of time alone to revive?

Discovering you're an empath can be a revelation. Putting a name to a very real intuitive experience legitimizes your perceptions. It also pinpoints where you're losing energy so you can regain it. The beauty of Energy Psychiatry is that it recognizes and treats this phenomenon. I can't count how many patients have said, "Judith, I thought there was something wrong with me! I felt like such a weakling." Not so. The problem is that traditional physicians lack the facts to correctly diagnose empathy. Instead of seeing you as an intuitively gifted person who needs proper coping skills, you were labeled "hysterical," a "hypochondriac," or a "complainer." Because no one knew what to make of your low energy, you suffered.

Throughout this program, you'll see how intuitive empathy enters into the energetics of relationships, health, and career. I know well how tempting it is to shut down around unbearable people or events.

The danger is that defending yourself becomes habitual. Armor turns into a straitjacket, restricting spontaneity and love. You don't want to risk this. Here's an option: instead of armoring, try centering yourself so negativity can't weaken you. This strategy will help you enjoy your own energy while remaining receptive. Consider it warrior training. When you cultivate a solid internal core, nothing external can usurp your power.

As a starting point, I'll share a centering meditation I teach my patients and use myself. I suggest you practice it once a day. Then when negative energy threatens to drain you, you'll know what to do.

MAKE CHANGES NOW

A BREATHING MEDITATION TO CENTER

YOURSELF AND BUILD POSITIVE ENERGY

Wearing comfortable clothing, settle into a quiet place with no interruptions—turn off your cell phone, shut the door. Think of it as erecting the cone of silence. Start with a few minutes; gradually increase the duration.

Sitting in a relaxed position, eyes closed, begin to focus on your breath to center yourself. Be conscious only of breathing in and breathing out. As thoughts intrude, notice but don't judge them—an ongoing part of the meditation process. Each time you catch your attention wandering, continue to refocus on inhaling, then exhaling.

Breathing activates positive energy. It's a lifeline to your center, to the earth. With each breath, extend your awareness downward, right into the ground. Picture your breath flowing downward through strata, bedrock, minerals, and soil. Mentally plant a root from your body into the earth's core.

Picture a long, strong tail stretching down from your spine, rooting you in that nurturing center. As you breathe, feel your connection with the earth deepen. Allow the earth's positive energy to infuse and stabilize you.

This meditation is an everyday survival tool. Try it out when you're rattled by a demanding boss, a needy friend, or new trouble in the Middle East. During the heat of the situation, focus on your breathing and planting your roots deeply, safe and secure. Being firmly grounded protects you from getting flattened by negativity. Centering is also stabilizing in crowds. For me, airplanes are the biggest test. When I'm jammed like a sardine in economy class, assaulted by stale air and perpetual chatter, centering has saved my energy. Anchored by the rhythm of my breath and my rootedness, I'm cocooned from the chaos. With practice, centering becomes second nature. It's a victory to remain open yet inwardly strong. Doing so takes you off the defensive; empathy becomes a pleasure. Visualize this: You're surrounded by negative energy, but it doesn't get to you. I want you to know such liberation.

Not everyone has empathy overload. If you're like my friend Linda, it's not a concern. An avid traveler, she's visited over seventy-five countries in twenty years. No jet lag; her energy stays high. After returning to Los Angeles from Antarctica (a seventy-hour haul), she immediately went to a movie! Marveling, I asked, "How do you do it?" "Eye shades, earplugs, and a good night's sleep," she said. Sounded reasonable—if you're not an empath. Practical tips do ease wear and tear. But clearly, the negative energy I'm so vulnerable to, earplugs or not, doesn't faze her. Though Linda is one of the most intuitive people I know, she just isn't predisposed to absorbing energy. Our constitutions differ. Define your instinctual style of interacting with the world so you can honor it.

THE ART OF PACING YOURSELF

Over the years, throngs of discombobulated patients have come to my office. Mothers, actors, teachers, dog groomers, all with their own reasons why life is out of whack. As an energy psychiatrist, I teach them about pacing: a basic energetic rhythm I train my patients to sense intuitively. Just as heartbeat and respirations tune our physiological tempo, pacing sets our subtle energy clock's timing. Often we get caught in extremes. Before they practiced the Positive Energy Program, my patients typically either tore around like maniacs or were at loose ends when things quieted down. I try to help each one achieve or at least approximate a pace that suits them, whether fast, slow, or in between. As a physician, I've long ago learned to give up preconceived notions about what rhythm is right for people. No one pace fits all.

Early in my practice, I discovered this the hard way. Izzy, in good health at sixty-eight, came to me weighing retirement. For thirty years, he and his brother, children of Jewish immigrants, had run a successful furniture business. A real character, Izzy was known for his big heart, but also for his rabid complaining. In sessions he'd swear, "I tell you, Doc, the aggravation at work's gonna do me in." Naturally, as an earnest novice physician, I'd ask, "Why not slow down a little, or retire?" For a moment, he'd be silent, mulling it over. Then, he'd wink at me, eyes strangely radiant, and say, "Nah, honey. I'd have too much time on my hands. I'd miss schmoozing with my customers." Still, Izzy's well-meaning wife and brother grew alarmed by "that much stress at his age"; convinced by his complaints, they got Izzy to retire. I supported their decision, though something off about it nagged at me. Three months later, his wife called, weeping: "This morning Izzy dropped dead from a heart attack. I found him slumped over in the yard with a gardening book in his lap." I was in a shock of remorse. All I could think was, "Oh God. By pushing him to retire, we killed him!"

In retrospect, I believe that Izzy's job, aggravation and all, fed his life force. I regret not urging he remain at the store at least part-time. Back then, I hadn't yet incorporated intuition into my practice, nor did I read patients' energy. I couldn't see that the wonderful twinkling in his eyes when he talked about work counted more than his words—or that complaining, for Izzy, was just a tic, not reflecting his true energy needs. I was then easily swayed by conventional wisdom, which argued for a universal curtailing of activity for "old age." Long since, I realized how the best intentions (without the correct information about subtle energy) can cause fiascoes.

Today, as an energy psychiatrist, pacing is the first thing I read in patients, an important aspect of the First Prescription. When Josie, a designer, came in "to learn to analyze dreams," she was comfortable with her pace. My reading of Josie's energy concurred. Our life force has rhythm: this is what I attune to. Sensing a well-paced energy field like Josie's is a delight. It feels like the perfect heartbeat, inaudible to my ordinary ear, but palpable to intuition. It also transmits a motion that's neither sluggish or rushed. My body relaxes around it. In contrast, Tracy, a fifty-year-old garden designer, came in to improve relationships. Her schedule was busy, yet Tracy was ploddingly obsessive, did everything soooo slow. Not surprisingly, her energy field had a weak rhythm, as if it were stuck in molasses. This told me that Tracy had the brakes on in her life and relationships, issues we'd have to address. Finally, John, a stockbroker at forty who suffered depression, hadn't thought to question his manic rushing around. Outwardly he seemed calm, but his energy field felt jarring, antsy. From this I knew that part of John's recovery from depression would mean slowing down.

Of all the pacing dilemmas, rushing tops the list for draining many of us. *Webster's Dictionary* defines *rushing* as "a violent forward motion; to act with haste . . . in a short time at a high speed." Energetically speaking, rushing means running on more cylinders than you've got. It's so toxic because the negative energy is cumulative. On perpetual overload, your physiology responds: cortisol, the "stress hormone," surges; serotonin, a chemical protector against depression and anxiety, plummets. That, in combination with an inevitable diminution of subtle energy, launches the downward spiral.

We rush for many reasons: To dull emotional pain. To flee from anxiety, depression, or feeling we're not enough. To respond to unrealistic expectations of what we can accomplish in a finite period. To dull our fear of stillness and silence. Whatever the reasons, rushing is different from operating quickly and efficiently when your rhythm's in sync with a busy yet balanced life.

The following intuitions give rushing away:

- Your energy feels scattered.

- You have little or no awareness of your body.

- You experience a subliminal or overt sense of panic.

- Your ability to listen is impaired, as is your memory for details.

For me, rushing is a consciousness-shrinking altered state. It blurs into a bad hallucination, as if my energy body fragments and races ahead of itself while the material me is trying to catch up—I feel a tinge of vertigo, a nauseating sense of disconnection. Be certain: rushing steals your well-being; it must never be construed as harmless.

Even so, I understand how addictive rushing can be. As a medical student at the University of Southern California (USC), my sixteen-hour days were packed with life-and-death emergencies. I was on call every third night. This grueling pace continued when I opened my private practice. The most maddening part was wearing a pager. Strapped to my belt, it'd go off so frequently I'd catch myself fantasizing it would self-destruct. One day, at my accountant's office, it started beeping while I was going to the bathroom. I reached for it—but not quick enough. It'd slipped off. I'd already flushed. I heard a splash. Aghast, I stood and stared as my pager, still maniacally beeping underwater, disappeared down the toilet. The absurd pace of my life was never more apparent.

After years of whirling like a dervish, it finally sank in: my energy was being stretched way too thin. Wound tight, I'd get terse, snippy, hurrying myself and others along. It's hard to be nice when you're frantic. Worse, I'd drive and rush: more than once I got a speeding ticket zipping from the gym to the market so I could get home to unwind in a tub. I was rushing to relax! Ultimately, I rushed my way right into an energy crisis. Refusing to slow down, my body intervened. A profound weariness came over me that lasted nearly a year. I was forced to cut back on speaking engagements and other commitments. Doing so made me realize how much I craved the nourishing sense of presence that being in the moment brings.

At the onset of this program, I'd like you to intuit if you're in sync with a pace that supports your energy. (It may vary with the phases of your life, age, or shifting priorities.) Subtle energy-wise, pacing sets the tone for everything you do. I know that when I'm in sync, I want to skip, dance, fly. I'm unstoppable. If my pacing is off, my stamina is obliterated. Your body is an astute intuitive barometer, the first place to look to evaluate pacing. Start with the "big picture" indicators, then we'll address the subtler ones. Here's a general checklist to consider:

WHEN YOU'RE IN SYNC YOU CAN EXPERIENCE:

- Emotional balance
- Physical stamina
- Patience
- Excitement
- Passion

WHEN YOU'RE OUT OF SYNC YOU CAN EXPERIENCE:

- Ongoing fatigue
- Emotional numbness
- Irritability

- Mood swings
- "Psychosomatic symptoms" (such as irritable bowel syndrome, headaches, or acid reflux)
- Decreased libido
- Sexual shutdown

Now, moving on to the more subtle energies, you'll apply the First Prescription to find a pace you're most in sync with. I suggest you try the following exercise, which involves active self-inquiry: posing a question and receiving an intuitive response. The exercise will introduce you to the intuitive center, known by ancient mystery schools as the Third Eye chakra, a small energetic opening located midway between your eyebrows. Mystics see it as a vibrant purple light. In a quiet state, the idea is to lightly bring your awareness to your intuitive center. This increases energy flow in that area, facilitating greater insight into pacing or any other issue.

MAKE CHANGES NOW
INTUIT YOUR PACING

PART 1: TAKE TIME OUT TO TUNE IN

- Set aside five minutes or more to be still, an official break from your usual thinking. Sit comfortably, eyes closed, and take a few long, deep breaths until you're relaxed. (Sometimes I'll do this exercise in the shower, which is like an intuitive phone booth for me; information pours through!)
- Begin to direct your attention inwardly to your intuitive center. To help it open, you may also gently place your finger there. (Think of this as revving up an engine.) This spot might heat up or form pulsating purple swirls you can see with your eyes

closed. Some people feel pressure or a slight headache until the opening is able to accommodate more energy.

- After a minute or two, ask yourself, "Does my pace feel good?" To find out, stay aware of body sensations or visual flashes. You'll know if you're in sync if you get an intuitive "yes." For me, this feels like a luscious warmth, an excitement and energy in my gut, a wave of goose bumps. Also note any uplifting images or memories, no matter how far-out they seem. Conversely, an intuitive "no" feels cold. When it happens to me, my gut tenses. I'm tired, sinking, or rigid like a brick wall. Negative images or memories may also surface. Don't censor. Just let yourself go. See how you perceive "yes" and "no"— information you'll use throughout the program.

- Then get more specific. Ask yourself: How does my pacing feel at work? At home? On vacation? With friends? One area may be more balanced than another.

PART 2: WORKING WITH SOLUTIONS

- *To realign with an in-sync rhythm:* Make gradual changes. Focus on one area at a time. Ask yourself: What kind of change would feel good? Focus on small, do-able chunks, not an instant overhaul. Say, your job. Try out ten minutes of a nurturing pace. If you're a perennial multitasker, use that time to do only one thing: answer e-mail; talk on the phone; or read a report; but don't allow yourself to scatter your focus. Savor how that feels. Then build on it. See if your well-being improves. Energy never lies. If you work at your right rhythm, you will be more productive; trust me.

- *If you're a rusher:* Let at least a few minutes each day be a meditation on energy focus. Rushing is best reduced in increments. Don't get ahead of yourself. Attempt to be totally

present. Open your senses. Take pleasure in tulips, cascading
fountains, the aroma of baking bread. Feel the breeze caress
your cheek. Listen well to people. Respond with your full
attention. If this exercise feels good, try it daily for five minutes.
Then increase the duration from there. At first, being present in
the moment may be a real challenge. Stay with it. To be really
bold, remain timeless for an extended period; remove your
watch, and head for destination unknown. What I especially
cherish about slowing down is that my sense of humor perks
up. There's room to laugh and get into the hilarious side of
people and the world.

- *If you're on deadline:* To survive these potentially oppressive
  time crunches, be sure to plan minibreaks to utilize this quickie
  subtle energy technique that has saved me: For just a minute,
  take a few deep breaths while touching your intuitive center
  between your eyebrows—this heightens focus and brings you
  back to center.

- *If your pace is too slow:* Intuitively tune into an activity that
  brings you joy. It can be anything: ice skating, gardening,
  volunteering at a soup kitchen. Once that memory is rekindled,
  plan to do it. If the activity makes you happy, begin to
  incorporate it into your routine. The aim is to jump-start
  positive energy if you're underperforming or shut down in
  another arena. Then tune in again to something else that brings
  you joy. Incorporate that too. One activity sparks others. This
  will lead to a more vibrant pace.

During this exercise you may receive surprisingly specific flashes
about energy. If so, act on them. Jack, a physician in his forties who's
on the go running a hospital cancer unit, saw a startling inner vision
of a beaming being in white who warned, "If you don't slow down,

it's time for your heart attack." No wiggle room there! Jack took the message seriously, has modified his pace. Sue, a young fashion buyer, adored her quick-paced job, but often felt jangled despite enough sleep and downtime. When tuning in, Sue's stomach knotted. Then, in a burst, she saw a rerun of her evenings: "I'm in bed with my husband watching a late-night talk show. He leaves for a while. There I am stuck with Jay Leno!" This exercise identified a conflict Sue hadn't told me or her sweet husband: that she despised having "that unhealthy TV" in the bedroom. The couple discussed the situation and the TV got a new home in the den. Now, every evening Sue reads quietly in bed, which relieved her jangled feeling.

The key to success is to ease into your new right pace. As some of my overzealous patients discovered, making giant leaps too quickly can sabotage this program. They ended up feeling like failures, demoralized, until they emotionally regrouped and began again. Please, no grand gestures. Just start moving in the right direction. This sends a positive message to your life force. Don't worry if you slip into old habits. We all do. Every minute you've succeeded renews vitality and awe.

BE IN THE NOW: HOW TO GET THERE

Getting in sync with your life requires being present for it, though many of us aren't. Our days flit past without us savoring the passage of time. By fine-tuning our focus, intuition conserves energy and restores awareness of the Now: a visceral, moment-conscious state your life force adores. When your energy isn't dissipated by dwelling on the past or future—no matter how many suicide bombings or "merely" personal demands you experience—you can view every situation with centered appraisal. For me this defines sanity. Building energy is important; so is knowing how not to squander it.

Energy Psychiatry 101 emphasizes the importance of being in the Now. This state of awareness is an energetic bulls-eye that intuition hits by heightening the connection to your body and environment. In the Now you're moving, grooving through the eternal present, physically and emotionally alive. Out of the Now you're cardboard, numb, distracted, imprisoned in your head; the intoxicating fragrance of a rose garden on a summer's night doesn't even register— a sorry state I urge you to rail against.

These days I revere the Now. I fight for moments and hours when I'm fully present whether at work or shopping at Home Depot. It's ecstasy to feel all that positive energy in my center where it belongs. Also, as an intuitive, I must be in the Now. I'm constantly scanning an influx of energies and impressions, including how "present" my patients are. Many who find the Now elusive energetically hover over their bodies, not realizing the disconnect. Seeing this, I can help reanchor them by methods I'll describe. My intuition short-circuits if my attention drifts, obscuring the wavelength I've tuned into.

Here's the dilemma: Many of us operate in a taxing world where we lose track of the Now. There seems to be a conspiracy of forces that fragment our attention. Expect this, but also know how to regain your presence again. For openers I'll offer four simple tips to help you feel more energized and present in a range of situations.

MAKE CHANGES NOW

TUNE IN TO THE NOW

OBSERVE MASTERS OF THE MOMENT

To viscerally grasp the power of the Now, observe those who're in it. This intuitively attunes you to vibes you can resonate with. Babies and young children are naturally in the Now. It's rare and precious to experience beings for whom past or future doesn't yet exist. Babies, especially, have totally focused energy when they zero in on you. Locking into their gaze will align your energy. If you don't have a baby you can commune with, watch children playing in a park. Let them be teachers of presence and wonder.

Similarly, observe creative people for whom the moment is everything. Watch Maya Angelou singing and strutting her poetry. Or Yo-Yo Ma stroking his celestial cello. Attend a performance by someone who gets you going. Immerse yourself in those timeless vibes. Memorize this feeling. Also recognize that during emergencies, you naturally, instantly revert to the Now. If your seven-year-old falls from a tree, your mind isn't going to roam; all your energy and attention will be with her. To intuitively hone such presence, observe yourself and others in these situations.

FOLLOW YOUR BREATH

There's nothing like following your breath to reel you back to the present during a busy day. Many cultures equate the terms *spirit* and *breath:* Latin, *spiritus;* Hebrew, *rauch;* Greek, *pneuma;* Sanskrit, *prana.* Many Westerners, however, are clueless that the breath is sacred until illness takes it away. Many of us walk around unconsciously holding our breath, which constricts energy. The miracle of breath involves inhaling oxygen and expelling toxic carbon dioxide—as well as assimilating your life force's energy. So you won't miss a moment of this miracle, I recommend conscious breathing. It'll ground you in the body and still your thoughts.

Take a few quiet moments to relax, eyes closed, focusing on each inhalation and exhalation: the softness of breath entering your nostrils, your lungs; your chest rising and falling. Simply follow your breath; don't control it. Feel the life force enter you. If thoughts intrude—and they will—intuitively visualize each one as a puffy cloud passing in the sky. Try not to attach to these thoughts, an ability that gets easier with experience. Just let them float by. Then, each time, return to your breath, your body, and the Now.

CHECK YOUR PULSE

An instant antidote for being out-of-the-Now is to feel your pulse. As a physician, I was trained to check this first in patients: to access the rhythm or to determine whether the person was still alive. Outside the Now, you're losing life force fast. To recoup it, locate and concentrate on the beat of your pulse: with one palm facing upward, gently align two fingers from the other hand on your wrist, just below the thumb. Violà—contact! You're in your body now.

Get used to how your pulse feels. Then, with each beat, intuitively visualize your life force as golden energy rushing through you, a splendid sensation. If you're initially squeamish about touching your pulse, like some of my patients, don't worry. It'll pass as you get used to how natural it feels to locate the Now anytime, anywhere, in this marvelously inconspicuous way.

ADOPT A MANTRA

A mantra is a sacred word or phrase that can cue you to return to the Now. One translation of mantra is "that which protects you from negative energy." In Tibetan Buddhism, a mantra is passed from teacher to student. It's recited either inwardly or aloud, a way to focus during meditation or amidst chaos. So, in the chaos of your universe, a special mantra can retrieve you.

See what grabs your intuition. It could be *om* or *shalom* for peace, the catchy Zen koan "If not Now, when?" or the Beatles song "Let It Be." A mantra I get deliriously happy saying as fast as I can, running all the words together, is "I am that I am that I am that I am ..." One comedian repeats a joke that always cracks him up. Laughter only happens in the Now, anchors you in a flash. Whatever mantra appeals, it's a grounding incantation.

The Positive Energy Program has maximum wattage when practiced in the Now. These tips will make this precious region less elusive. Additional resources I recommend are Ram Dass's classic *Be Here Now* and Eckhart Tolle's *The Power of Now*. I promise: Your journey home to the moment will kindle the energy you're looking for. I hope you love the moment as much as I do. As you continue this program's exercises, remember the Now's the right place to be.

TWO COMMON ENEMIES OF THE NOW

Twenty-first century America presents us with two unique maladies that obscure the Now: workaholism and technodespair, the burnout from being enslaved to e-mails, beepers, faxes, and phones. (Worry, fear, and other presence-dulling emotions are covered in Chapter 4.) What's scarily malignant about both energy leechers is that they can readily become habitual. If you're frazzled, these enemies of the Now might be the cause.

Enemy of the Now #1: Workaholism

Workaholism is the Puritan ethic gone haywire, an addiction to doing more, going nonstop until you drop. If you don't work at least eight hours a day, you're likely to feel ashamed. An American sickness, workaholism perpetuates negativity by exhausting subtle energy; it drowns out the Now in an adrenaline rush. The result: a plague of burnout. We workaholics are everywhere—in demanding jobs, racing between family and career, sacrificing every last ounce of energy to our children. Our "to-do" list, like some mutating life form, just keeps on growing.

The irony is that we haven't been taught to guard positive energy, to see slowing down as a virtue. We're socially reinforced to go faster, do more. In fact, we're bludgeoning our subtle energy reserves, inviting dis-ease. We push on, robotic in our mania to achieve. Because of workaholism's tenacity, I am adamant: If you keep pushing through fatigue when your intuition screams, "Rest!" you're inadvertently punishing yourself. As you'll see, fostering positive energy is about respecting your body's signals.

A tricky symptom of workaholism is multitasking—twenty-first-century lingo for juggling many tasks at once, either serially or simultaneously. Suddenly everyone is multitasking, and proud of it. My patient Meg, a young mother, regularly watches the kids, makes dinner, and cares for her elderly mother until her husband gets home. (When she describes this, her energy field is quite a sight! I see an after-image flurry of many arms around her body—like Kali, the four-armed, skull-wearing Hindu goddess, bearer of both life and destruction.) Despite Meg's mounting fatigue, she's still at the stage where being superwoman has allure.

Indisputably, multitasking lets us manage a deluge of very real duties, but it jeopardizes the Now when it invades our lives. We forget the satisfaction of doing one thing at a time, take multitasking for granted. (Being put on hold especially infuriates me; one click decapitates the conversation energetically.) When we do too much multitasking, we'll end up energetically floating above our body rather than fully inhabiting it, a limbo that promotes chronic drain.

Most of us are starving for quality time. Our full attention is a gift we must give ourselves and each other. To regain such presence requires not pushing so hard. This prescription offers a multi-pronged approach to workaholism that uses both psychological and intuitive strategies. For maximal benefit, combine them.

MAKE CHANGES NOW: STOP PUSHING AND BREAK
THE WORKAHOLISM CYCLE

INTUITIVELY IDENTIFY CAUSES OF WORKAHOLISM

Below I've listed some common causes of workaholism. Tune
into each one and see if it resonates. As you did before, see if
you get an intuitive "yes" or "no."
The causes are:

- A need to control
- Loneliness
- Self-worth tied to your accomplishments
- Ambition
- Masochism
- Financial pressures
- Greed
- An "inner slavedriver"
- Family conditioning
- An escape from emotions: loneliness, anxiety, depression
- An unsatisfying marriage
- No role models for showing self-compassion

If I missed one, feel free to fill in the blanks. Then start by
addressing an issue at a time. You can journal about it—noting
when it began, why it's sapping your energy, and how to
correct it. (Consulting a skilled therapist can hasten the
process.) One quick correction is to reframe your job, whether
running a gas station or a corporation, in terms of service and
surrender rather than compulsive activity. How does what you
do make the world a better place? When your goal is to be

helpful to others or humanity, you'll derive more positive energy from work. To combat workaholism, you can also apply the following solutions.

PRACTICE SELF-COMPASSION

Compassion, a subtle energy that comes from the heart, will help you stop pushing yourself. As a psychiatrist, I'm well aware that it's much easier to be compassionate with others than with ourselves. This is how to learn:

- *First:* Even if your strenuous schedule doesn't seem to give you a moment to breathe, you *must* carve out quality personal time. Commit to at least one self-compassionate action a week. For example, indulge in a short afternoon nap. Hire a babysitter to free up an evening. Decline listening to a friend's problems and go to the movies. Treat yourself to some mini restorations, five minutes here or there of Mozart, jellybeans, whatever appeals. Planning regular downtime nurtures positive energy.

- *Second:* Self-compassion means realizing not everything has to be done today, prioritizing essentials, then stopping there. From this perspective, much of our to-do list seems more obviously self-inflicted. Understand: If that dreaded list becomes an excuse to beat yourself up and inflict suffering, it's symptomatic of compulsion. Self-compassion can release its grip.

- *Third:* Self-compassion means being able to keep saying "no" to the crazed slavedriver within who'll push all your buttons to hook you. Realizing the certifiable insanity of the slavedriver's prodding will make it easier to resist.

SAVOR THE ECSTASY OF DOING ONE THING AT A TIME

As a respite from multitasking or for just pure pleasure, get totally involved with one activity a day. Whether playing golf or filing papers, fully inhabit your body and lightly focus on your intuitive center. Awakening intuition in this way attunes you to a natural high, a surprise feeling of ecstasy that comes from mindfully doing one activity. Our spirit rejoices in this coming together of our energy field; it becomes ecstatic when we focus enough to feel the holiness of the everyday. During mindful activity, expect ecstasy; revel in this in-the-Now sensation.

GET AN INTUITIVE DEATH-BED PERSPECTIVE

Workaholic pushing can become so entrenched it's not totally solvable in current time. To outwit this conundrum, intuition gives us special powers: the ability to project into the future and observe ourselves from a death-bed perspective. Sometimes, seeing through the eyes of our mortality is necessary to clarify our priorities. To do so, I suggest the following technique whenever the need arises.

A PERSPECTIVE-SHIFTING VISUALIZATION

Imagine you're on your deathbed looking back on your life. Really get into it. Picture your face, your clothes, your surroundings. Pay witness to your life; notice the real highlights. Was it love? Family? Friends? That summer afternoon planting petunias with your son? How does your to-do list compare to those times? Do you even remember it? What about the all-nighters you pulled at work? Or the constant rushing? What was it all for? What was truly meaningful? Take these insights about how you expended your energy back to the Now to restore a more enlightened perspective.

You don't have to retreat to a desert island to heal workaholism. Shifting from victim to victor by taking even the most modest, constructive action recoups positive energy. The change I'm suggesting is as much inner as outer. Empowering yourself by internally alleviating pressure is a radical act of self-love. For me, showing self-compassion—setting boundaries on my energy and leaving plenty of time for fun—has been an ongoing meditation. The sweet rewards I've felt are a happy body, clarity, and positive energy to spare. I urge you to have mercy on yourself too.

Enemy of the Now #2: Technodespair

My patient Stuart, a detail-oriented finance analyst, labors at his computer all day somewhere on the edge of the Now. Within arm's reach are a fax, two phones, a scanner, and a copier; he also carries an electronic appointment book and a pager. Amidst beeps, buzzes, whirrs, and rings, he's surrounded by machines. He's grown dependent on them for his job. If, God forbid, one or more break down, he's been known to freak out. Stuart had initially sought therapy with me for anxiety in social situations—but missing deadlines due to a computer malfunction could push him over the edge. Practically crazed, he'd tell me, "I'm utterly helpless. It's beyond my control. I can't stop trembling. I'm chewing out my coworkers and snapping at my wife."

I appreciate that Stuart's anxiety has many origins. But one is a Now-numbing energy affliction I call technodespair. How do you know if you're a sufferer? The clincher is that you experience mild to intense nervousness, depression, or fatigue after bouts with the complexities of technology. (I still get frustrated trying to program my VCR to record shows!) Relief from technodespair comes from limiting contact with machines, or by learning to cope more productively with them. The upside to technology: it makes life easier. The downside: mishaps can grate on your mental health.

Let me explain. First, negative emotions, which contaminate your serenity and energy field, can be set off by externals. For instance, a computer hard drive with what you think of as "my entire life" on it crashes. It's natural to be upset, even devastated. And those "minor" foul-ups—a printer that keeps jamming or a defunct "mouse"—are irritants that erode positive vibes. Secondly, machines give off electromagnetic fields that can jangle or zap energy. See if this is true for you. Though technology is miraculous, it can also dehumanize, spurning negativity.

To guard against technodespair, watch out for the following energy-sapping instigators, and work toward solutions.

MAKE CHANGES NOW

STOP LETTING TECHNOLOGY SAP YOUR ENERGY

AVOID INFORMATION OVERLOAD

In our rapid-fire world, we're hit too fast from too many sources. The Internet. Voice mail. Cell phones. Assimilating all this information takes energy. We're constantly processing positive and negative input. Everything adds up. It's easy to max out. Chronic energetic assault from a torrent of information emotionally burns us out.

The solution: To recenter in the Now, get in the habit of taking mini technology fasts, energetic breaks from machine or cyber exposure. For instance, go a few hours without faxing; take a walk instead. Check your e-mail less frequently. Watch a goofy movie instead of reading news updates on the Web. When you tune into the Now again, your gut relaxes, lightness and presence return. To clear your energy field you must purposely restrict the volume of incoming information.

DON'T CATASTROPHIZE TECHNOLOGY SNAFUS

Overdependence on machines is a setup for despair. A crucial file mysteriously gets erased from your hard drive before you saved it on a disk. As a writer, I know the terror of forever losing my words to some black hole in cyberspace. Even after hours of backtracking, my computer whiz still can't locate the file. Meanwhile, an entire day evaporates, as do my creative juices. When I write the check for his fruitless search, I begin to dream of typewriters, of pen and paper.

Technology fiascoes incite negative energy by ripping off patience and peace of mind. To not succumb, be prepared.

The solution: Above all, practice self-compassion and center in the Now: Breathe deeply, repeat a mantra, take your pulse. This expels flipped-out vibes, awakens the positive. Also adjust your attitude. Don't catastrophize. Remember: Even if a technical snafu occurs, you'll probably be able to at least piece things together.

Sometimes a feeling of being out-of-control or helpless may escalate because of flashbacks to earlier traumas—being unjustly fired, romantic betrayals, even childhood abuse. Still, keep your eye on the present. Later, it's important to address and heal the past. For Now, the point is to counteract this setback by tapping into your positive emotional energy.

COUNTERACT THE ENERGY DRAIN OF MACHINES

Just as fluorescent lights have been shown to agitate hyperactive children, the negative energy of machines can intuitively unsettle us too. For instance, computers emit a degree of electromagnetic radiation. As you sit inches from the screen, your energy field will be encroached on by it, which may compromise your emotional and physical well-being. (Some scientists now argue that there's a link between radiation from prolonged use of cell phones held right next to the ear and brain tumors.) Fluctuations in your mood or energy level could be machine-related.

The solution: Observe your intuitive reaction to machines. Do you get tired? Spaced out? Remote? We all respond differently. If you are machine-sensitive, reduce your exposure or take regular breaks. It's also wise to purchase a computer screen that reduces electromagnetic transmissions. To minimize drain, flush toxic vibes from your system as you would a virus so they won't energetically congeal. Drink lots of water. Inhale fresh air. Breathe and center yourself. Boost your immune system with positive thoughts and laughter. These actions keep toxicity moving so it can be dispelled.

RECOGNIZE THE EFFECT OF YOUR EMOTIONAL ENERGY ON MACHINES

Some of us get along with electronic devices better than others. I'm utterly convinced, far-out as it may sound, that they register our vibes, just as we intuitively register theirs. (Consciousness researchers call this psychokinetic energy.) To my dismay, I've found that often when I'm very upset, it's as if I become a poltergeist. Everything around me seems to break. Answering machine. Printer. Clocks. Lightbulbs. Toaster. Garbage disposal. One by one, they go down; my angst seems to jam their circuits. Your emotional energy, especially anger and frustration, may also disrupt appliances and technology. If so, pinpointing the link lets you contain potential mayhem.

The solution: First, recognize this is just a phase. It will pass. Next, do whatever possible to work through your angst. Intuitively pinpoint the source. Talk it out. Rail at the universe. Go to therapy. Scream. Do anything that gives release. Machines react to your energy field; you can't pull a fast one on them. They'll remain kaput until you've resolved your agitation. Without fail, when my emotions smoothe out, I can gladly send the throngs of service people home.

AS YOU CAN SEE, the Positive Energy Program's First Prescription—awakening your intuition—presents solutions to a range of dilemmas. It illustrates how the many forms of intuition catalyze energy by magnetizing you toward your center. Do everything you can to find intuition. Whether you're following your gut, scoping out someone's vibes, or grounding yourself in the midst of turmoil, be fierce about your inner listening. From that center point, feel your life's rhythm. Synchronize with it and watch your positive energy grow. Resist the rhythm and see how your energy dwindles. The art of living is to listen to signals. There's an ease to letting your instincts guide. Intuition isn't a luxury; it's mandatory for a joyous life. Risk trusting it. I guarantee: your energy will flourish.

Treat Yourself:

Indulge in an activity that intuitively rouses your energy. Try singing aloud, reveling in a rainbow, or doing the rumba in the wee hours of the morn. The only "must" is that it feel right deep down in your cells, a sure sign you're in sync with your life's rhythm.

INTERVIEW: QUINCY JONES ON INTUITION

QUINCY JONES IS A MUSICIAN, COMPOSER, AND PRODUCER OF
NUMEROUS GRAMMY AWARD-WINNING RECORDS, INCLUDING
MICHAEL JACKSON'S "THRILLER" AND "WE ARE THE WORLD,"
TWO OF THE BIGGEST SELLERS OF ALL TIME.

※

I've counted on my intuition for fifty years. I wouldn't be here if I didn't
trust it. To me, intuition is paying careful attention to God's whispers. It's
the most natural part of us—listening gives us energy and inner power.
What you feel, not what you think: that's what it's all about. I live by goose
bumps. I get them everytime something really touches me—music, movies,
poetry, an emotion. Then I know I've got the right take. Nothing to talk
about unless I get the goose bumps!

I totally subscribe to the theory of divinity, that you just let yourself
become a medium. I let intuition tell me what it wants to be. When I first
started doing scores for television, I had a lot of music to write. Before I'd go
to sleep I'd program my subconscious mind to help me. I'd leave a pencil and
music paper by my bed. In the morning, I'd jot down songs, colors, contours,
or ideas that I'd wake up hearing. My hand would just move. I'd keep on
writing. Using this information, I'd look for an entry point. Then the other
little rascals would come together to create an entire orchestration. I believe
all the answers to our questions are out there in the universe, if we just slow
down enough to hear. Coltrane always used to say that. It's all right there.
You just have to grab your little piece.

Most jazz people feel the same way. Jazz is all about intuition. Jazz
musicians improvise, take gigantic leaps into space. It brings amazing
energy to music. It's like skydiving without a net. When I listen to Miles
Davis or Dizzy Gillespie, it's unbelievable. They just bend intuition into
pretzels. Jazz people really trust intuition. They have to. They live off of it.
They exist because of it.

Look at the connection between energy, nature, and intuition. African music is so vibrant because it's based on the natural elements—the sound of rain, thunder, the movement of animals. Birds do not imitate flutes. Nor does the thunder imitate drums. When I worked with Michael Jackson on the *Thriller* album, he'd study the slow-motion movements of cheetahs and gazelles. He intuitively observed the natural world. That's a very African truth. It's a life-force music.

When inspiration doesn't come, it's miserable. When I first started writing for film, a few us formed a club in L.A. called the Rollers. The Rollers were rolling around under the piano trying to get just the right inspiration. It can happen anytime. Inspiration doesn't deal with verbal orders. When it's ready it says, "Let's get busy."

Sometimes majority decision can squash intuition—for instance, when I was producing an event at the Clinton inauguration. On multiple outdoor screens we'd show film clips of John F. Kennedy's speech "Ask what you can do for your country," then have John Jr. appear. For the clip of Dr. King's speech "I have a dream," I wanted to put LL Cool J there—linking the '50s protests to the '90s protests. The other producers didn't want to hear about it. This was before rap was where it is now . . . the power of it. I held my guns. My intuition was so right on. Five hundred thousand people in the Mall jumped to their feet when [LL Cool J] came out. Talk about energy! What a feeling. Damn! I'm glad I didn't get rolled over by that decision.

Positive energy is like a glass that's half full. Or it may be love at first sight. It feels good, intense, a strong intuitive affinity. Some people give off a glow, like angels. You can feel it. You can almost touch it. It's amazing. My eight-year-old daughter Kenya is like that. On the other hand, negative energy feels like a glass that's half empty, off-putting, draining. It may be because a person doesn't like themselves. But you must be careful of projection. If you have strong negative stuff going on, you may project it onto someone else and think, "I don't like him or her." That's what racism is all about. I'm careful to investigate projection in myself, to make sure where I'm coming from. If someone is really draining me—for instance with small talk, if they're not using their brains, or if I'm bored (which is rarely)—I'll find another place to be. Feeding or confronting it is just a waste of time.

My children give me energy. Seven kids, from eight to forty-eight. Six girls, one boy. They've got tremendous energy. Close friends also give me energy because we fill holes in each other. We make a strong unit. I meditate and exercise. I love food, books, music. Staying curious is always good. I'm nosy about everything. Always be nosy. That will energize you.

My masseuse talks about qi, the subtle energy of the body. I believe it exists. Sometimes she holds a hand under my leg and my neck. Her energy connects the two in a way I couldn't do myself. I can feel it. Since my brain operations I believe in this even more. They opened my head twice. Aneurysms. I really started to trust my intuition—to the point where I knew who was going to call on a day when I would get thirty calls. It was really funny and strange. I talked to my neurosurgeon. He said, "That's the way we're supposed to project." Maybe the brain surgeries cleaned the cobwebs out. A lot of it is that I was just happy to be alive.

A great doctor listens to intuition. I would ask doctors to open their minds. My neurosurgeon talks about the brain as God's art. Also, a lot of men think of intuition as feminine; it isn't macho enough. Please! Creative people depend on this feminine side. You're missing half your life if you ignore it. If a man feels intuition is too "soft" I'd say, "Try it! If you think you're okay now you'll be twice as good with intuition." We should be proud to be intuitive. Intuition is God's gift to you. Your gift to God is to take care of it. That, in turn, can nurture your energy.

2

THE SECOND PRESCRIPTION:

FIND A NURTURING SPIRITUAL PATH

IMAGINE AN UNLIMITED SUPPLY of energy at your fingertips. A powerhouse that never wanes. It's an experience I want you to get used to having. A spiritual practice makes it real in an ingeniously simple way. How? You tap into love, the most irrepressible source of positive energy in the universe. Untainted by guilt, conditions, or fear, it's pure power we can wield as individuals and collectively. Even the biggest, baddest demons within or without ultimately shrivel in the face of it. Love is our destination. It is waiting just for you.

Energy Psychiatry reveres spirituality, and all the numinous energy that flows from it. Too often traditional medicine lops off this crucial part of us, a totally unacceptable casualty. (I once left an analyst with a brilliant mind because he went scarily brain-dead at the mere mention of my spiritual side.) If, indeed, a psychiatrist is a doctor of the soul, as the ancient Greek stipulates—*psyche* means "soul"—my profession could surely be enriched by revisiting our purpose. In the dictionary, I was amused to find the term *psychiatrist* between *psychedelic* and *psychic,* a hilariously inspired ordering. I'm a little of each—minus the hallucinogens—and proud of it. Patients appreciate my many hats. Psychiatry frightens some because they fear being pathologized or seen as only fragments of the self. As an intuitive, I can't not "see" my patient's spiritual side: it'd be like ignoring Vesuvius. Our life force is stoked by spiritual energy, a loving essence I'll teach you to access in a way that feels natural.

In my second prescription, a nurturing spiritual practice gives this essence a vehicle to express itself energetically. The deliciously sublime vibes you'll contact are typically outside the radar of ordinary experience, outside the worries and distractions. To perceive them you must become still, then open to something larger, a higher power of your own. A spiritual practice catalyzes this energetic shift. It'll take you beyond your small self, what Buddhists call the "monkey mind"—the myopia of insecurities and ambitions that perpetuate negative vibes—and give you a wider field to play on. An unbounded vastness surrounds your tinier identity. This is where love lives.

Many paths lead to the heart—the antithesis of extremist "spiritual" ideologies based on hate. A wise Sufi teacher once said, "Love is the religion, the universe is the book." The type of practice is a matter of choice. It can be traditionally religious: church, synagogue, or mosque. Or like me, you may be more private, preferring meditation or communing with nature. (One patient's Christmas Mass is spent at midnight stretched in a God-lit meadow overlooking the Pacific.) For some, spirituality may be nameless, the silent place within. Mary Oliver, a poet who's a beacon for me, sanctifies the details of our humanness. In one poem she writes:

> *Bless the fingers,*
> *for they are darting as fire . . .*
> *Bless the eyes*
> *for they are the gifts of the angels,*
> *for they tell the truth.*

Using the spiritual models I've mentioned, or no models at all, find a loving approach to spirituality that rings true. This will help you override the negative and provide positive energy to draw on. Energy

Psychiatry is a melting pot of unconventional and mainstream wisdom. It honors that Spirit means different things for different people. Here's how some friends I respect of various ages and traditions define it in relation to energy:

BUDDHIST PRIEST WENDY EGYOKU NAKAO: "[Spirit is] Breathing in wholeness . . . the aliveness of feeling interconnected."

RABBI DON SINGER: "Love that doesn't discriminate. It makes us joyful and full of life."

MUSLIM PRACTITIONER DR. NEVIT ERGIN: Breathing exercises (*zikr*) and fasting twice weekly makes me clearer, and close to a divine energy.

BENEDICTINE MONK BROTHER JAMES: "Rituals in the Catholic Church strengthen me by focusing my soul toward God."

JORDAN HOBSON, A FOURTEEN-YEAR-OLD GIRL: "We have a spiritual stomach as well as a digestive one. They both process energy we don't need, and leave us with what helps the most. Spiritual indigestion is awful!"

ELSE JOSEPH, AGE ONE HUNDRED: "God gives me energy, hope, and makes miracles. In 1938 God helped my husband get released from a concentration camp in Nazi Germany."

WAVY GRAVY, CLOWN: "Popcorn is the Lord!"

I've been lucky. Since I was a little girl, I've strongly sensed Spirit. I'd feel it most lying on top of our garage roof staring at the night sky. The canopy of stars, the moon, the velvet darkness—all were my friends. Something above was loving me: a mysterious, ever-present radiance. Though I didn't realize this was energy, when I closed my eyes, when I was hurting or happy, that love sustained me like the finest food. My parents hoped I'd find God at temple. I really wanted to. But all those fancy women in mink coats and the gold-plated mechanical Ark that cranked open for the Torah reading made me long to escape. My way has always been more solitary and off-beat. I've come to respect that.

I've never been one to take anybody's word for anything, especially about God. Yet, still, I longed to find a guide. In the early 1980s I sampled a smorgasbord of gurus, from an ex-housewife who channeled age-old entities to a celebrity astrologer, but for me they all lacked a certain depth. Then one day, a friend told me about a Malaysian teacher whose meditation techniques had helped her. A week later I walked up a flight of creaky stairs in a modest office building in Santa Monica. A man in his mid-forties, wearing a cotton shirt and pants that could've come from Sears, he just sat there, so still, waiting for me. No fanfare, no hoopla. Looking at him, all I could see was his eyes, two luminous pools I'd known from somewhere before. Those eyes saw my every hiding place, faults and gifts too, all before he even said a word.

That day I found my teacher, with whom I've studied the last seventeen years. Our practice comes from Taoism, which venerates the power of the heart, unseen subtle energies, and the cycles of nature. It also emphasizes compassion and helping others. I'll share with you the pearls of wisdom I've learned. This path fits for me because it's utterly simple and irreverently devoid of rules; you do only what moves you. And thankfully, not a mink coat in sight! My teacher introduced me to a regular meditation practice, my direct line to spirit and the heart. He showed me how to keep loving despite feeling broken and afraid so many times. For all these gifts and more, I am grateful beyond saying to him.

No one can dictate your spiritual identity for you. If you were turned off or made cynical by early religious upbringing, start fresh. Try not to get mixed up by other people's opinions. From an Energy Psychiatry standpoint, spirituality is a viscerally experienced energy that opens your heart, enabling you to feel a higher power. It has nothing to do with intellectualizing, expectations, politics, or social norms. You're the only one who'll know if your connection is viable. Here's how to begin.

FIVE GUIDELINES FOR DISCOVERING YOUR OWN SENSE OF SPIRIT

Use the following guidelines with the Steps to Opening Up Your Spirituality that follow.

Guideline #1: Appreciate That Questioning Is Healthy

Feel free to question everything you've ever learned about spirituality, and continue to do so. There's no one to satisfy but yourself. As I do, sniff out hypocrisy or the inauthentic. If something sounds good, but doesn't move you, it's not for you. People can talk until the cows come home about how spiritual they are, but if you can't feel their heart, all that rhetoric means nothing.

Guideline #2: Permit Yourself the Freedom to Explore What Moves You

This is not necessarily what your friends and family follow or condone. You may link Spirit with God, Goddess, Allah, the Universe, or the wildness of a wind-blown sea. To begin exploring, get your hands on books, from William James's classic *Varieties of Religious Experience* to the Dalai Lama's *The Art of Happiness.* Also see the Selected Reading section at the end of the book. Notice what descriptions of spirit intuitively resonate with you and scrap the rest. A part of you will feel curious, wake up, or affirm your discovery with a "Yes!" If, however, you're bored, untouched, or offended, keep on exploring.

In the same way, gauge your intuitive reactions when trying out different types of services. For instance, I'm consistently stirred by the low-key, nondressy Jewish High Holiday services at the Los Angeles Zen Center. (I attend these in addition to my Taoist path.) There's no pretense: we all sit on wobbly white plastic chairs in an outdoor garden. The rabbi is also a Zen roshi—and as it happens, an old college boyfriend! At the Passover dinner, celebrating emancipation from Egyptian slavery, I just melt watching a glowing monk punctuating the traditional "Four Questions" by striking a gong. Why is this night different than other nights? *GONG*. Why do we eat only Matzoh? *GONG*. Who'd believe it? We can't not giggle. And so it goes. We're a quirky conglomeration, and that suits me fine.

Similarly, you'll find an open-minded environment at the New Thought churches. I've been privileged to speak at many nationally. A safe refuge for the religiously traumatized, these churches embrace all forms of spirit and respect intuition. They're heartful, fun, with fabulous music and a variety of cross-denominational speakers.

Guideline #3: Know What a Spiritual Connection Feels Like

Don't convince yourself of anything. Go for where the energy is. How? You'll sense this connection in your body, whether it's a slight spark or a major epiphany. Expect to feel warm, comforted, uplifted. Intuitively, spiritual connection feels like a "coming to," a clearing. While meditating, I sometimes get shivers or goose bumps, or am moved to tears. Two specific subtle energy centers (chakras) drive this experience, the crown or "halo" at the top of your head, and the heart in the midchest. You might feel a growing heat in these areas, an opening, or sense a cap being lifted from the crown.

As you experiment with different practices, notice: Is something in you stirred? Do you feel more centered? Compassionate? It may be an instantly positive reaction—as Tennessee Williams writes, "Sometimes there is God so quickly." Whereas other practices may just feel wrong. With some, though, you may intuit a vague affinity, so stick with them a few weeks; see if the energy grows. There are also cycles of connection, times when we feel spiritual energy more or less. This is natural. Don't expect the peak moments to be sustained. Even if you never have one, don't worry. Bottom line, with a successful practice you'll feel more energy and love.

Guideline #4: Know What a Spiritual Connection Doesn't Feel Like

There isn't a mystery to this. Lack of spiritual connection is evidenced either by no energetic response (what I call spiritual flatlining) or an off-putting one. Your mind—or your mother!—may be trying to convince you of the merits of some path, but nada is happening. A positive energetic bond never needs to be coerced, nor does it make you feel worse about yourself. Guilt, judgment, and condemnation are all man-made—not a by-product of a compassionate intelligence.

Guideline #5: Flush Out Your Resistance

Opening to spirituality requires vulnerability, which can make you resistant or afraid, particularly if you've been disappointed by this issue before. It's important to articulate resistance and fears so they don't stonewall your energy. I want my patients to express the whole diatribe to me—an energetic purge that's necessary to find their own way. They've told me that they're resistant because spirituality can be elitist, dogmatic, repressive, abusive, saccharine, wishful thinking, not scientifically based, confined to conventional religions, or too "fire and brimstone." Whatever your reservation, honor it, but don't get mired there. Seek an apporach that feels right to you.

I treat a young stockbroker with chronic fatigue whose parents dabbled in everything from shamanism to Orthodox Judaism. Growing up, she was surrounded by a variety of spiritual paraphernalia and people. Their home served as base for rotating "gurus of the month," as my patient terms them. She loved her parents but, understandably, came to consider spirituality "flaky"—so she swore off of it. Starting Energy Psychiatry, she was desperately tired of being tired, ready to make a tentative reentry into this sphere. Though spirituality and religion were ruined words for her, she was open to having the experience of "whatever this is." So I kept it really simple: I taught her a heart-centered meditation (which you'll learn) to connect with love. She felt the boost, continued the practice. Love is an energy she increasingly cherishes. It helps buoy her spirits and lessen fatigue.

For years, one of my resistances was attaching myself to any spiritual tradition. I feared losing freedom, perhaps because of being raised by conservative physicians who very much wanted me to conform to the mainstream. I'll never forget one night as a teenager when my father, furious at me for sneaking off with hippie friends, chased me down our street like a madman, literally waving a yardstick! (How a yardstick was in his possession at that moment I'll never know!) Understandably, to this day, I loathe anything that smacks of measuring me.

Many of us fear being abandoned by Spirit if we open up. Once, after a really hard year, I despaired that I was losing my spiritual connection, which had always been as steady as Old Faithful. Then I had the most loving dream: A voice came to me that said, "Sometimes God holds your shoulders so lightly that you don't feel it." I awoke experiencing the utter truth of this in my bones, terribly grateful and relieved. Whenever my fear of spiritual abandonment creeps in, I remember my dream's message. I hope it brings you comfort too.

Be honest with your resistances. List them in a journal, or read them to someone you trust. Get ready to revamp or eliminate outdated notions. Give yourself full permission to transcend what didn't click for you spiritually in childhood and to reinvent a new way that works. Spirituality can help you access massive energy if you're willing to remove the obstacles that stunt your liberation.

HOWEVER YOU DEFINE spirituality, hundreds of scientific studies have shown it catalyzes energy. Research associates traditional religious practice with a decreased risk of heart disease, lowered blood pressure, and increased longevity. A National Institute on Aging study showed that geriatric patients were more active and less depressed if they attended regular spiritual services. Recently, an entire volume of the *Psychiatric Annals* was devoted to spirituality and patient care. Their verdict: the new generation of psychiatrists must be well versed about spirituality, which is already being taught in seventy-five American medical schools.

Spirituality is more than belief. It's a potent conductor of energy with real-world implications. Polls indicate that as many as 95 percent of Americans—hundreds of millions of people—believe in God; two out of five report having life-changing spiritual experiences. What a collective font of energy! Learning to activate spirituality and harness it for the good is a win-win proposition. You gain a lifetime energy source. Your health improves. You exude a lightness of being others can feel. Even if you've previously written spirituality off, I hope your experience in the Positive Energy Program can supplant any past debacles.

The following spiritual practices are everyday energy-shifting devices. They'll take you past the black hole of swirling thoughts and emotions to the larger terrain of the heart. Don't count on this happening spontaneously; you can get sidetracked in a flash. Accessing the boundless energy I'm talking about requires a well-strategized stance.

FOUR STEPS TO OPENING UP YOUR SPIRITUALITY

Step #1: Discover the Power of Meditation

I'm so pro-meditation, I'm convinced this practice can help solve a whole array of seemingly unfixable woes, personal and collective. In Energy Psychiatry I've seen how, many times, a problem cannot be solved on the problem's level. To achieve clarity, we often must see it from higher ground. Meditation lifts us there—out of the rat-maze of circular logic to a place of vistas.

Meditation is a technique of calming the mind to access energy and insight, utilized by traditions from Zen to Judaism. In this receptive, nonanalytic state, you're using more of your intuitive equipment, particularly those sensors that let you detect your higher power. Meditation has been proven to relieve pain and stress, and to boost our immune system. It also yields quick results. In just minutes, meditators have shown increased alpha activity—the relaxed brain waves—plus less anxiety and depression. Not to worry. You don't require an hour twisted in the lotus position to feel energized (though feel free to meditate as long as you want). A little quality time can revive you.

For we humans with overactive minds, meditation works by mercifully quieting inner chatter. Lucky for us. Scientific data prove that too much thinking can be exhausting, particularly as we age. We can think our life force right into the ground by depleting glucose, a key brain nutrient that sharpens memory and concentration. To recoup energy—and glucose—meditation offers a healthy relief from the drain of excessive thinking.

Everyone can meditate, though like some of my patients, you may be certain you can't. Over the years I've heard rocket scientists, cyberwizards, and others with hyperimpressive intellects swear, "It's hopeless. My mind just won't turn off." I'm proud to say I've proven them all wrong. Be careful not to misconstrue a busy mind for an inability to meditate. Inner chatter needn't hold you hostage.

As an energy psychiatrist, I serve as a kind of lifeguard of the heart. My duties include teaching meditation, a way to make our hearts grow. In the subtle realm, love resides in the heart chakra, a main energy storage and production site. It's about two inches in diameter, located in the midchest. (The physical heart is to its left.) In most of us this energy center lies dormant until triggered by outside forces such as meeting someone with whom we fall in love. That rush of warmth, wellness, or ecstasy is what we're yearning for. The heart has no boundaries. It's the place from which true power flows.

Opening your heart will nourish you and replenish your energy. I'm flabbergasted by how most of us graduate to adulthood without learning to consciously utilize the heart as an energy source. For me, the heart is a timeless sun that emanates energy, optimism, and healing. You must go within to find it, a happiness independent of externals. Then you can shine it everywhere.

Use the simple "Three-Minute Mini-Meditation" I suggest to open your heart. Geared for busy people who need quick tune-ups, it will help you counteract negative energy. The intention is to create a high-quality heart-focus in a short, uninterrupted period. Set a timer if necessary. Meditate for three minutes only! More is not better here. See how rapidly energy builds. In this meditation, you will once again follow your breath. The word *spirit* comes from the Latin, *spiritus,* to breathe, to give passage. Inhaling and exhaling provide a rhythmic focus to contact the sacred. For beginners, this meditation is a place to start. For the more experienced, a chance to deepen. Taking you beyond the boundaries of your conditioning, meditation reveals new forms of energy.

MAKE CHANGES NOW
OPEN YOUR HEART WITH THIS THREE-MINUTE
(ONLY!) MINI-MEDITATION

1. *Settle down in a peaceful place.* Separate yourself from any possible interruptions—phones, beepers, people. Then get comfortable. For example, prop yourself up in a cozy chair, warmed by the sun in your garden. My heaven is being submerged in a hot bath with candles all around. Make it as sensual as you like. Get very quiet. Relax your body. Slowly inhale. Then exhale. Allow your breath to bring you back to center.

2. *Gently rest your palm over your heart chakra.* Concentrate on a person, place, song, or memory you cherish. You may want to

start with nature. Visualize a sublime dawn. Or picture a puppy napping in your lap. If you prefer, focus on your higher power, whatever your definition. The purpose is to feel love in a general sense, then specifically as a localized energy in your midchest.

3. *Visualize any thoughts as clouds drifting in the sky.* As always during this practice, try to detach from thoughts; just let them float by as they pass in and out of your awareness. Keep returning to the breath to center yourself.

4. *Observe the sensations in your heart center, dramatic or subtle.* Heat. Coolness. Tingling. Vibration. Expansion. Bliss. Pressure releasing. Compassion. Let it happen. Don't hold back. With time, you'll feel a vortex of positive energy growing in your heart that spontaneously flows out into your body.

The "Three-Minute Mini-Meditation" is a lifelong reenergizing tool if you're tired, out of sorts, or need to increase your well-being. I depend on it to restore my grip on sanity in this insane world. It's easy to become devoured by negativity. Tuning into my heart lets me come from a more positive place. When I start slipping, I tune in again. The goal always: counteract negativity with love, the best medicine of all. Keep practicing the mini-meditation. I want you to know that you can depend on this energy-builder when life is so frantic you only have a few minutes to spare.

Though a serene setting is ideal, meditation is portable. Once you've got the hang of this technique, you can do it in phone booths, airports, parks. A friend meditates on a bus-stop bench beside the restaurant she owns, a handy escape from the daily lunchtime frenzy. (I'd be thrilled if a stall in every public bathroom was designated for quiet time and meditation!) Forget formality. Close your eyes, put your hand on your heart, then go for it. Mini-tune-ups are lifesavers. I meditate between patients to recenter, as a midafternoon lift from fatigue, and to restore composure if someone aggravates me.

Opening your heart with family can do miracles with turning around negative energy. My patient Zoe, a graduate student at thirty, was raised in a family known for venomous screaming matches. It'd gone on so long, they were all poised to fight. Recently Zoe told me, "I got into a nasty argument with my sister. I got defensive, started to explode. I wanted to kill her! But instead of wearing myself out with rage, I forced myself to close my bedroom door, and meditated on my heart for three minutes. This let me cool down and not attack back." Zoe has learned to use this strategy to ward off arguments. Also, once a family member can change, it disrupts the dysfunctional system. Zoe's move into her heart both spared her own energy and improved how her family relates.

Meditation is also a potent negativity diffuser at work. Watch how attorney Danny Sheehan uses it. As a civil litigator, Danny's crusade against corruption has repeatedly brought him to the front lines. He was there when his client, the *New York Times,* decided to print the Pentagon Papers, revealing secret government involvement in the Vietnam War. Later, he was the first witness before Congress to implicate Oliver North in the Iran-Contra scandal. He has tried cases against the Ku Klux Klan and the American Nazi Party.

Talk about confronting the negative! Imagine deposing the Grand Dragon of the Klan. The mere thought of looking into what Danny calls "reptilian eyes" makes my bones chatter. I wanted to know, "How do you stay energized and not let such negativity consume you?" Not at all self-important, he replied, "Spiritual practice and meditation." A graduate of both Harvard Law and Harvard Divinity School—surely a rare combination—Danny brings a spiritual sensibility to litigation. "To maintain an elevated perspective, I meditate each morning and evening. This keeps me attuned to a loving higher consciousness. It helps me concentrate, think a problem through, and also strengthens my energy to deflect negativity. If I don't meditate I'm emotionally shaggy. I lose my temper, become passionately inflamed. Despicable people get to me more."

Danny stresses, "When we're spiritually renewed, we're better able to perceive everyone with compassion, even a Grand Dragon." Be sure: Danny doesn't condone hate crimes, but he empathizes with the psychological damage that impels them. A peaceful heart would never wreak such destruction. Warrior in his field, Danny models how spiritual values organically inform social justice work. Without such values the danger is he'd resemble his enemy, perpetuating the negative energy he was combating.

No matter our profession or predicament, meditation helps us relax, center, and cultivate compassion, with exciting ramifications for our energy fields. Personally, you become a positive-vibe generator, and not only while meditating. People just fall in love with you. You develop a heart presence that puts others at ease. It can also trigger a chain reaction. Your loving energy sparks a coworker, who sparks a client, who sparks a boss: suddenly everyone is smiling. Now you know why.

You can use my meditation approach with negative people or spaces too. Your heart can transform the energy field of any environment. I've learned this well from years of giving talks on intuition to the statistics-equals-reality constituency of traditional physicians. Some staunch rationalists can feel so threatened by an "inexact science" that they go bonkers. I truly empathize with the fear behind such resistance, and have at some cost become expert in transmuting it. But to protect myself from such exhausting negativity—it can feel like rounds of energy bullets being fired at me—I must prepare.

Consider the time I was invited to speak at the American Psychiatric Association meeting. I was the very first "intuitive" and psychiatrist to be asked to give a workshop at their prestigious convention. Of course I was honored, but I didn't know what kind of reception I'd receive. This is where all the bigwigs in the profession go—the most conservative of the conservative. But thankfully there were the more open-minded too.

To conjure some positive energy in the drab hotel conference room, I arrived ten minutes early to meditate. Though it looked as if I was resting, I was really disseminating heart energy to add sweetness to the space. Then the psychiatrists, mostly older men properly suited-up, marched in. As I spoke, I was pleased to watch even the most rigid ones soften in this loving atmosphere, though I'm sure they didn't quite know what hit them. As always, a few arrows were shot, but overall the group left grateful to have learned new skills; a useful dialogue had begun. Of course I, too, felt grateful this connection had been made. It was an experience I will always treasure.

On a larger scale, potential collective gains from meditation are compelling. Studies at Fairfield University on Transcendental Meditation (which uses the repetitive phrases called mantras) showed that when a test group in high-crime neighborhoods regularly meditated on nonviolence, crime rates decreased. The stunning implications: the positive energy field emitted by meditators can be felt by people nearby. Picture a thief getting a whiff of that tranquil energy as he's about to vandalize your car. What a deterrent! Also consider the ramifications for world peace: the real possibility of overcoming violence with love by reconfiguring the negative energy field around people, cities, continents. Hatred leaves a residue of energetic pollution that meditation can help clear. Love invisibly insinuates itself in even the hardest of hearts. By consistently mobilizing it, as groups or individuals, we can potentiate a more peaceful atmosphere. Food for thought. Just know that your love travels far. Meditation, as a spiritual practice, is the launching pad.

Step #2: Nurture Yourself with Silence

I can never say enough about the power of silence! It is pregnant with positive energy, magnificently evident when noisy clutter disappears. Our spirit thrives on quiet, has vast spaces to breathe. Unobscured by noise, you can return to yourself, and the love you carry. In the quiet waits the divine. Silence, though, means more than not talking or watching television. It's a time-out from mental stimulation to partake from the well of energy within. Making silence part of your routine will revitalize you.

We may not realize the drain we can suffer from noise pollution. In our hectic lives, we can barely hear ourselves talk, let alone listen for our higher power. Sirens. Boom boxes. Jackhammers. We're inundated by noise. Sound can have a negative energy field we react to. On an unconscious level, we energetically seal ourselves off for protection. Instead of being open, we walk around defended. All this takes gigantic effort. Silence offers a healthy reprieve, gives a much-needed chance to recover. Oliver Wendell Holmes had it right: "Silence comes to heal the blows of sound."

Incessant talking also depletes our energy. From childhood we're taught to feel awkward around silence. A lull in conversation can seem intolerable. As if on cue, someone inevitably chimes in to break the silence, easing tension. Speech is a wondrous form of communication, but too much of it numbs us. Society's conspiracy against silence is counterintuitive to our energetic needs. A spiritual practice gently desensitizes your discomfort. It'll help you talk less, enjoy the energy from silence more. For me, silence is a relief, a space in which to collect my inward forces and diffuse negativity. With friends, I relish the pauses in conversation, and longer periods of being quiet together. Although this may be a new style of relating, in this program, I urge you to try it too.

MAKE CHANGES NOW

PLAN REGULAR SILENT TIME

Begin with at least five minutes of silence a day for the first week. Gradually build on that. Actively protect this respite—it's too easily stolen. Schedule this time in your planner with no interruptions. Make it sacred time, a break from e-mails, faxes, phones. I put a "Keep Out" sign on my office door, and anyone in the house knows not to come in. (I had a boyfriend who was so supportive of silence, he bought the sign at the hardware store for me.) If you have kids, plan to be silent when they're at school or arrange for your mate or babysitter to take them. Then you won't always have one ear open to their needs.

You can be silent in your office, hoeing your petunias, or gazing at the Milky Way. Like some of my patients, you can plan longer periods to be silent either alone, or with friends—away from the city's hubbub it's especially magical. (The Insight Meditation Center in Barre, Massachusetts, offers superb group silent retreats from a weekend to three months!) Silence isn't supposed to feel like a muzzle, or physically inhibit you. My patient Hilda, at seventy a social activist who refuses to sit still, communes with Spirit while walking the Santa Monica beach at dawn. Do whatever feels natural. Sit. Hike. Soak in a tub. Silence is meant to clear life's negative debris so that your energy can settle. With no noise distractions, Spirit is more easily sensed.

To quiet the overactive voices in your head, remember to breathe and to use the meditation techniques I've gone over. It may take a while to become at home with this practice, but with time it'll provide an enduring energy refuge.

As a psychiatrist, I understand our aversion to silence. Especially at first, it can feel odd not to talk—lonely, anxious, strained. You're used to being on the go. Your mind keeps nagging, "I'm wasting time. I have too much to do." Or you may encounter old fears. This is not your intuition—rather a knee-jerk response to unfamiliar terrain. To your task-oriented mind, being silent can feel like going to Timbuktu. Even many people who relish experimenting with the Positive Energy Program's other exercises resist being silent. Accordingly, I suggest you ease into this practice. (Some of my patients who'd felt the most skittish with silence now request that we begin each session in this meditative mode.) Once you know the replenishment of silence, the energy itself will be reinforcing.

You may even yearn for more. In a week-long workshop I gave at a remote Montana ranch, I had participants spend two days in silence. The intent was to connect deeply with a sense of Spirit and energy, without social distractions. Fifty lawyers, psychologists, switchboard operators, CEOs—all not saying a word. It was a delight watching them wander through acres of ponderosa pine, paired or alone. Such precious time, to be with oneself honing energy and inner power. When we reconvened, I was captivated by their experiences. Having led many of these workshops, I've developed a special soft spot for lawyers, who initially seem to get the most flummoxed. This time, one shared, "I felt like a dog squirming around trying to find the right position. I felt lost." The anxiety he and others felt typically turns into calm on the second day. Then more calm. Then joy, even bliss. When the silence ends everyone looks renewed, radiant—not supercharged from adrenaline, but strengthened by an inner fire.

I was never more struck by the potency of silence than after the World Trade Towers assault. A few days later, in reverence for the terrible loss of life, one minute of synchronized silence was called for around the globe. That evening on television I was in tears watching a montage of film clips: members of Congress, people on the streets, crowds in front of Buckingham Palace and the Eiffel Tower, all silent. In the faces was sorrow, but also profound love. For sixty seconds, silence amplified the hearts of the world.

Step #3: Open to the Energy of Prayer

Beyond the miracle of this planetwide silence, it was undeniable that in response to terrorism there was also planetwide prayer. It happened instantly across races, ethnicities, and religions. Even in this moment of despair, one saw an extraordinary universal reaction. Clearly, this was an instinctive gathering of the positive against the horrific. Prayer was the world's immediate attempt to transmute unthinkable negative energy, a vast impulse toward peace.

Prayer is an attitude of the heart, a reaching to the divine. It reattunes you to the positive, the way a tuning fork gives correct pitch. Prayer brings love closer, energy you can resonate with. When you're confused or tired, love can feel far away. To pray is an act of opening to love, then of being filled. Poet C. K. Williams writes: "I'd empty like a cup; that would be prayer, to empty, then fill with a substance other than myself." Through prayer we are infused with energy.

A national survey reported that nine out of ten people pray, and nearly all feel their prayers are answered. One thing is certain: there's a lot of praying going on—many, many kinds. Catholics say the rosary. Jews daven. Protestants use centering prayers. Muslims practice *salat,* prayers five times a day. My patient Jerry, a banker who's "allergic to formal religion," prays "from my heart to the universe in a sanctuary of eucalyptus." However you pray, it must feel alive.

Prayer increases positive energy in specific ways:

- **PHYSICALLY**: Nearly 1,200 studies have been done on how prayer improves health. Harvard scientist Dr. Herbert Benson found that it initiates a relaxation response: heart rate, breathing, and metabolism slow down, promoting healing and boosting your immune system. People who pray get sick less often. Columbia University also showed that women in a fertility clinic were almost twice as likely to get pregnant when, without their knowledge, complete strangers prayed for their success.

- **EMOTIONALLY**: The relaxation response during prayer has been shown to reduce stress, so you're more optimistic. Your link to a higher power lends purpose and meaning that makes life worthwhile.

- **ENERGETICALLY:** Prayer, as an expression of goodness and love, opens your heart, activating healing vibes throughout the body. It tips the energy balance from negative to positive by instilling hope, well-being, and compassion.

- **SPIRITUALLY:** You establish ongoing contact with a higher power, whether perceived as "out there" or "in here," which allows you to access an energy reserve larger than yourself.

In my medical practice, I've been awed by how our prayers can also help others heal. My scope as an energy psychiatrist often reaches beyond my actual sessions with patients. In certain situations, prayer is the most powerful intervention I can make. (I always provide it when needed unless a patient says otherwise.) I've prayed for patients undergoing surgery or chemo, or in coma. Also for those with pain or illness. My intuitive prayer-process is that I get very quiet, and close my eyes while focusing totally on the person. I feel her with my heart, and articulate a prayer such as, "May she heal speedily and without suffering." I can sense loving energy cranking up in my chest as warm waves emanate from me into the invisible realm with impeccable direction. Many patients have independently said, "I could feel prayer lifting me over a hump so I could get well faster." One man in coma after an auto accident said he felt my presence near him, urging him toward consciousness. This elegant energy we call prayer has more functions than medical science knows.

Our prayers are not isolated acts. They generate an energy field that the prayed-for person can benefit from at a distance. Cardiologist Randolph Byrd found in his groundbreaking study of cardiac patients that those prayed for had a higher survival rate, required fewer antibiotics, and had fewer complications than the group not prayed for. I never cease to be amazed by such findings: the energy of our prayers can affect the energy of someone else's body. Over the years, having prayed for many patients, friends, and family, some in dire circumstances, I've seen that it can augment recovery.

As part of this prescription, I'd like you to try prayer, keeping an eye on how it affects your energy or another's. You can pray in a religious sense, or not. The point of prayer is to link you with love and make it travel to a target. Conceiving of it this way may make it easier to for you to contact a compassionate energy larger than the personal. Don't get stuck in terminology. Send love outward, and watch the results.

MAKE CHANGES NOW
PRAY WITH AN OPEN HEART

Take a few calm moments to lovingly center yourself and focus on what you're praying for. Choose any prayer position you like. Some of my patients wouldn't be caught dead on their knees again—they associate it with being coerced into a religious straitjacket that didn't feel right to them. (When I pray, the flatter and closer to the ground the better. It's a position that magnetizes me.)

Try praying for health, love, joy—either personally, for others, or the planet. Such prayers aren't sacrilegious or inappropriate. Or you could simply ask for the highest good, not presuming what that might be. This requires a trust that your needs will be met, but perhaps not as you'd envisioned.

Be aware: prayer's positive energy is often cumulative. Social injustice might not be instantly defeated, but our ongoing prayers tip the balance toward success. Let prayer energize you. Then feel your prayer take flight into the ether, heading toward the person or situation you named.

Realize, though, that prayer may not always cure every dilemma or disease. Psychiatrist Elisabeth Targ, pioneer in the healing energy of prayer, lived this intimately. Shortly after receiving a grant to examine the effects of prayer on a rare form of brain cancer, incredibly, she was diagnosed with this same cancer herself. A few months later, it took her life at forty. I believe that Elisabeth somehow unconsciously foresaw this possibility, and was setting up an experiment to heal both others and herself. I'd known her for years, had great respect for the intuition she consistently showed professionally and personally. Friends started praying for Elisabeth, but were our efforts too little, too late? Perhaps. Or else, perhaps there's a Mystery that knows more about such sychronicities than any of us. I don't presume to understand the whys or wherefores, but I do know this Mystery exists. And I am sure Elisabeth was held in its arms, while alive and always. Ultimately, this could prove the greatest blessing of all.

Also, as I remember our prayers for Elisabeth, I remind myself we don't always get what we pray for. Though I've come to grasp the intelligence of this, I've done my share of railing against it. The wise irony of the poet Rumi's words continues to sink in: "I plot to get what I want and end up in prison. . . . I should be suspicious of what I want." For example, at thirty-nine, my biological clock had become a time bomb. I desperately wanted children, but my relationships always seemed to fall apart. Being a single mother didn't feel right. So I prayed for a man I could have children with. The clock kept ticking. I prayed. Still, no one. At forty, I'd had it with prayer. I figured, "If my dearest wish hasn't been granted, there isn't a God. Fine. I won't believe in one." The strange part was, my declaration of disbelief didn't matter. Much as I tried, I couldn't shake the sense of the same loving energy that had always been there. I hadn't gotten what I'd wanted, yet the bond was stronger than ever.

Today I have the life of my dreams—teaching, seeing patients, time for friendships, love, meditation. It's a balancing act, but I can do it. With children, the way I utilized my energy would have been different. I'm not saying I wouldn't have had a good life. It just wouldn't have been the one I have now.

The Serenity Prayer, my mantra, helps me intuit when it's appropriate to accept a situation—whether my ego likes it or not—or strive for change. The prayer's message speaks volumes about energy, the graceful interplay of the personal and the spiritual: when to act, when to let go. (Your higher power won't leave you stranded!) Then we can make discerning use of resources and time. I keep these spare, potent words taped to my refrigerator door:

> *God, grant me the serenity to accept the things I cannot change, the courage to change the things I can, and the wisdom to know the difference.*

I consider this my "flare prayer"—no big to-do about saying it. It's quick, to the point, effective; when necessary, I repeat it many times a day. The Serenity Prayer's strength is in addressing our power as well as our limitations; we're let off the hook of having to be super-human. Wisdom dictates: We do what we can to change things for the good—personally or globally—but we don't waste energy trying to bulldoze the impenetrable. As a regular practice, I suggest you say this prayer too, to teach yourself to channel your energy wisely. But also realize that where you may be limited, your higher power is not.

Prayer can create miracles. Several years ago, Buddhist priests in a South Korean temple reported tiny white flowers blooming on the statue of Quan Yin, beloved Goddess of Compassion. A first in the monastery's thousand-year history. Botanists say it's impossible that a wooden statue, regularly refinished, can produce flowers. Nonetheless, pilgrims were flocking to view them. Monks kept a prayer vigil by the statue, performing healings, and saw the flowers as an auspicious sign for our troubled planet. If you're not the type to believe in miracles, you can write this off as a fluke. But there the Goddess of Compassion's flowers were. I couldn't help but feel the wonder. And the hope: where there's compassion, there's peace.

Step #4: Trust the Wisdom of Flow

Flow is perfect attunement with a larger-than-self energy that carries us through our lives. I view this energy as Spirit, compassionate and wise. Trusting the wisdom of flow means going with what's presented to us as gracefully as possible, rather than flailing around in opposition. Our life's flow propels us in certain directions. Of course, we do everything possible to create optimal outcomes, but we also must know when to ease off. The art is learning to go where the current takes you rather than maniacally micromanaging every detail of your existence. If you've ever swum against a powerful ocean current, you know how your energy can be futilely depleted. The same thing happens when you fight the flow in life.

Going with the flow safeguards your life force. Thus, to keep flowing, you have to know when something is in your power to control or not. The Serenity Prayer helps clarify this, as do the deep-listening practices of meditation, silence, and prayer. I'll offer other ways too. As you try them, please appreciate: Letting go doesn't mean giving up. It's having the sense to know when it's optimal to explore new possibilities. This frees energy, whereas forcing breeds negativity. If you can't directly influence external events, you can always influence your attitude.

Producer Norman Lear exemplifies how going for what you believe in keeps you in the flow. During our interview he said,

> *If something excites me I jump on it. Take* All in the Family. *I got the idea from a British show about a father and son-in-law who fought about everything. I thought, 'My God, that was my dad and me.' So I fell in love with the idea. I didn't know it would be a smash. But there was a larger force at work too. It was a miracle that four actors were available who turned out to have chemistry no one could've imagined. That's in the lap of the Gods. Energy came from every direction. Edith with Gloria. Gloria with Mike. Mike with Archie. How do I explain this? Emerson said, 'We live in the lap of an immense intelligence and we are receptors.' It was this little group of receptors that took the energy from the Gods. That's what flow can be.*

Sometimes, though, you may believe in yourself but try too hard. One of my patients, who'd named himself Z, wanted his boy-band to make it big. At nineteen, a gentle, pierced-tongued punk rocker who wore a T-shirt saying "Planet Weird," Z had hit every dive from Seattle to L.A. According to reviews, Z could really play guitar; record labels had begun to seek him out. But each time he'd come close to a deal, it'd fall through. Despite these excruciating letdowns, Z not only persevered but became obsessed. He told me, "I wouldn't take no for an answer, despite what anybody said. I made people nervous. I was turning them off but couldn't stop myself. Finally I burned out and collapsed in bed depressed." That's what led Z to me. I felt for him. I know the physical and emotional exhaustion that comes from being overinvested in something you desperately want. He'd fallen into a common trap; Z crossed a line; the death grip of too-relentless an ambition strangled the possibility of achieving it.

Here's a basic law of energy: To realize your dreams, you must give them some breathing room. Do the footwork—but also stand back a little, let the universe work its magic. Usually Z was antipsychiatry and "programs" of any kind, but I slipped past his censors. My intuitive approach to energy fit with how he experienced music. Our sessions focused on Z finding energetic balance, with an emphasis on tuning in to flow. At first, he was too splayed to even pick up his guitar. But with rest, and moderation of his maniacal will, Z's energy returned. In therapy, one nonnegotiable truth I underscored was that going with the flow creates positive energy; going against it creates negative energy. To know the difference, I helped Z recognize certain signs that I'd like you to watch for too:

INTUITIVE SIGNS YOU'RE IN THE FLOW

- You're happy, or at least able to accept what is, without engaging in an unrelenting internal battle.
- You go after what you want, but back off if you're pushing too hard—dodging that tense, obsessive sense of being in overdrive.
- Your energy is high; you have an ease in relating with people and

yourself. If conflicts arise, you breathe deeply, work toward resolution instead of getting rigid or retaliating.

- Hours pass, and you may not even notice. Kids get into a flow-consciousness when playing, artists when creating.

- You evaluate the timing of situations, rather than simply trying to break doors down.

- You feel like you're coasting in a deeply spiritual state because you're trusting the energy of the Now.

There's an energetic line between happiness and misery that you must recognize. When you go beyond being healthily assertive to forcing the flow, you immerse yourself in a form of insanity in which you do something over and over again with the same negative results.

INTUITIVE SIGNS YOU'RE PUSHING AGAINST THE FLOW

- Your well-being suffers; your energy is frazzled, physical symptoms are aggravated, you're impatient or desperate. A constant uphill battle can make you sick, instigate a cycle of frustration, blockages, and emotional pain.

- You can't tolerate giving the issue you're fixated on a rest without feeling tremendous anxiety.

- Others are irritated by your pushing, and relationships linked with the desired outcome are strained.

- You deal with conflict by fighting it and clenching, instead of working toward the best possible compromise. In unavoidable, stressful situations you hate every minute of the "ordeal"—rather than flowing with it—and thus inflict suffering on yourself or others.

- You feel an overall drain on your life force. You cling fearfully to self-will, and lose temporary touch with a compassionate intelligence, your Higher Power.

In the Positive Energy Program, paying attention to these signs about flow gives you a choice in how to behave. It did for Z. Like many of us, it wasn't that he didn't want to go with the flow. He simply got swept up in a frenzy with no tools to counter it. These days, Z's a flow devotee; it fuels him. Z likes where the flow is leading. The promise of new people, opportunities: he's hopeful, but not as fixated. He's begun to allow something larger than himself to carry him to his dreams.

MAKE CHANGES NOW: FLOW, DON'T CLENCH

Identify an area of your life you are struggling with—where you're pushing, but not getting desired results. For at least one week, cease and desist "making things happen." Do your best to tolerate the anxiety it may cause. During the time-out, list all your "what-if-this-never-happens" fears. For instance, I'll never get love, success, or recognition. Then inwardly ask Spirit, however you conceive of it, to lift these fears from you—a process of energetic unburdening. Be ready for relief. Repeat this as much as you like. It clears the way to feel where flow wants to take you.

Also, to groove with the flow, practice doing what you're given in a day without complaining. In addition, say the Serenity Prayer regularly and listen to your intuition—not just your head. Then see what new insights you gain about the blocked issue. You may discover a more effective approach to take, or decide not to move forward until the tides are more favorable. Either way, your choice will come from a flow-centered place.

Energy moves in mysterious ways. You may labor on projects for years, yet nothing externally affirming happens. Then suddenly energy changes. There's an explosion of opportunities. Or you may notice a wave phenomenon. In one week you get a new job, a new boyfriend, and payment of a long-owed debt. Energy has many phases. Just because your dreams aren't manifesting now doesn't mean they never will. There's an integrity to how our lives flow. Releasing attachment to expectations takes you to places grander than you envisioned.

Risk trusting the flow. Whether it's bumpy or smooth, take every chance to nurture your heart or be loving to another. Spasming around negativity steals stamina and insight. Savvy body-surfers know to relax when massive waves crash on top of them. If they fight the flow, they'll be ravaged by the force. If they don't tense up, they fly though the waves. Similarly, we must remember there are cycles to life: turbulent and calm, dark and light. Try to breathe deeply through it all. It's vital to constructively direct your energy.

THE POSITIVE ENERGY PROGRAM'S Second Prescription—find a nurturing spiritual path—presents you with a loving day-to-day theology of energy. Beyond any specific beliefs, I'm advocating a full-souled plunge into the experience of the heart—knowing love from an energetic view that supercedes intellectualization. Consider the spiritual practices of meditation, silence, prayer, and flow as compass points toward love. Even when you're floundering, your heart energy is a mighty defense against dark forces. When a monster—our own or someone else's—looks goodness in the face, it becomes aware of its own ugliness. A spiritual path is a way to keep cultivating goodness. You may feel afraid yet still you close your eyes, and reconnect. This is no small action; it's a gargantuan energetic leap.

Our species' survival is contingent on the awakening of the heart. Nothing vague or theoretical about it. We must become intimately versed in the energy of love. You can't afford to be a stranger to this realm, or put love on hold because you're too busy. These days we need all the heroes we can find. Activating this love is both heroic and revolutionary. It illuminates your positive energy and all that is good here on Earth. Brightness, by nature, expands. Remember Emerson's words: "Thou art enlarged by thy own shining."

Treat Yourself:

Visit your favorite special place: the ocean, hot springs, a secret backyard alcove. Then close your eyes, and make a wish or say a prayer (personal or for the world), straight from the heart to your higher power. Let this loving energy permeate you.

INTERVIEW: AMY GROSS ON MEDITATION

AMY GROSS IS EDITOR-IN-CHIEF OF *O: THE OPRAH MAGAZINE*
AND A PRACTICING BUDDHIST.

✳

My meditation practice has helped build my energy and create a more compassionate, positive way of responding to others. It's provided access to what's going on inside me in a much clearer way. In any situation I'm better able to pick up the truth, so that saves lots of energy. I'm far less confused. I'm not going left-right, left-right when the answer is forward. There's much more of me available when I'm with people.

I practice Vipassana insight meditation. The focus is on getting as close as possible to the truth of this moment. I prefer not to use the word *spirituality,* which probably means something different to everyone. I start by sitting and paying attention to my breath. I try to observe my mind, to really stay in the moment. If a thought comes, instead of trying to push it away, I look at it. Then it shifts. A huge amount of our brain energy is spent trying to block things out. The other day I was walking down the street with a friend and heard rap music blaring from a car. It took so much energy to put this out of our consciousness, we couldn't keep track of our conversation. It was exhausting. In my meditation practice, nothing is an interruption. I observe my thoughts, but I don't judge them or act on them. When you're not expending effort fighting things off, you have much more energy left over.

In the magazine business, where there's always so much going on, I use my practice to center myself. If I don't meditate, my energy dissipates. I get edgy. A raggedy feeling. Scattered. Since I've been meditating I'm much more patient, not nearly as reactive. I'm still doing five things at once, but I've got a lot more energy to give.

My interests in meditation aligned me with the mission of the magazine—Oprah's values. I think the magazine's strength is that we're all on the same page about what we feel is important, which is apparently in harmony with a lot of people out there. When this job came up, I was very happily not working much. I was taking a psychology course at NYU, thinking about going back for a master's degree. I was reading. I was studying. I loved it. I'd spent my whole life postcollege doing magazine work, including being editor of *ELLE* and *Mirabella*. It wasn't a challenge to me anymore. But when I met Oprah and she offered me the job, I knew I had to take it. I was really clear: there was no question, no agonizing. I was totally in sync with the magazine. Oprah's exhilarating to be around. Very high wattage. An incredible intelligence and sense of purpose. We started talking as if we'd known each other for years. It was just really easy, comfortable, and fun.

To replenish my energy I love to be quiet at home. (Oprah talks about escaping into her "closet," though her closet is probably the size of my office.) I also regularly plan retreats away. In the beginning of a new magazine, it's hard to take time off. This year I've been on a one-week-long silent retreat. I'm scheduling a ten-day silent retreat later on, and I slip in a few days at a time here and there. Silence is medicine. After a draining day, the silence in my apartment feels like a balm, this softness surrounding and filling me. It's the most delicious thing in the world. I have a saying on my wall, from a friend who's a psychotherapist: "My remedy for everything is to be quiet." The older I get, the more valuable silence becomes.

Energy also increases when your heart is open. There's a special lovingkindness meditation that has helped me with this. It begins, "May I be happy. May I be healthy. May I be safe. May I live with ease." It then goes on to wish the same for other people. Meditation trains you to recognize when your heart is open or shut off. When mine is open, I feel harmony, energized, happy. When it clamps down, I feel like I'm cutting off my circulation. The radiant feeling leaves. It physically hurts. As our hearts open during meditation, our kindness toward ourselves and others grows. It gets energy moving so we can have more of it.

3

THE THIRD PRESCRIPTION: DESIGN AN ENERGY-AWARE APPROACH TO DIET, FITNESS, AND HEALTH

ENERGY PSYCHIATRY can revolutionize your approach to wellness.

It did for Liz, a heroic social worker counseling death-row inmates in the inferno of an Alabama men's prison. Working there the past five years, Liz had failed diet after diet. Severely overweight, she was desperate by the time she traveled cross-country to my workshop on energy: "Every doughnut seems to have my name on it. I can't control my eating! I lose weight, then it creeps back on!" I quickly developed respect for Liz. She'd tried like a trooper to heal why she binged: family strife; equating food with love; the daily angst of confronting inmates who'd committed heinous crimes, seeing in them the smaller savageries all humans are capable of. Despite admirable progress, including more self-compassion—lacerating herself less— she'd have demoralizing lapses when she ate. And ate.

Here's where Energy Psychiatry saved the day. In my practice, I've identified a previously undefined but widely prevalent eating disorder that's energetically based. Until we address it, food abuse by many adults and children simply cannot be solved. What Liz and most of us don't realize is that overeating often constitutes an unconscious defense, an attempt to buffer negative energy at work, home, school, anywhere. Liz had drained all her energy reserves. Her beyond-strenuous job was her life's passion, but she needed tools to help her avoid absorbing the despair that oozed from the energy fields of both murderers and guards. For Liz, these indispensable tools, along with learning to eat with attunement, were the "miracles" that broke the horrific cycle of her energetic eating disorder.

Liz's situation was extreme, but you may well face an energy-overwhelming scenario that drives you to overeat. Perhaps you've been stuck in some nightmare slump about food or another wellness concern. Energy Psychiatry offers breakthroughs, facilitating awareness of both the physical as well as energy fields, a domain still alien to conventional wisdom. In this prescription, you'll grasp the ways that diet, exercise, how you sleep, and who you sleep with shape your subtle energies. By choosing what affirms your whole self, you'll feel and look healthier, a striking congruity that prevents a scattering of focus. (My read on people with "perfect bodies" but stunted inner growth is that they're energetically distorted, off-kilter.) When your insides match your outsides, positive energy increases; you emanate wholeness in an erratic world.

Extraordinary times require extraordinary health. To actualize the best in ourselves and humanity, our immune system must be robust. If we're ill, we'll need to cope and heal. Even if you've failed miserably at various wellness makeovers, put the past behind you. Allow yourself to assimilate the new data I'm presenting. Then follow what makes inner sense; it's the gospel for me.

WHY DIETS FAIL: DO YOU HAVE AN ENERGETIC EATING DISORDER?

Humans beings are watery creatures; we're two-thirds water. Sound waves, movement, and the tides pulled by the moon's gravitational force ripple through us. Similarly, we're permeated by subtle energy, too. A glaring void in traditional weight-loss programs is a recognition of our reaction to the subtle realms. At any age, when weight becomes a subconscious weapon against negative energy, an eating disorder can result. I've defined and named this disorder Energy-Defensive Eating. Think of Brünnhilde, the famously fat Viking warrior—an armored woman with a winged helmet and spear—who became an untouchable tank. ("It ain't over until the fat lady sings" refers to her Wagnerian operatic finale, and to a long lineage of overweight opera-divas.) Trouble is, obesity may offer the illusion of protective armor, or act as the sole knee-jerk barrier to threat. This program offers healthier alternatives to counteract Energy-Defensive Eating.

Of course, multiple factors contribute to obesity. Genetics plays a role, as do emotional triggers. It's crucial to uncover the psychological roots of overeating, and also to find nourishment for emotional hunger other than food (such as spirituality, the basis of Overeaters Anonymous). But don't stop there. For many, discovering that you're an intuitive empath may provide the missing key to emotional binge-ing, and how to stop Energy-Defensive Eating. Chronic bingers like Liz are intuitive empaths—she answered "yes" to every question on Chapter 1's "Am I an Intuitive Empath?" quiz. (I advise parents to ask overweight children these questions.) If you struggle with weight, see if you identify yourself as an empath on this quiz. Whether your sensitivity to vibes is minimal or intense, for a diet to succeed you must determine if you experience Energy-Defensive Eating.

Here's the energetic premise of obesity: When empaths are thin, they have less padding, are more vulnerable to soaking up untoward vibes. Early-twentieth-century faith healers were renowned for being grossly obese to avoid absorbing their patients' symptoms—a common trap I've seen modern-day healers unconsciously fall into; food is a convenient grounding device. Similarly, many of my patients pack on pounds to protect themselves against overwhelming vibes. Energy imbalance is at the root of an empath's hunger.

The third prescription offers many overeaters the Holy Grail: how to cope with negative vibes without abusing food. In this chapter, I'll describe emergency and long-term interventions to combat Energy-Defensive Eating. You can apply them immediately, whether accosted by an angry colleague or a global threat. Try them all, and stick to those that work best for you.

MAKE CHANGES NOW

HALT ENERGY-DEFENSIVE EATING

When the impulse to overeat hits, try some of the following emergency interventions.

- *Distinguish an addictive craving from a true need.*

  - Addictive craving, a symptom of nutritional abuse, is a frequent response to energetic overload. You feel compelled to eat certain foods like a drug addict, leading to obesity. The cravings feel intense: whenever you keep lusting after sweets and carbs especially, be suspicious. (I've yet to see someone binge on brussel sprouts!) For instance, chocolate turns from simple pleasure to crutch when you gorge on it, use it to self-medicate stress, or to get a sugar high. You're eating addictively if you experience mood swings, sugar hangovers, can't control your intake, or feel sick afterward. With cravings, you eat to relieve stress, not to build energy. You may be able to indulge in addictive "comfort foods" occasionally with no harm. One friend craves a chocolate square when she's premenstrual—her body is seeking the antidepressant serotonin found in chocolate—but doesn't devour the whole bar. You may be the type, however, for whom even limited intake sets off a destructive, downhill cycle. For now, identify which foods prompt addictive cravings, try to limit them, and practice these emergency interventions to thwart the cravings that do arise. Later, you'll learn how to eat with attunement, a longer-term solution.

- A true nutritional need lacks the *Sturm und Drang* of an addictive craving: there's no lusting or lunging for food to guard against negative energies. A true need comes from a centered place, has nothing to do with soothing your emotions (comfort foods) or obsession. For instance, you may prefer the taste of mashed potatoes to cauliflower, but you eat the potatoes in a balanced way, not to anesthetize anxiety. Eating healthful, nurturing food never causes mood swings—sedation or elation—rather an even feeling of satisfaction. Gratifying a true need lets you enjoy your meal, optimizes energy, and doesn't lead to obesity.

- *Quickly pinpoint energetic stressors that trigger addictive cravings.* Immediately ask yourself: Have I been exposed to bad vibes? A loud-mouth neighbor? The ordeal of passing through airport security? A siege of overbearing phone messages from my mother?

  Don't write off the "smaller" incidents which notoriously send empaths motoring to the refrigerator. Avoid panic. Methodically pinpoint cause and effect. You don't have to be victimized by negative energy. The trick is to clear it as soon as possible once you've been slimed.

- *Breathe negative vibes out of your system.* Take a five-minute break for damage control. Slowly inhale and exhale. As you've learned, breath activates positive energy; it also releases negative vibes. Notice if they get stuck in a specific part of your body. For instance, negative vibes go straight to my gut; I feel irradiated by a toxic stun gun. Identify your vulnerable points. Then practice the following visualization:

  Just as your lungs take in oxygen and expel toxic carbon dioxide, you're going to breathe in light and clarity, breathe out stress. Breathe in vitality. Breathe out fear. I also visualize negative vibes exiting through the spaces between

the vertebrae in my lower back. You can try this too.
Breathing out toxic vibes is a proactive cleansing process.
You're in charge of the flow. Allow well-being to permeate
every inch of you. Repeat this exercise until you're free of
negative residue. (Also use this with Chapter 1's "Breathing
and Centering" meditation.)

- *Pray to release the addictive craving.* If you're gripped by a
  craving, go into praying mode. For a few quiet moments,
  breathe slowly. Bring your awareness to your heart, and aim for
  self-compassion. The craving may feel impossible to handle, but
  that's okay. In this calm state, ask your higher power to lift it
  from you. No mental nudging needed. If you surrender your
  ego-involvement, this simple heartfelt request works like a
  charm. What you're doing is calling on a cosmically influential
  positive energy to supplant a material-world negative drive.

- *Take a bath or shower.* A speedy way to dissolve negative vibes is
  to immerse yourself in water. My tub is my refuge after a busy
  day: it washes away everything from bus exhaust to long hours
  of air travel, to personal unpleasantness. Water works on you
  while you relax. It has alchemical cleansing properties that will
  purify your physical body and energy field.

- *Burn sage.* Just because vibes are invisible doesn't mean they
  don't make you overeat. Try burning sage to counteract the
  negative energy someone deposits in your office or home—a
  strategy that has kept pounds off my patients who have a lot of
  people invading their space. Sage comes in the form of "smudge
  sticks," which are available in New Age stores. Burning a few
  small stems of sage in a plate can purify a room. Vibes
  accumulate, can cause stress if not eradicated. You may not
  realize that leftover subtle energies trigger addictive eating

patterns, but these vibes subliminally wear at you. Sage has been used by ancients cross-culturally to purify locations. Burn it, and the desire to eat because of lurking negative vibes will wane.

Food is no place to be passive. These emergency interventions offer the first line of attack against Energy-Defensive Eating. You don't have to let poisonous energy lodge itself in you. To stay on top of your eating, do a daily check-in. Stay alert for cravings prompted by negative vibes. Watch your responses. Also, combine the above interventions with the options I'll describe in Chapter 9 to combat energy vampires, a companion problem. Below, I'll present long-term interventions for Energy-Defensive Eating that teach you to tune into the vibes of food.

FINDING A DIET THAT WORKS: HOW TO EAT WITH ATTUNEMENT

Do you eat to appease a craving? Chase a sugar high? Stifle boredom, loneliness, or anxiety? You may be suffering from a subtle energy deficiency, a hugely overlooked reason why diets fail. Whatever diet you choose—high-protein, low-carb; low-fat; low-calorie—can't fully satisfy you if it doesn't build subtle energy, and most of them don't. To discover what truly nurtures you, you must pinpoint foods you attune with and which support your subtle system.

Food is a primary energizer: it's downright negligence that most psychotherapists aren't schooled in this core aspect of mental and physical health. For many of my patients, especially teenagers, food carries a hyperintense emotional charge. Initially, some can't even bear talking about it—they get that anxious. In our culture, so much shame and confusion revolves around weight. Given this, it's no surprise that supermarkets are a notorious site for panic attacks. Part of the panic, though, stems from lack of information about the energetics of diet, which can demystify this mortifying, painful problem.

I want you to think of food differently. Mechanically, we ingest food as fuel and use it for energy, but the benefits of eating go beyond kilocalories: food contains the subtler essence of life force, which we also metabolize. This force forms an energy field in and around everything from cantaloupe to trout. We are starving for high-energy foods, not just quick carbohydrate fixes.

Of course, for a well-rounded diet, you have to balance protein, carbohydrates, and fat. Also, to reduce heart disease, you need to stick to unsaturated fats such as those in olive oil, salmon, and sardines. These increase "good" cholesterol, and reduce saturated fats, the "bad" cholesterol from meat, cheese, and other high-fat dairy products. (*Dr. Dean Ornish's Program for Reversing Heart Disease* is a superb dietary guide.) But for optimal health, you must also feel energetically sated by what you eat. By combining foods that build subtle energy with good-sense nutrition, you can design a "high-vibe" customized food plan.

I'm going to guide you through the steps of eating with attunement, an intuitive strategy to augment subtle energy and combat Energy-Defensive Eating. Food is alive inside you, not just an inert substance you ingest. As an intuitive, I read food as I would any life form. This diet will show you how to reorient your eating in energetic terms. The beauty is that you'll feel healthier, and find a weight that really suits you.

SEVEN STEPS TO EATING WITH ATTUNEMENT

Step #1: Take a Food Inventory

Make a survey of what's currently on your shelves. Are they lined with bags of potato chips or processed foods? Is your freezer stacked with pepperoni pizzas? Is your refrigerator brimming with fresh vegetables, but devoid of chicken, fish, or meat? Ask yourself why you've fallen into these buying/eating habits. Are they based on what your parents used to serve or deny you? Tantruming children having their way at the market? Obsessive dieting crazes? A hectic schedule? Also reflect on if you feel better or worse after eating these products. If you're on a special diet, how is your energy affected? Attend not only to how food tastes but to how it alters your well-being.

Step #2: Eat for Energy

This is the motto of our food program. I'd like energy to become the raison d'être of why you eat, more important than taste or any dietary dogma—a priority to impart to children. It'll take some reconditioning, but give it a try. Whatever you put in your mouth, run by your energy meter; see what truly nourishes or depletes you. I've been lucky; I mainly eat this way. Maybe because my doctor mother served me delicious, healthy meals—not restricting anything or rewarding me with treats—I'd no reason to sneak or rebel. Whatever your food history, I'll train you in this dietary stance. Even foods you've shunned become more attractive when you experience their energy lift.

Step #3: Recognize Alive from Dead Food

To glean the most positive energy from food, you must reorient how you look at it. Don't be fooled by appearance. The most obvious example is the tomato. Superficially, all tomatoes may appear the same, but in terms of subtle energy, some are alive, others are dead. How do you know? Try an experiment. Put a supermarket tomato— that pitiful orange tennis ball wrapped in cellophane—beside an organic or homegrown tomato. (Organic foods, though slightly more expensive, are available at health food stores, farmer's markets, and most large markets in the "Organic Produce" section.) First, take a bite of the mass-market tomato. How do you feel? To me, this kind of tomato is an android imposter without fragrance. It's tasteless, I get no pleasure or boost from it. Now compare it with the organic tomato: I savor every morsel of this vibrant vegetable. Get used to feeling the food's life force in you, a satisfaction the following steps will deepen.

A QUICKIE GUIDE TO ACCESS THE LIFE-FORCE CONTENT OF FOOD

POSITIVE-ENERGY FOODS (ALIVE FOODS): Radiate a glow, are fragrant, filling, energizing, organic, chemical and preservative-free. They won't give you the impulse to overeat.

NEGATIVE-ENERGY FOODS (DEAD FOODS): Appear limp or tired, lack fragrance, are unsatisfying, sap energy or add none, contain preservatives and chemicals or are enriched; make you bloated or ill; stimulate overeating and sugar/carbohydrate binges.

Step #4: Visually Tune in to the Energy of Food

Food is constantly talking to you, but you must know how to listen. You're going to visually intuit the energy of food to tell if it's dead or alive for you. Sensing in this way enables you to create a diet you resonate with, one that won't seduce you with addictive cravings.

Like nurturing people, all positive-energy foods, from fruit to beef, give off a light field or energy, an aliveness that draws you to them. You may see or sense this energy—a halo that's independent of a grapefruit's shine or a lovely display. Around positive foods your body responds by getting happier, lighter, hungrier. In contrast, negative foods are energetically drab; you feel nothing around them, or are repelled. It's not only that they're brown around the edges or wilted—there's something else operating, a death vibe, announcing "no nutrition here." Think of it this way: If you're around an exhausted person, his low energy can drag you down. The same is true for "tired" foods, but more subtly.

With a playful spirit, make an expedition to the market—for me, a sacred place (our abundance of food is a true blessing) where everything emits energy. This can also be turned into a game for children. Start with unwrapped produce, fish, chicken, and meat; they're more readily observable. Then go on to packaged products. Practice sensing one food at a time, an intuitive habit that'll soon become second nature.

For instance, tune in to the vegetable section. Your linear self may protest, "You're losing it!" but be bold. Take a few deep breaths; quiet your thoughts. Try to set aside self-consciousness about other shoppers, and taste preconceptions. First, observe outer appearance: Which vegetables look vibrant? Fresh? Or withered? Also smell them; fragrance is a sign of high energy. Then, beyond this, practice intuiting their vibes (useful in reading organic produce, which may not look as blemish-free as chemically treated produce). Does a vegetable emit a glow, an aliveness? Do you feel drawn to it? Lusciously alive food can shoot spotlights of joyful energy toward you that open your heart—especially palpable when you slice these delectable morsels at home, releasing their inner energy.

In contrast, a dead vegetable seems sad, listless, or lacks attraction, indicators of waning life force. To get a full vibe assessment, also be sure to hold the vegetable. While doing so, cup your palm a few inches above the surface to sense its energy field, just as you do with people. Alive foods emit heat, tingling, even ecstasy. Dead foods feel more like lumps. Then, notice where you're physically drawn, a magnetic feeling. Your body knows where to go. Don't force it, but pay attention: Are you pulled toward the watercress? Does okra repel you? An artichoke beckon? Reading energy is initially visual, then feeling which *healthy* foods attract you. If you keep gravitating to candy bars or other comfort foods, be suspicious. As in the previous section, determine a craving from a true nutritional need, a distinction elaborated on in "visceral sensing."

Also know: Anything you buy in packages—pastas, soups, cheeses—has lower energy than fresh, organic food. In the store, packaged foods can be harder to connect with because they're so often hidden and sealed. But if they're your only option, here's what to do. For foods wrapped in cellophane, say chicken, try to sense the most alive vibes of all the possibilities through the coverings by feeling the surrounding energy field with your palm. See which item calls to you. Alternatively, canned and packaged goods are better sensed in your kitchen once you've opened and prepared the food.

A practical hint. Visual sensing gives you an energy read on foods so you can establish a hierarchy. Naturally, it's ideal to eat the most energy-charged foods—but also have second or third choices ready if the best isn't available or practical. Changing your diet isn't an all-or-none proposition. For instance, if you adore the energy you get from organic carrots or salads, but they end up rotting in the crisper because you loathe peeling and washing them, prepare them just occasionally. Alternate with the jumbo bags of packaged carrots, or bagged prewashed salads if you'll eat them. Or if you can't get to the fish market, but salmon nourishes you, buy it in cellophane. In general, though, the most supercharged energetic foods are lean, fresh, and organic. Eat them whenever possible.

Step #5: Viscerally Tune in to the Energy of Food

Testing out your energetic responses to food lets you discover a nutritious "alive" diet that pleases your body—another way food communicates. At home, over time, experiment with all ingredients of your diet, including organic foods versus those sprayed or with preservatives. Keep a food journal to log which satiate you or set off addictive cravings. This will clarify your energetic food compatibilities.

Start the Process.

Pick two foods to compare on consecutive days. For example, chicken versus fish. Eat them slowly and with mindful awareness. Ask yourself: How does each one feel in my body? Am I energized (not wired) and happy? Or do I feel sick or enervated, or have no lift at all? In your journal evaluate your response on a scale of 1 to 10: 10 is highest energy, 1 is lowest.

Similarly, note if the food sets off addictive cravings or mood swings: 10 is most intense, 1 is least (see "Distinguish an Addictive Craving from a True Need" on page 90).

Also evaluate on a 1–10 scale: Do I like the taste? Smell? Texture? One by one, rate everything you eat.

Here's what a sample food journal entry might look like:

FOOD JOURNAL ENTRY	CHICKEN	FISH
How do I rate my energy response?	7	9
Does it set off an addictive craving?	2	2
Do I experience mood swings?	1	1
Do I like the taste?	10	5
Do I like the smell?	9	5
Do I like the texture?	8	6

Apply Your Results.

You've hit the jackpot if a food—say, chicken—is high-energy, non-addictive, and aesthetically pleasing—the Positive Energy Program's definition of a true "chicken person." However, if the criteria don't all track, as with fish above, here's how to interpret them. Hands down, your energy response alone has the most clout in this food plan—you'll benefit most if you stick to foods you've rated as 5 or higher for your energy response. Eat only these foods for a week or longer to see how much better you'll feel. Some of my patients have a blast eating this way routinely.

The difficulty is we're conditioned to value taste over energy, a habit that can be gently reprioritized. For instance, you may prefer the taste of chicken to fish, but steamed fish makes you feel lighter and energized. How do you weigh your taste preference against the energetic boost? Again, think balance. Eat chicken occasionally, but allow fish to supply the bulk of your energy needs. With foods you "know" are good for you, like broccoli or cauliflower, but whose taste may not appeal, see if the boost they provide can compensate for your aversion. If so, incorporate them gingerly into your diet, mixing them into a stir-fry or soup, using other ingredients and seasonings to mask the flavor. However, if you find any food unbearable, don't force yourself to eat it.

Scrutinize Your Body's Reaction to Sugar, Carbs, and Comfort Foods.

To combat Energy-Defensive Eating or any cravings, you've got to impeccably assess addictive foods. Go for the big guns: ice cream, pasta, potato chips, or bread. Pick the most irresistible brands. Test out a small amount, say a spoonful of butter pecan ice cream, a handful of chips, or a slice of warm sourdough. Then, as it digests, notice whether your energy increases, decreases, or stays the same. Use these more specific questions to nail down your cravings: Do you feel a craving for more? A desire to binge? A change in mood or personality? Are you wired or tired? Or do you enjoy what you've eaten, feel even-keeled and satisfied? Also watch your reaction to caffeine and alcohol. Some people can drink them moderately; others can't. (One glass of wine with a meal may promote digestion and health, but more can dehydrate.)

If you've rated foods as 5 or higher on the addictive and mood-swing scale, eating them will erode your energy and sanity. Above all: Do not keep addictive temptations at home. Foods lower on these scales present less of an emergency but pose a chronic energy threat because you're not eating with attunement; plus, they can activate your addictive circuitry, setting off dietary cravings you've rated as above 5. Limiting or weaning yourself off addictive foods (don't go cold turkey) helps break the craving cycle. But even more important: Create an overall high-energy diet. When your body's energetic needs are consistently met, addictive cravings have less power and frequency.

Honor Your Energetic Read on Foods—Never Coerce Yourself to Eat Anything.

The Positive Energy Program differs from others because it values your body's intuitions about diet above any other dictums. For example, when a petite dancer-patient tells me that she derives energy from regularly eating meat, even though the American Medical Association suggests more limited intake, I respect her needs. (Still, she keeps an eye on her cholesterol.) Or if you told me, "Okra makes every cell of my body nauseous," I don't care if the whole world says to eat it—okra isn't for you. Even health food products might not be right if they don't spark your energy.

Expect eating with attunement to bring sustenance, even joy. You'll feel gratified with average servings, won't want to stuff yourself. Periodically reevaluate and update your diet.

Step #6: Consciously Drink Water

I am an unabashed water-lover. Water is an energetic purifier, re-places toxins with subtle energy. Whether you drink it, soak in it, gaze at it, or dream about it, your health will benefit. I keep bottled water with me at all times to stay hydrated. Water keeps our skin moist, bowels moving, and mind clear—and also washes away stress or other negative vibes. Water is a precious balm, will help you heal faster, and supports wellness.

You require more water than you may think. One friend who prides herself in being a "camel" feels fine for eight hours without a sip. She's misinterpreting this as her body's intuitive need. Many people only start craving water when dehydration sets in. In truth, we need six or more glasses of water daily: bottled or filtered (which removes chlorine and other pollutants) are best. Intuitively gauge the amount that yields the most energy. Most of us don't know about the regenerative proper-ties of water, so we don't drink enough. Water is a sacred, life-force-rich substance. Subtle energy swims in it, and thus we're nurtured. As you did with food, sense the effects of water in your system. An organic ele-ment that composes two-thirds of our bodies, it has a primal resonance. In the words of the poet Rumi, "We know the taste of pure water."

Step #7: Eat for Your Body-Energy Type

Working as an intuitive has allowed me to more deeply appreciate the energetic aspects of diet. Tuning in to my patients' energy fields,

I get a read on which foods would ideally match them. Over twenty years, I've observed three common body-energy types and the foods that balance them. Knowing your type enables you to ward off cravings and eat with attunement. Further, it opens dormant energy centers and their associated qualities, such as intuition or grounding.

Body-Energy Type 1: The Floater

I am the epitome of this type. See if you relate. My frame is thin, small-boned, more like air than earth. It needs grounding. As an intuitive empath, I have a highly sensitive system that picks up everything, *though I don't cope by overeating.* I'm an avid dreamer, ethereal, and naturally hold my subtle energy in my upper intuitive and spiritual centers (above the shoulders), where I energetically gravitate under stress. My ongoing challenge has been to be more centered in my lower body, more connected to the earth.

Foods that balance your body energy. As I do, for energetic anchoring, I suggest eating protein—meat, chicken, or fish daily. (Tofu alone, though protein, is energetically too light for grounding purposes. Combine it with other protein sources.) Once, for eight months, I was vegetarian (airier foods) and nearly floated away. I feel best when I'm thin, so I prefer a low-fat diet, and a mix of vegetables, whole grains, and fruit. My body flourishes on what's fresh and fragrant, loathes grease and chocolate hangovers. Typical of this type, I'm sensitive to sugar. Too much overamps my energy, then wipes me out. Similarly, if you fit this type, limit sugar and regularly eat more protein (denser food). This solidifies your link to the physical world so you don't drift off; people will find you more present and available.

Body-Energy Type 2: The Earth-Centered Eater

My patient Kevin, a practical-minded thirty-five-year-old contractor who's over six feet, has a sturdy (not obese) Earth-bound frame. Physically, he looks glued to the ground—no floating going on here. Kevin is emotionally aware, but he's no intuitive empath. Negative energy seems to bounce off him, without any effort to repel it on his part. Kevin naturally holds his energy in his trunk and lower body, the earthier energy centers. His challenge is to open to more intuitive, ethereal realms.

Foods that balance your body energy. Like many people of this type, Kevin opts to be vegetarian. It suits his energy preferences. Meat or excessive protein makes him sluggish and causes weight gain. Though he doesn't consume much sugar, it doesn't throw him off. If you fit this type, I suggest trying a vegetarian diet for a week, then monitoring how you feel. Or if you prefer, for that time, eat a balanced diet of vegetables, fruits, and whole grains with minimal meat or fish. Because your subtle energy is weighted in your lower body, lighter healthy foods will lift and balance it. Make them a dominant part of your diet. Though you may be less susceptible to sugar or carb highs and lows, cravings still signal addictive eating and cause added pounds—so limit intake in this case. With such dietary shifts, you'll shed weight, and your intuition and dreams will deepen.

Body-Energy Type 3: The Energy-Defensive Eater

Obesity gives this type away. As I've discussed, you cope with overload by reaching for food. You may lose weight, but it always returns. Like all intuitive empaths, you're ultrasensitive to toxic vibes, including people's anger, depression, and pain. When you're thin, you're especially vulnerable to absorbing this negative energy. Thus, to build a protective buffer (fat) you reach for sugar, carbs, or high-fat comfort foods as a quick fix—a short-lived, unhealthy solution that you repeat addictively.

Foods that balance your body energy. Altering your diet will complement the Positive Energy Program's other interventions for an energetic eating disorder. The best dietary defenses for this type are (1) Drink at least six glasses of water daily to keep flushing out negative vibes. At the first sign of them, step up your water intake—try this first, in place of comfort foods. (2) Eat miniportions of lean protein for meals and snacks three to five times daily—for instance, two ounces of chicken, beef, or fish. Protein mounts a subtle energetic defense against negative energy, including stress. Protein's energetic benefits may take a few weeks to kick in, but gradually, you'll feel quick-fix cravings lessen. (3) Consume unlimited vegetables, with some whole grains (but beware of carb addictions). (4) Limit or avoid sugar, comfort foods, anything fried or fatty—this will be easier with regular miniprotein meals. With these new eating habits, you'll feel energetically stronger and safer in the world.

AS YOU GO THROUGH and hone the Seven Steps to Eating with Attunement, it's also vital to address the energetics of meal preparation and serving. Food is sensitive to vibes. You can't chop a carrot or slice a turkey and have them remain unaffected. Food is energetically porous, becomes saturated by the positive and negative fields of those around it. How it's served and prepared alters the energetic content.

Have you ever wondered why homecooked meals prepared with love taste so sublime? Or why fast foods, hastily handled, seem cardboard in comparison? Though some food is inherently healthier and packed with subtle energy, when meals are lovingly assembled they're more delicious and energizing.

Creative chefs attest to this. The chef of an Italian restaurant, Brava, in Santa Monica, told me, "Each morning, our waiters and cooks form a circle around the food and send it loving energy." The patrons of Brava know about this ritual, return because of it. The meals are especially alive, reflect the handlers' love. For Weaver D, an evangelist-turned-chef in Athens, Georgia, cooking with love is automatic. His family-run restaurant is called Automatic for the People (REM, a famous local band, titled their CD after it). A friend took me there. I resisted going. I feared it was a greasepit—which it wasn't. But what did I know? My barbecued chicken, mashed potatoes, and collard greens had magic in them. Weaver D's exuberance filled the food and the packed, cafeteria-style room. Though the food had sky-high cholesterol, not at all what I'd eat every day, I left his restaurant in a state of bliss.

But don't get me wrong. Even though love can improve the energy content of any food, a consistently greasy diet isn't good for you. Based on both my intuitive reading of foods and basic nutrition, I recommend some energy-aware cooking rules to follow. You want food to be natural, lean (for example, skinless chicken), and not drenched in salt: light steaming, broiling, wok cooking, or eating vegetables and fruits raw preserves nutritional content and subtle energy. In comparison, frying kills off life force. Even a subtle-energy-rich food like fresh asparagus can be obliterated by globbing it with fat. Whether you're cooking in or eating out in a restaurant, meals give more energy when life force is preserved.

There's also an art to serving food energetically. Much healing can go on from an exchange of positive energy between the waiter, the chef, and you. (Picture the snippy waiter who slaps your loveless sandwich down. Those vibes in my lunch make me cringe!) For years I've had a fantasy about taking time off and waiting tables—temporarily setting aside my M.D. to just *BE*. Some small café by the ocean. I'm sure it's hard work, but it would be an opportunity to spread good energy around.

As you can see, to me, food is a sacrament, never trivial—a view that sheds new light on how you eat. Your earthly body won't be around forever. For more energy here, forge an intuitive partnership with the fuel you feed it. Such cooperation, with diet and in all areas, increases your life force, which wants you to be vibrant. Expect results. The positive changes that come from an energy-aware diet are proof of success.

DEVELOPING AN EXERCISE PROGRAM: FOUR STRATEGIES FOR INCREASING POSITIVE ENERGY

My mother began walking five miles a day when she was sixty.
Now she's ninety, and we have no idea where she is.

NASRUDDIN, THIRTEENTH-CENTURY JESTER-SAGE

The purpose of exercise is to feel good, to be healthy—and to look healthy. When exercise is really grooving, as Nasruddin, mystic Middle Eastern joke teller suggests, our Spirit is set free. A "must" for a rewarding fitness plan is listening to your body's subtle energy cues. Without this, exercise can become torture—a masochistic pushing through pain (not a pretty sight when I intuit this in people at my gym) or else drudgery you avoid. This prescription gives you more tuned-in, effective exercise options.

As an intuitive, I'm clear that exercise works best when it harmonizes with our body, a law of Energy Psychiatry. Otherwise, it's beyond me how we can fully benefit from exercise's touted perks, including the reduction of heart disease, stress, depression, insomnia, and bone-wasting. If your workout has become a squeeze-into-a-size-two marathon you abhor, you're creating negative energy and burnout. It's fine to exercise and lose weight, but find a regimen your body loves. As my patients learn, some exercise yields positive energy, other negative. Also, sticking to a program involves more than following the right instructions or using the right equipment; it's about finding the right vibes in your exercise venue.

The following four strategies will help you find the right kind of exercise for *you*.

Strategy #1: Find an Energy-Compatible Environment

Where you work out can make or break a program. You must feel comfortable there—otherwise you won't go. Begin by asking yourself: Do you prefer exercising at home? Outdoors? At a yoga studio? Traditional health clubs may be convenient or get you going—terrific incentives. I myself have a hard time even walking into them. The loud music blasts through my spine. Adrenaline-hyped model-types are crammed together, eyeing one another. Talk about chaotic energy fields!—a nightmare for me, as an empath who absorbs vibes. These gyms are devoid of intuitive sensitivity to my body's needs. Though each of us may react differently, many people such as empaths get scared away.

There are alternatives. For instance, I'm in nirvana jogging by the ocean, a freedom I first felt as a child. During family trips up the California coast, my parents would pull over to a field of wildflowers and just let me gallop around. They called it "letting off stream"—a glorious release of pent-up energy that jogging gives me today. For variety, I also work out at a small, quiet rehab gym for people recovering from orthopedic injuries. I first went there for a neck problem. I like that everyone comes to get stronger. No big singles scene. I prefer the pleasure of not socializing when I exercise. Sometimes, at closing time, it's just me and a sweet, schizophrenic man who babbles to himself—sometimes brilliantly—about everything from OJ to Shaq to George W. Bush. A strange compatriot, but somehow perfect.

You, too, must find your ideal spot—either inside or out in nature. On workdays, one accountant patient walks a few miles near his home, but on weekends hikes the sage-strewn Chumash trails of Malibu Canyon, a balm for the excessively civilized. Other patients flock to women's gyms: they like the *yin,* or feminine energy—more pliant, soft, warm. High-testosterone or aggressive *yang* energy is difficult for some (not all!) people to take. One timid librarian patient who was new at exercise would consistently get sandwiched between two yang jocks on a row of treadmills in her gym. She huffed and puffed while they just trucked along. It was demoralizing, so she switched to a woman's gym with gentler vibes.

Also, never exercise with people who are energy drains. During a workout, avoid whiners or gossips. Their words and energy fields will invade your space and drag you down. If someone at my gym gets wind that I'm a psychiatrist and starts pouring out her life story, I don't hesitate to say, "I'm relaxing. I'd rather not talk." Sensitively set your boundaries too. Or if you enjoy socializing during exercise, choose elevating people and conversations, vibes that enhance your energy.

We're in dire need of a new paradigm for fitness centers, places with vibes truly conducive to getting in shape. I see peach tones, curves, ample space between machines, designated "silent" sections, BB King in the background—a place mellow enough to be healing, but motivating too. I see these chains all over the country, safe havens for energetically sensitive people to work out in peace and adhere to a regular regimen.

Strategy #2: Make Exercise a Moving Meditation

One of my fitness heroes, Phil Jackson, former champion coach of the Chicago Bulls and now coach of the Los Angeles Lakers, has a philosophy called mindfulness basketball, which he modeled on Buddhist precepts. In *Sacred Hoops,* he accentuates the power in sports of mindful awareness, spirituality, compassion, and selfless team play. I'm tickled that he adorns team rooms with prayer totems and an owl feather symbolizing energetic balance and harmony. To me, many professional sports have long seemed a depressing macho spectacle, despite my male friend's patient explanations of the finer points. I applaud Jackson for articulating a long-overdue, more enlightened set of values.

This program also presents an alternative model for fitness. Unlike traditional fitness models, it doesn't equate exercise with purely physical energy, but spiritual too. It's not fixated on outer results—though they occur. Nor is the primary impetus to compete or get thin—but don't worry, you'll lose weight. Rather, my approach emphasizes strengthening your life force from the inside out.

Here's the mindshift: Whether you're Roller-blading or poised in a Yogic Sun Salute, start by envisioning any exercise as a moving meditation: a consecrated time to connect with your body, breath, and life force. Such in-the-Now focus quiets noisy thoughts and counteracts negativity. It also synchronizes you with a transcendent energy that, if you surrender to it, will transport you to what athletes call "the Zone"—a noncerebral place of perfect flow.

In any meditation, kindness is called for. Exercise entails harmonious energy building, not a lunatic lunge to the finish line. I've seen the sweetest patients emotionally put themselves under the whip of the Marquis de Sade during workouts. They want to get healthy, but instead poison their energy field with an inner tirade including "I'm too fat" or "I'm not going fast enough." As I advise my patients, set your intention to be compassionate. Don't allow exercise to become a free-for-all to scourge yourself about weight or anything else. If negative thoughts arise, be quick to banish them. Find a routine that includes days off, but also improvise. If you've got a virus, rest. If you have a chronic illness or pain, go slow. Sometimes, though, an extra nudge to exercise can rescue you from a funk. Your body gives energy feedback as guidance.

Strategy #3: Intuit the Right Exercise

Discovering exercises to which you're attuned changes everything. Some techniques, such as yoga from India and qigong from China, specifically cultivate subtle energy—twin systems for body and soul fitness that each culture invented autonomously. However, even humdrum sit-ups can become a spiritual high where you're carried by a greater flow. An aerobic workout and simple stretching can be scintillating when executed with an energetic eye.

How do you find the right exercise? Let me describe the remarkable journey of Carl's fitness transformation. College wrestler turned Zen monk turned massage therapist, this huge-hearted bald Buddha now happily practices yoga and Aikido. Raised in an abusive, alcoholic home, Carl got his aggression out through wrestling. "Sometimes I'd be mean," Carl admitted. "I'd squeeze my opponent's skull and put him in a head lock not just to win, but to hurt him." After college wrestling, he drifted homeless for a while in New York City, drunk, "in survival mode." Then, while living in the Village with a girlfriend who had pet boa constrictors, he started reading spiritual material. Incredibly, this led to his becoming a monk. Though he eventually left the insular world of the Zen Center, his quest for spiritual awareness continues to be his passion.

Spurred by his Buddhist training, Carl wanted to find an exercise that complemented Zen and nurtured more than the brute force of wrestling. As if meant to be, soon after departing his monastic community in New York, he was walking down Broadway and stepped on a flyer for "Zen and Aikido." His intuition practically broke into song: "Yes!" it bellowed, "Yes!" The next day, Carl began studying Aikido, a martial art that strengthens the body by activating subtle energy; the movements resemble ballet. "I knew it was right: I was excited; my body felt happy; I looked forward to going; plus, by directing my breath, I began feeling an incredible inner energy flow through me. I let it lead. Initially in Aikido, though, I tried to throw this guy down, as I did in wrestling. I felt like a barbarian! I had to learn that Aikido is about blending with energy. Wrestling is all self-will and physicality, so unsatisfying in comparison." These days, Aikido offers Carl a vigorous workout, "a healthy way to energetically disperse leftover aggression so I don't act on it." Alternating this with gentler yoga exercises, Carl has formulated an ingenious fitness scheme catered to his temperament.

Now you're going to find a regimen to fit your needs. The right exercise builds positive energy, even joy, and releases physical and emotional toxins. Some of my intuitive-empath patients who tend to absorb anger and frustration go for more strenuous routines to purge stress. You may respond to slower movements. No matter what workout you choose, it must harmonize with your body, Spirit, and yes, schedule.

Begin by asking your intuition:

- Am I at least curious about a new exercise, or does it leave me flat?

- Is an exercise convenient and workable with my daily routine?
- Does an exercise make my body happy, or am I doing it because it's a fad?
- Does an exercise improve my energy or leave me neutral or spent?
- Does an exercise lift my Spirit, or is it just a physical slog?

You're on the right exercise track if your gut answers "yes" to every question. If not, consider change. Experiment. Try the following exercises or others that draw you. Pace yourself. A few minutes a day is a heroic start! The criteria for success is more energy, alertness, and connection with body and Spirit. As an intuitive, watching someone doing an exercise to which he's energetically attuned, such as Baryshnikov's flying ballet leaps, or Tiger Woods's gliding holes-in-one, is a breathtaking dance of light. Following are several types of energy-enhancing exercise you might want to test out.

Stretching.

A gentle way to begin exercising, especially if you've been away from it, stretching centers you in your body, releases stress clogged in joints, gets energy moving. I'm crazy about stretching. It takes the creaks out of our being. Sometimes, after the flu, a round of toe touches returns me to the land of the living. Stretching is an ideal bridge between inactivity and working out. In addition to preventing injuries, it discharges negative energy, makes you feel more open.

Aerobic Exercise.

The rhythm of aerobics calms the mind, calibrates you with a renewing energy flow. Just moving and breathing hard is pleasurable, primal; we often forget we are physical animals. Movement amplifies our sense of the body, liberates confined energy, and opens us to the divine. Dance your Spirit free. Run like a wild mustang into the heavens. Make that hoop with a guided hand. If you're hiking up a mountain or by a hundred-year-old oak, bow inwardly with each movement; let the power of nature imbue you.

Yoga.

Sanskrit for "union with spirit," yoga originated in India five thousand years ago as a holy path to realization. It stimulates the life energy called prana through breath and postures. Hatha yoga, the most common type in America, uses poses, stretching, and breathing to enhance the mind-body connection. Other kinds involve meditation and chanting. Yoga has gone mainstream, making the cover of *Time* and being featured on *The Oprah Winfrey Show*. Western physicians advise it for those with heart disease, cancer, depression, and stress. Model Cheryl Tiegs told me, "Yoga has changed my life. It brings a calmness to my body and spirit. I don't push myself to the brink anymore. I'm a strong German. I've always forged ahead. Now when my energy is low I'll do yoga. To keep my energy high I try to schedule it three times a week. When I'm consistent the calmness is always there."

Many of my patients who've avoided exercise have fallen in love with yoga once they've given it a chance. One busy decorator resisted yoga for years, though now she can't wait to go. Initially, she told me, "I only have a limited time to exercise, so it better burn calories. Yoga sounds like it won't do much for my abs or heart." She needed to have a myth about yoga demystified: just because it doesn't always raise your pulse as much as aerobics doesn't mean you're not getting a good workout. Learning this and seeing results helped her over the block.

Qigong.

These ancient Chinese self-healing exercises—which combine movements, massage, breathing, and meditation—ground your energy and strengthen you physically. The goal is to cultivate positive life-force energies and release the negativity that causes disease. My patients laud qigong as a stressbuster and cure for pesky chronic symptoms that baffle doctors. Studies have shown that qigong improves digestion and hypertension, and boosts the immune system—you heal as you work out.

Tai Chi Ch'uan.

An exercise involving graceful movements, it's the most widely practiced form of qigong. Besides giving a good workout, tai chi helps you find a balance point, a place of inner stillness. This allows you to center during turmoil and deflect negative energy. Also, research has shown significant balance and coordination improvement in elders who practice tai chi. As I age, this has increasing meaning for me. Eventually a time will come when my joints will appreciate an alternative to the wear and tear of aerobics. Whatever your age, though, tai chi is an elegant fitness choice with an energetic flair.

MAKE CHANGES NOW
ADD A SUBTLE-ENERGY PERSPECTIVE TO YOUR
EXERCISE ROUTINE

A subtle-energy perspective can enhance any routine. For exercises like yoga or tai chi, it's already built in. But for more traditional exercises, also incorporate the following intuitive pointers:

- Remember to frame exercise time as a holy moment.
- Practice Conscious Breathing (described in Chapter 1). Staying aware of your breath during any exercise will keep you in the Now and intuitively attune you to subtle energy. This is a miraculous chance to intuit your life force. Whether you're on the treadmill or playing ball, practice inhaling life force, and

then exhaling stress from your system, a energetic purification your body will thank you for.

- While focusing on your breath, try to intuit signs of subtle energy flowing in your body: waves of heat; an exhilarating buzz; a flash of clarity, or ecstatic tingles. Sometimes I get creative flashes while lifting weights—exercise can desludge stagnant channels—so I keep a notepad nearby. To keep track of unsolicited inspirations, you can do this too.

- Periodically place your hand over the energy center two inches below your naval. It's associated with the ecstasy of the earth, the sensuality of grounding, and the color orange. Touching or lightly rubbing this place for up to a minute will balance your energies and enhance the pleasure you feel from your routine.

Strategy #4: Melt Your Resistance

With exercise, resistance goes with the territory. Resistance comes from the mind, not the intuition. It's the part of you that fears change and newness, the voices that talk you out of something before you give it a chance. Generally, unless you're too ill or tired to function, resistance isn't an intuitive message to stop. It may be fear, anxiety, shame about your body, or, if you live in your head, avoidance of being in the body. Even if your weariness is real, five minutes of exercise that harmonizes with your subtle energy can perk you up. Or if you have an ongoing illness such as chronic fatigue or pain, take baby steps—the tinier the better (toddling along can feel marvelous!). The point is to slowly get energy moving. We're creatures of habit, but once in a routine, an energetic rhythm propels us. As our stamina mounts, the endorphin surge increases our well-being and energy: potent reinforcers.

The novelty will wear off of any program. It's helpful to rotate exercises you enjoy. When my enthusiasm sputters, I remind myself how magnificent it is to have a body that moves, that exercise is even an option—not a morbid musing, but reason to celebrate. For the handicapped or bed-bound, taking just one step would be the answer to their prayers. Sometimes we forget the blessing of mobility. Use exercise to revel in your body and the glory of its movements.

YOUR ENERGETIC HEALTH: TAKING WELL-BEING TO A NEW LEVEL

Well-being is a state of high-caliber health—the crown jewel of living—not just making it through the day. Well-being is the refined interplay of physical and emotional realms as well as energy fields. A doctor's kindness or healer's touch can activate your immune system. This part of the third prescription emphasizes the energetics of sleep, health, and healing. Fine-tuning them takes well-being to a new level.

The Nourishment of Sleep

A skilled, caring therapist I know once fell asleep during a session with one of her patients. Both overtired and lulled by the monotony of this particular patient, she didn't see it coming. "My eyelids got heavy," she said. "For a few seconds I just nodded off." Then the wobbling started. By some incredible fluke her chair's leg suddenly collapsed. She was flabbergasted: "Before I knew it I'd landed on the floor!" (It could've been worse. As poet Bill Matthews writes, his friend's "analyst died in midsession, nondirective to the end.") Fortunately, her patient was a narcissist. She plunged; he barely blinked. Though she tried to discuss the incident, he kept right on talking about himself. So the session continued.

My therapist friend badly needed sleep, a healing force that recharges our physiology and subtle energy. Mental babble subdued at last, in sleep we energetically percolate in our life force and the greater mystery of realms beyond the waking consciousness. Deep rest purifies the day's toxic remnants. Anger or pain can soften, even evaporate the next morning.

As an energy psychiatrist, I'm a sleep fanatic. We spend at least a third of our lives asleep, so it better be good. I help my patients, especially overachievers, determine and attain their ideal amount of sleep. Chronically working at the expense of sleep is a culturally sanctioned insanity I never condone; sleep deprivation can literally cause psychosis! (Overtired workaholics are scary—they drag into my office like the walking dead, completely energetically detached from their bodies.)

Some of us require more sleep than others. To pin down the amount that gives you maximal energy, do a test: For a few days or longer—the weekends may be easiest—pull the blinds, close the door, turn off the phone and alarm, and allow yourself to sleep until you naturally get up. (For new parents who may lack this luxury, remember your prebaby needs to approximate your sleep baseline.) Since childhood, I've required at least eight hours. With less, I'm irritable, askew, half-here, my intuition foggy. Regularly achieving your nightly ideal is a battle well worth fighting for. However, if a hectic schedule impinges, other options include taking naps to compensate or sleeping longer on other days. A saving grace for new parents is to nap—not catch up on work—when the baby naps; also to grab sleep when you can, not just after obligations. Over time, this juggling of total sleep hours will help balance out your energy quotient—a tactic that prevents years of debilitating fatigue for parents and all busy people. (For more on getting a good night's sleep, I suggest Janet Kinosian's *The Well-Rested Woman* and Dr. Joyce Walsleben's *A Woman's Guide to Sleep*.)

Other subtle-energy measures I suggest for better sleep and to relieve insomnia are:

- **MAKE SLEEPING COZY.** Sleeping is sensual. You may want to wear a silk negligé, comfy pajamas, or nothing at all. Also, make sure the weight of the covers and temperature are right for you. When you're nestled under soft blankets and sheets, your bed is creating an energy womb—a warm, nurturing protection.

- **OPTIMIZE ENERGY FLOW IN YOUR BEDROOM.** *Feng shui,* the ancient Chinese energy-art of object placement, can improve the vibes where you sleep. Here are some pointers. To increase harmony and energy balance, place a bouquet of flowers by your bed, or position your bed pointing north to make your body parallel to the Earth's magnetic axis, a peaceful, sleep-inducing alignment. Unmade beds, clutter, and electronic equipment wear down energy; televisions or computers should be covered during sleep.

- **CALM YOUR MIND.** The biggest obstacle to a good night's rest is a brain that won't turn off. Before bed, avoid anything that smacks of stress. To quell thoughts and banish the world's uncertainties, a few minutes of deep breathing or meditation helps. Turn the lights off. Sit upright in bed, eyes closed. Then, to conjure positive energy, envision what's loving and peaceful. It could be a placid beach or a wind-borne eagle. (My father used to see himself making the perfect tennis shot.) If anxiety or fears arise, keep breathing them away. Another calming device is to read some really boring literature. Once I had a boyfriend, a poet himself, who lulled me to sleep by reciting Victorian poetry. A few minutes of Tennyson and I'm gone!

You want everything about sleeping to feel safe. How you sleep, where you sleep, and who you sleep with affect your quality of rest. Sleeping can be more intimate than making love. I advise patients to spend a full night—no sexual activity necessary—with a partner before committing to live together. The reason: When you sleep, the intellect recedes and your energy field, which is wide open, overlaps with your partner's. Whoever is near, you will feel. Hopefully, you wake refreshed. If not, tenderly try to address and heal the impasse. Otherwise you'll risk chronic energy drain and health problems.

My patient Lulu, a psychology student who's a vibe magnet, told me, "I can't sleep with my husband when he's angry. It intrudes on my space; I go to another room." Her husband knew about subtle energy from our family sessions, though he didn't feel it like Lulu. Even so, because he respected her feelings and also missed her terribly at night, he agreed to seek help. Once he dealt with his anger, Lulu's sleep became tranquil again.

Sleep styles can't be stereotyped. What we're partial to differs. Some loving couples I've worked with opt to spend the whole night together just occasionally, or not at all. Their sex life is gratifying, but they prefer separate beds or rooms. For whatever reason—a snoring or restless spouse, or an energetic preference to be alone—they simply like their own sleep space. I've treated intuitive empaths who avoid intimate relationships because they can't get used to sleeping with anyone, no matter how caring. If this is you, give yourself a break. Speak up. With a sensitive partner, there are many creative ways to honor your energetic necessities.

Practitioners and Energy Healing

As an energy psychiatrist, I feel privileged to be part of a Renaissance that is sweeping modern health care. Physicians, nurses, and therapists are bringing Energy Medicine into patient care. Increasingly, more of us are speaking out. We're becoming less of a secret society.

Take Mehmet Oz, a gutsy cardiothoracic surgeon at Columbia Presbyterian Medical Center in New York, who brings energy healers into the operating room during open-heart surgery. These healers send energy to patients through their hands, a technique shown to accelerate postop recovery. "Energy fields definitely impact our lives," Oz says. "Understanding what energy is gives us a new grasp of how the body functions."

As a physician, I'm a big believer in utilizing the best of both traditional and alternative medicine. There's *always* more than one way to attack a problem; don't let anyone tell you otherwise. Healing can be like ordering from a Chinese menu, mixing and matching to find an ideal blend. In the Positive Energy Program, to maintain well-being or hasten healing, you can choose an Energy Medicine practitioner who'll work along *with* your traditional health care team. This can get you over the hump if treatment has stalled and prime your system for swifter recovery. When energy is freed up, medications work better, and your healing system kicks into higher gear. Also, sometimes Energy Medicine is the only treatment modality necessary. I've seen it cure many a "mystery disease" and pesky chronic ailment in my patients. Since Western physicians aren't trained to identify subtle energy imbalances that cause illness, it's good to have another set of eyes. I know the frustration of consulting a doctor with a real complaint and being told, "The tests are normal. Don't worry. You're fine." This response is crazy-making. I've grown clear about the merits of traditional medicine, and also its limitations. Sadly, I've seen empathic people who absorb energy be misdiagnosed as hypochondriacs. If this is you, don't give up. When the energetics of health are understood, the "unexplainable" can be resolved.

How to Find an Energy Medicine Practitioner

What to look for. What all energy practitioners share is that they treat both the physical and energy body. The various Energy Medicine specialties include Energy Psychiatry, holistic medicine, acupuncture, therapeutic touch, homeopathy, qigong, and massage. Most are associated with a professional organization with qualifying standards, such as the American Holistic Medical Association (see the Resources section). Consulting these groups or medical centers with complementary medicine programs helps weed out quacks—essential in an era when "healers" can include both sidewalk swamis and board-certified M.D.s. I look forward to an even more comprehensive peer-review system. Meanwhile, look for credentialed practitioners—a licensed acupuncturist or a nurse certified in therapeutic touch. Sometimes, though, a healer may lack credentials, but patients rave about the results. In this case, you may want to try him or her out. See how you respond. Also, seek referrals from either a trusted health professional or friends. What impresses me most is a practitioner's track record.

How to spot a quack. As an informed consumer, be suspicious of grand claims of "miracle cures." Don't be bamboozled by anyone who insists that his or hers is the only "enlightened" way or that you must divorce yourself from other medical approaches. Some quacks suggest they have an exclusive line to God. Or worse, that they are beaming down wisdom to only a select few. Watch for subtle racism or gender preferences signifying the "chosen ones"—dangerous beliefs. Beware of those who charge exorbitant fees or who try to hook you emotionally or financially, seeking to control, not empower you. Go toward practitioners who are humble. Follow your intuition. Use good common sense. Always tell your physician about any recommendations from your energy healer.

What to expect from treatment. We are busy people. If you're like me, the last thing I need is to make time for a health appointment and not get results. With Energy Medicine expect to see some improvement in the first couple of sessions. At mimium, your energy will perk up, or the change can be more dramatic. Over a few weeks, expect symptom relief, gradual or extreme. I usually give a practitioner a three-week window. By then, if healing isn't moving in the right direction, I consider seeking other help.

I love Energy Medicine because it's gentler on my highly sensitive system than traditional modes. Like many intuitive empaths, I'm the queen of side effects—I've had some doozies that my doctors claim have never been reported. It can drive a by-the-book M.D. crazy. Nevertheless, I require a fraction of the usual dosage of most medications, and my reactions to toxicity are energetically real. As you can imagine, if I can avoid allopathic prescriptions, I'm thrilled.

Energy Medicine isn't daunted by "psychosomatic" symptoms. My patient Peg, an office manager who'd seen scores of doctors for unrelenting fibromyalgia (chronic pain in muscles, joints, and tendons), improved with holistic medicine. With this added help, the pain cycle was broken; she could reduce her anti-inflammatory drugs. Plus, once she felt better, her joy of living returned. Peg's family was awfully grateful. Illness had made Peg short-tempered, testy. She said, "When I'm sick it's hard to even be civil. It just takes too much energy." I knew what she meant: one day of feeling poorly, and my patience has been known to snap. Peg and all long-term symptom sufferers deserve a hero's medal for endurance, but Energy Medicine can offer relief.

I've had other patients with chronic fatigue, irregular heartbeat, and pain respond well to acupuncture, which increases energy flow along pathways called meridians. (One patient tells me she goes to a blind acupuncturist who's a genius at needle placement!) I'm also happy to report it cured my recurrent sinusitis. After a few life-force-battering courses of antibiotics—which I counterintuitively tolerated because it seemed like the quickest fix—I finally relented and made time for acupuncture. This simple solution enabled me to avoid possible surgery, and ultimately saved time and expense.

For life-threatening illnesses, including cancer, Energy Medicine bolsters the immune defense and mutes conventional treatment's toxicity. A friend undergoing chemotherapy for leukemia swears by her Chinese herbs, which miraculously reduce nausea and allow a quicker rebound from treatments. Personally, I find it inconceivable to go through a serious illness without energetic support. At the least, it sustains our clarity to make sound decisions, and our emotional resilience to overcome disease. Optimally, though, it accelerates the remission of symptoms, augments our response to traditional therapies, and heals.

Awaken Your Own Healing Power

As an energy psychiatrist, I offer patients healing sessions to program their bodies to access positive energy, a method similar to biofeedback. Although I am the catalyst, it's never just about me doing it. I also teach patients to self-heal, a skill you'll also learn when stress or other symptoms strike.

In my office, here's how a typical healing session goes, and my expectations. A patient removes her shoes and lies on my velour couch, eyes closed. Kneeling on the floor, I say a silent prayer. Then I place my hands a few inches above her body and sense where healing is needed. I envision what I do as slow dancing. Not imposing my step on you, but seeing what your step is. Energy centers have little voices. They say, "Come here," or "Go there." If someone has a migraine and I get pulled to the knee, I do as I'm told. I don't think about it. My role is simply to be a vessel through which love flows. I trust my patients' bodies will utilize this energy well. Then I wait for roses to sprout. Sometimes it's immediate. Panic melts. Eyes sparkle. Depression lifts. More often, though, improvement is a gradual brightening that comes with balance.

Using this technique, you can mobilize healing energy too. I'll show you how to transmit loving vibes to yourself or another, the basis of Energy Medicine. Love fortifies your energy field from the inside out; this protects against stress, flu, smoke, anger, noise, and other pathogens. Negative thoughts weaken our defenses to everything from colds to depression. Buddhists believe that compassion, our heart's expression of subtle energy, powerfully guards against stress and disease.

The following exercise extends Chapter 2's "Open Your Heart" meditation into healing. You'll learn to direct energy in your body, and how to be a healer for another. A loving touch ignites energy and tension-releasing neurohormones. (If it wasn't for a caring technician who once held my hand through a sixty-minute—it felt like forever!—MRI scan, I would've bolted out of that claustrophobic contraption.) As my patients do, use this exercise to counter stress or any discomfort.

MAKE CHANGES NOW
USE ENERGETIC FIRST AID TO REDUCE STRESS
AND HEAL YOURSELF

Three-Minute Self-Healing Meditation

Practice this exercise alone. Set aside at least three stress-free minutes, as regularly as possible.

Quiet yourself. Let your body unwind. Slowly inhale . . . exhale. Your breath will bring you back to center.

Gently place your hand over your heart chakra in the midchest. Then, to activate positive energy in this area, focus on whatever makes you feel love, as you've done before. Become a love-sponge. Luxuriate in these vibes.

If you're ill, visualize this energy going from your heart to saturate specific locations. No straining. Just let it flow! Target your focus. For spastic bowel syndrome, aim love at your gut. For congestion, at your chest. For cancer, at your tumor. Ditto for all aches or pains.

What to expect? At a minimum, positive energy will revive you if you're stalled. I've also seen dramatic shifts. Back pain resolves. Fatigue relents. Try not to fixate on outcomes. Whether your zest returns or a symptom remits, trust your body's response.

Share Energy with a Friend

This exercise is about sending and receiving healing vibes. Identify problem areas with each other. Then sit beside your friend as she relaxes comfortably on her back. Take a few deep breaths, releasing tension. Next, place one hand on her midchest, the heart chakra. Simultaneously, feel your heart opening. Spend at least a few minutes allowing love to go freely from your heart, down your arm, out your palm. Be a conduit for loving energy. No ego or effort.

When you're finished, reverse positions. Have her direct energy back to you. (Receiving, especially for us givers, can be the difficult part!) Sharing energy aids in maintaining health and regaining it if you're ill. The more you practice, the more love you'll feel.

IN THIS CHAPTER, I've hammered home the import of the Positive Energy Program's Third Prescription—design an energy-aware approach to diet, fitness, and health. Bringing a consciousness about energy to these areas means you won't waste an iota of your precious life force. Appreciating the subtle mechanics of energy equips you to conserve and augment your life force so it won't seep out erratically. Before you know it, you're bone-tired yet again. You don't want to reach that point.

The thrust of my approach is to prevent these subtle energy breaches, not simply scramble to manage them. The glory of experiencing self-care from an energy stance is that life force becomes palpably familiar in your daily routine. Knowing what it feels like helps you expand it. Exploring what energy is, where it comes from, how to use it, is an evolutionary leap in awareness we can all achieve. Energy is exquisitely woven into the details of our days, making the mundane holy.

Treat Yourself:

Gift yourself with a healthy activity that feels divine. Perhaps it's taking a tai chi class and letting the power of the universe flow through you. Or placing a bouquet of fresh roses by your bed to improve the feng shui of your sleep space. Or sitting on your back stoop, getting lost in the ecstasy of a juicy peach. Take pleasure in this energy!

INTERVIEW: NAOMI JUDD ON ENERGY
AND HEALTH

NAOMI JUDD IS A GRAMMY AWARD–WINNING SINGER-SONGWRITER AND
PART OF THE COUNTRY MUSIC MOTHER-DAUGHTER TEAM THE JUDDS.
SHE'S A FORMER NURSE, SURVIVOR OF HEPATITIS C, AND SPOKESPERSON
FOR THE AMERICAN LIVER FOUNDATION.

※

I'm grateful that I've been able to sense energy since I was a child. Growing up in Ashland, Kentucky, I felt safe and balanced around certain playmates and teachers; other people overwhelmed or drained me. As a young woman, my energy awareness shifted to safety issues. In my twenties, living off Sunset Strip, I was near danger constantly. I was so naive going from Appalachia to Hollywood in one fell swoop. I had two babies, Wynonna and Ashley. I was alone, on welfare, working minimum-wage jobs. I didn't have a car. I walked everywhere. Reading energy helped me survive. From yards away, I could sense if someone was a predator, on the edge, or if I could give an open smile, say, "Hey! How are you doing?"

At the time, though, my infatuation with a man made me misread his energy. He turned out to be an ex-con heroin user who beat me up. I directed all my nurturing instincts toward him. He was a bottomless pit of need; his negative energy was destroying my health. I started getting colds. I felt drained. My shoulders were up to my ears. I believe you're only a victim once—then you become a volunteer. Eventually I moved on.

The link between energy and health became even clearer when I was diagnosed with hepatitis C in 1990. Wynonna and I were at the height of our singing career as the Judds; we'd won five Grammies. I loved being on stage. It completely energized me. But as I got sick, I became exhausted. After a concert, in our bus, I'd collapse still wearing my fancy outfit and high heels. I was shocked to find out I had hepatitis C. I'd never done IV drugs. I'd been monogamous. I'd never been drunk in my life. Even though I was an R.N., I knew little about the virus.

So my healing journey began—through allopathic medicine and beyond. When I was initially diagnosed by a couple of real patriarchal physicians, I was mortified. It was my first time being a patient. I'd never been sick before. Hepatitis C is a life-threatening disease that poisons you. I remember sitting on the doctor's table with my little paper gown, with this guy telling me I had three years to live. I was so angry at him and what he represented. I wouldn't accept a death sentence. I started looking for the right people who could help me. With a lot of research, I found them.

Today, I'm a medically documented miracle. I have completely cleared hepatitis C from my body. In the nineties I was treated with interferon, the only game in town. It stops the virus's ability to replicate, but doesn't kill it. I benefited from traditional medicine—and continue to respect it—but to totally heal I also needed something more. If I hadn't used energy healing combined with prayer, walking in nature, and herbal supplements, the doctor's grim prognosis would have been fulfilled. I'm sure I wouldn't be here.

Energy healing is amazing. It strips everything down to qi, the vital life force. All languages have a word for qi, whether it's soul or Spirit. We're all composed of biomagnetic fields. When we don't acknowledge our emotions, we encode unresolved conflicts on a subtle level. Energy healing helps clear this. I'd have regular sessions with a practitioner, who'd send qi through her hands as I'd rest on my bedroom floor. I'd feel deep stillness within, a comforting warmth. Receiving energy is not only relaxing, but I'd realign with God's goal for me to be healthy and whole. I've also felt the same thing with acupuncture.

I am very vocal about asking scientists to open their minds about energy. Remember: A hundred years ago, a guy got run out of town trying to tell his fellow medical community that hand washing prevents the spread of infection. My momma used to say, "Wash your hands and say your prayers. God and germs are invisible, but they're everywhere!"

The invisible world is more real to me than the physical world. Love is an energy we can't see, but it can boost T cells and support the immune system. I'm sure the love of my fans helped me heal. The reason I did a farewell tour when I was told to go to the farm and die was that intuitively I knew being on stage at the Houston Astrodome with sixty thousand people sending me waves of positive energy would jump-start my recovery. I've also built a room in my barn with cards and knickknacks from fans. These tangible manifestations of invisible energy buoy my spirit. Miracles happen when there is love.

Love can make food healing too. My husband and I cook a lot together. We eat dinner at six o'clock every night. Wy and Ashley, who live on either side of us, know that Mom and Pop's restaurant is always open then. We pray together over our meals. It sanctifies food and gives it positive energy. What a difference between healthy food prepared with love and food pumped with preservatives! Some food is energetically dead, like the supermarket tomato, a symbol of our culture: disposable, tasteless, incomplete. It's worth it to pay for alive organic produce, which is better for digestion.

I've always talked to my daughters about energy. When Wynonna and I would sing in harmony, we'd become a third entity. A beautiful golden warmth filled us with light. If I try to describe this to Joe Six-Pack, he's not going to get it. But Wynonna did. As an actress, Ashley learned she physically takes negative energy on. Once we talked with a mind-body researcher who analyzed the immunoglobulins of an actor when he played a villain versus when he played a hero role. The good guy had a more positive immune response. It explained why when Ashley was cast in a dark role she got sinusitis.

I've also been known to strike up conversations about energy in the aisles of Wal-Mart. Recently, in the automotive section, I was looking for a holder to put my drinks on in my car. A woman recognized me, just started talking. My intuition told me to ask if someone was sapping her, a person she felt obligated to but resented. Beaming, she said, "Yes! My sister-in-law." I told her a story about how I handle energy vampires, gave her a few suggestions. She thanked me. Then we parted. The fun thing was I didn't even know her name.

4

THE FOURTH PRESCRIPTION:
GENERATE POSITIVE EMOTIONAL
ENERGY TO COUNTER NEGATIVITY

AT THE VERY MOMENT my Aunt Sylvia died, lightning struck her family home during a freak thunderstorm. Somehow it figured. Growing up, I'd always been slightly scared of Sylvia: her opinionated bun; those cryptic instructions she'd slip under my teenage bedroom door citing how I could be nicer to my mother; her insistence on having the last word. Though Sylvia also had an endearing softer side, I wouldn't put it past her to make one final obstreperous exit from this life. *Crash! Zap! Sizzle!*—then gone! Astonishingly, her son, who lived in the house, told me this bolt from Beyond managed to bypass the surge protector and fittingly destroy his computer's motherboard!

Emotions are a dazzling expression of energy. As an energy psychiatrist, I know they contain stupendous life force, negative or positive. Medical school taught me only a fraction of their power. A rush of ecstasy, flash of rage, or flare to defy anyone who doesn't honor how awesome you are: emotions can either uplift or discombobulate. The warrior tracks her emotions and recasts negativity; the victim is beaten down, oblivious. Garnering positive energy requires moral courage, heart, and *chutzpah* (nerve). I'll show how to outsmart fear and other Spirit-sapping emotions so they don't devour you. Being wishy-washy won't do. In this program, you decide, "Do I want an angst-driven life or can I achieve more?"

It's time to feel something other than tired. My Fourth Prescription is a manifesto on how to counter negative emotions so you can let positive ones reanimate yourself. In terms of energetic wattage, optimism, self-acceptance, and compassion make you glow; shame, envy, and vengeance dim brightness by short-circuiting power. Cultivating positive emotional energy is an ongoing pursuit of opening your heart, striving for lovingkindness if you've lost it. Doing so isn't Pollyannaish or saccharine; it's an authentic life stance that unshackles joy.

Science dictates that energy is produced by cellular metabolism, but Energy Psychiatry recognizes it also comes from the firing of emotions in our surrounding fields. The emotional energy center, seen by mystics as yellow, is located in our solar plexus—the processing hub for both fear and joy. From this center, our moods generate positive or negative vibes. When you say, "I feel peaceful," it reflects positive energy flow in and around your body. You're aware of peace; others get a contact high from it. Or take the soul-sickness of terrorism. Imagine feeling so much hatred that killing your enemy becomes more important than saving your own life or even the love of your children. Such poison energetically infects the carrier and the field of everyone he or she contacts. Also, if you repress negative emotions, they'll congest your system. But when dealt with, the emotional release emancipates energy. Thus, our goals are to accentuate the positive and heal whatever thwarts goodness.

Emotional energy has consequences in any physical space: vibes are palpable and accumulate. Have you ever noticed the sweetness in a room where immense love is present? Perhaps in your grandmother's kitchen, a classroom with children playing, or an ashram where years of heartfelt meditation have occurred. Happy vibes are like fairy dust that get scattered around. You sense them and feel better. They also prime a space for good things to happen for everyone there. (A friend rightly said after our vacation at her farm, "Your loving this house so much feeds it.") Not so with negativity. One of my patients and his wife, looking for their first home, were offered an unbelievable deal on a Beverly Hills listing where a notoriously grizzly murder had occurred. They tried to convince themselves this was a chance of a lifetime, but finally concluded it was just too "creepy." There's an energetic explanation why we instinctively don't want cherished mementos or our families in a place where violence has occurred. A residue of emotional darkness can be felt. We shouldn't depreciate our reaction to it as mere superstition.

Knowing the many dimensions of emotional energy gives you a jump on mastering it. This program is about choice, not victimhood. For most of us humans, though, inner peace doesn't just magically descend; we must keep fighting for it. In fact, the Buddha taught eighty-four thousand ways to tame and pacify negative feelings! I'll teach you to pinpoint the energy of emotions: how they impact you, and tacks to turn difficult ones around. As an energy psychiatrist, I chase monsters from the dark so they don't loom before my patients. Naming the positive and negative forces within makes us immune to surprise attack. Then, as unproductive behaviors are overcome, we find freedom. Even if it's been dark for ten thousand years, we can always begin again.

BREAKING THE TRANCE OF FEAR

Whoever can see through all fear will always be safe.

TAO-TE CHING (TRANS. STEPHEN MITCHELL)

Fear is the biggest energy thief there is. A master seducer, it shamelessly robs us of everything good and powerful, preys on our vulnerabilities. Many people become mesmerized for a lifetime, letting negative attitudes seize control. Enough! Though some fears are intuitively protective, as I'll discuss, we can't let the irrational ones bamboozle us. Fear never stands alone; it inflames every vampiric emotion from worry to shame. This program shows you how to break fear's trance and reacquire lost energy.

As a psychiatrist, I know we *all* experience fear. Me. You. Your mother. The president. No one escapes. The wise ones admit it and, eyes open, confront and heal fear. The ones who're in trouble look the other way and, bit by bit, get eaten alive. The point is to stay conscious. When we know what we're dealing with, we decide who's in charge.

For new insight into fear, consider how it operates energetically. Let's say a boss visciously berates you. Instinctively, you're on guard. This sets off an adrenaline cascade, flooding your body with the "fight or flight" hormone and putting your body on high alert. Compounding this biochemical stress, on a subtle level fear pulses through your system, overriding positive energy. It all comes down to vibes. You can feel both positive and negative emotions resonate; they're like interior music. Emotional well-being occurs when positive vibes dominate and optimal resonances blend. Fear has a vibe just as delight does: one brings you down, the other elevates. When fear amps up within you, it's more like Mahler than Mozart. Some fears are short-lived. You feel the fear, sort through it; then it's gone. Others energetically inhabit you for decades, replaying the same tape.

Fear may spout from an external source. Since childhood, my patient Flo has contended with a near-demonic mother who'd drum into her head, "You're a good-for-nothing, unattractive slouch." Flo, a lovely caterer who was plenty successful despite her mother's virtual hex, felt nauseous and knifed in the solar plexus with each attack. Flo practically lived on antacids because, over time, the message had been seared into her emotional center. Words have energy to heal or harm. Flo couldn't shake the life-force-crucifying effect of her mother's words until she learned the Positive Energy Program's antifear tactics.

Sometimes we take on other people's fear. Intuitive empaths, receptors wide open, are particularly prone to absorbing it. As I've discussed, empathy intensifies in crowds. Each person emits emotional vibes, including fear. Magnify that by a hundred in the movie theater. Or a thousand in the symphony hall. To an empath it wields quite a punch. No wonder agoraphobics (people who panic in crowds, many who are undiagnosed empaths) never want to leave the house again. If you identify, I'll describe ways to stop being inundated by free-flying emotions.

Even for nonempaths, an overdose of fear can be lethal. A colleague was caught up in a tragic chain of events. When walking her poodle in a "safe" Beverly Hills suburb, she witnessed the murder of a man in a drive-by shooting. The shock was so severe, she suffered a heart attack there on the spot. While recovering in the hospital, she became agitated; she couldn't sleep. This extreme stress caused a previously undetected brain aneurysm to rupture, which abruptly killed her. I'm hard-pressed to envision a more snake-bitten scenario. What it can hammer home, though, is that negative energy is synergetic. To stop our fears from provoking one another, we must nip them in the bud.

Many fears are self-induced. We don't mean to, but we inflict an emotional terrorism on ourselves when we let our dark side run amok. The self-sabotaging messages we send, including the "I'm-not-good-enough" harangue, distort reality. To ensure we're perceiving ourselves accurately, we must look through the lens of love. I'll explain how. The truth is, each of us is magnificent, but our fears keep us from knowing it.

If we want to have high energy, we must expose fear's seductive but draining ploys. Fear gains a foothold when an authority figure's pronouncements get branded on our thoughts and energy fields. When the high school principal says, "Forget about college. You'll never make it," it's easy to buy into that hex. In addition, fear is our defense against being let down. If you expect the worst, energetically creating a negative force field around you, it's harder to be disappointed. Also, fear drowns out our intuition; it's a stronger, noisier energy than the nuanced vibes of the positive. Consider: Isn't your attention drawn more to the train wreck than a smoothly running system? The same is true of your thoughts. Fears leap out at you; serenity's quiet strength is often harder to discern.

There's a misguided expectation that if you're "evolved," you won't have to grapple with fear or negative emotions. Well, maybe in nirvana, but not on this planet. Here is where we learn: it's a training ground to hone positive forces and conquer negative ones, both as individuals and a civilization. Our daily lives—our choices— are an enactment of the fabled contest between dark and light. Exciting, yes—but a true test of the heart. Every time you choose love over fear, the good guys win. There's an old saying, "You're never given more than you can handle." An open heart is the greatest ally of all.

SHRINKING FEAR WITH POSITIVE ENERGY

When it comes to defeating fear, we're all in this together. Sharing solutions gives us more clout. In my interview with composer Quincy Jones (see Chapter 1 for his insights on intuition), I was moved by his tenacity in overcoming a fearful, troubled upbringing. Let his words spur you to greatness, too:

I grew up poor, on the streets of Chicago's Southside. My mother was schizophrenic, in and out of mental hospitals. Many people, like myself, have had horrendous childhoods. Lord knows many stars have. We make up a dysfunctional army. For years Oprah and I have talked about it. We both come from screwed-up families. She can take darkness apart, convert it in a New York minute! Then she gives the healing to so many people! It's important to blow darkness away with light. We've had to take pain and process it into something beautiful, positive, creative. You have a choice. Turn it on yourself or turn it around.

There is a demon inside the heart of the Buddha. There is a Buddha inside the heart of the demon. To protect your joy, you must be prepared to lock eyes with fear and say, "You're not going to run me. I'm stronger than you. Beat it!" Do this again and again. Fear is a merciless pursuer. You're really onto something when you see every experience—depression, loss, loneliness—as a way to grow larger, more compassionate, instead of shutting down. Banishing fear and its companions makes negativity wither. Life is only uncomfortable if you're afraid of it.

Our emotional history has many sides. Traumas and happy times are stored as memories in brain cells. They're also registered in neurotransmitters, which relay information between mind and body. Further, our emotional past is recorded in our energy fields, as it would be on film. Impressive evidence is surfacing that organs such as the heart literally possess cellular memories. Some heart-transplant recipients have reported new likes, dislikes, even food cravings that they later discovered matched the donor's. Subtly, either in our DNA and/or as energetic imprints, emotions reside in us. The harrowing ones latch on until they're healed. Walling them off takes energy.

Although you can't undo difficult events, the following tactics can unhinge the fear associated with them. (They also banish other negative emotions, which I'll give special instructions for later.) Use which ones work best. Ultimately, what matters is that love triumphs. In my life, fear has been one of my greatest tests and teachers. When I've really gotten sucked under, these tactics have reemerged me. My Energy Psychiatry patients live by them too. As they do, I suggest you keep a "Journal of Solutions" to record which tactics are most effective for you. Fear is feisty; count on it to reappear, though with awareness its trance will weaken. Get in the habit of referring to this journal. What has succeeded will succeed again.

SEVEN TACTICS FOR DE-ENERGIZING FEAR

Tactic #1: Name Your Fears So They Can't Ambush You

To de-energize fear, you must name it. Identify the whole gamut, miniscule or monstrous. Don't censor. (Submerged fears have more negative power than those expressed.) For instance, "I'm not smart enough, pretty enough . . . I'll never find a soulmate so I might as well not try." Some of my biggest fears include ending up drooling and alone in a nursing home; or that I'll suddenly die at home and just lie there unmissed until my cleaning lady finds me. Give each fear a name; describe it thoroughly.

Breaking the trance. Don't drift into denial. Scary worst-case scenarios need a positive retort. After you've named your fear, say to your nemesis, "Thank you for sharing." Then make a conscious move into your heart. (Impediments to love block energy flow.) Do this by verbally reframing your dilemma from a compassionate perspective. For instance, to replace fear with faith, I affirm, "I will be taken care of, not abandoned, in my time of need." To further cement your new affirmation, I suggest meditating on your heart (as you did in Chapter 2) to reconnect with whatever you love. I do this by focusing on Spirit—letting all that renewing energy fill me. This reminds me I'm not alone—nor are any of us. It releases me from the spell of my fearful myopia, and substantiates the integrity of the path I've been given. Conjuring positive energy in these ways collapses fear.

Tactic #2: Listen to Your Intuition

Once you've identified the fear, tune into the actual truth of the situation. Some fears are protective, others are not. Sometimes we must anticipate danger to survive, but too often unlikely or untrue fears put us on a draining high alert. We must question fears tied to low self-worth: we're all entitled to an extraordinary life, whatever form that takes. We also must question fears that we're unable to love. Even the severely traumatized can have enormous capacities. Fear seduces most when we doubt ourselves.

Breaking the trance. The following guidelines will help you to distinguish intuition from fear.

- **TRUSTWORTHY INTUITIONS WILL ENERGIZE YOU.** They are either neutral, simply conveying information; compassionate, never beating you up; or felt in the gut, tipping you off that something feels right or off. For instance, if late at night you notice an unkempt man approaching you and your gut senses negative vibes, it's prudent to avoid him. Or if the person you're dating has terrific qualities and your family and friends adore him, but your gut yells "Beware," don't marry the guy. At the very least, take the relationship slow.

- **IRRATIONAL FEAR, ON THE OTHER HAND, EXHAUSTS YOU.** It's so emotionally charged that you can't pick up neutral information. The content is often cruel or demeaning, *with no gut-level confirmation.* Irrational fear lacks the clarity of feeling on target. One good thing: its denigrating rants give it away. Knowing your fears can keep you from getting hooked.

Tactic #3: Say a Prayer to Lift Fear

Sometimes fear grips your spirit and just won't let go. You do everything right. You pin down the fear. You tune in. You know it's irrational, but still can't shake it. Now, ask for another kind of help. You may believe in angels, or that your grandfather is watching over you (mine is!). Whoever your emissaries of positive energy are, get ready to call in the troops.

Breaking the trance. Take a breath. Close your eyes. Be innocent, not cynical. Know that the nonmaterial world holds much magic our rational mind can never understand. Then say a prayer from the heart. It could be very simple: "Please take this fear from me." Meanwhile, just stay open. No tensing up. Let the positive energy you're summoning do its job. Requesting such intervention brings phenomenal results.

Tactic #4: Make a Gratitude List

Concentrating on what you're grateful for shifts fear. Gratitude is a form of positive energy. If you want it, you've got to seek it out. Gratitude doesn't just happen. By accentuating blessings, not problems, you're supplanting negative thoughts with positive vibes. Writing down what you're grateful for solidifies your sense of gratitude. If you're riddled by fear, however, the last thing you may feel like doing is counting your blessings. Nevertheless, take "contrary action"— even if you resist, make a list anyway. Until my patient Toni, a busy entrepreneur, broke down and wrote a gratitude list, all she could fixate on was the 10 percent that wasn't working in her life, rather than the 90 percent that was. I want to emphasize that Toni's absorption in her complaints was not so very different than how most of us behave. But an accounting of blessings is hard to argue with, and Toni had plenty. Viewing them on paper loosens fear's seduction.

Breaking the trance. Take at least ten minutes to compile your list; keep adding to it later. You may be grateful for your health, that miracle we too often take for granted. Or your home, a relative who truly listens, a trusty pair of combat boots, or your granny's sweet-potato pie. High up on my list is friends—when I've been overwhelmed by fear, a loving circle cocoons me in positive vibes and mirrors my own power. An attitude of thanksgiving is a mighty trance-breaker. By enlarging your list and reviewing it daily, fear doesn't have a chance.

Tactic #5: Visit an Energetically Uplifting Place

When fear takes hold, brooding in isolation isn't the answer. Get out of the house. It's all over if you become fear's captive audience. Go to a setting that makes you happy. Positive vibes will rub off on you. Soak them up. One of my patients goes to an aquarium. Another to a cathedral. Another to a Malibu bluff. Drinking in the energy of places you cherish offsets fear.

Breaking the trance. Visit places that feed your soul. When I'm depressed, I read in a corner of a bookstore, go to animal shelters and melt at all those sweet eyes, or if I'm really lucky, visit the circus when it comes to town. My love of books, animals, and the enchantment of carnival tents circumvents fear and returns me to my heart. Your special spots will do so too.

Tactic #6: Heal Energetic Scars

If fear persists, it may be rooted in the past. Unlike traditional psychotherapy, Energy Psychiatry doesn't view old traumas simply as memories; it acknowledges that they lodge in our fields forming energetic scar tissue that blocks our life force. Fear is locked in these scars, but it can be scattered when scars break up. Traumas must be retraced and healed for energy flow to resume.

One of my patients, a fifty-five-year-old man, was tormented by one fear: that his girlfriend of two years, whom he was crazy about, was cheating on him. From knowing her, I was certain he was wrong. (Also, he'd shared that he'd had similar suspicions about *all* his former girlfriends.) "Nothing I can say or do makes a dent in his suspicions. Even when he's not talking about them, I feel them orbiting around him," his girlfriend told me in desperation, about to call it quits. Fortunately, my patient was determined to try to get beyond this barrier. "I'm too old for this. It's killed my relationships so many times. If I've been wrong, I think now I'm willing to see it."

With his commitment, our therapy went deeper. He remembered as a boy walking in on his mother in bed with another man. A crucial moment: we'd uncovered his fear's origin. He sobbed and sobbed, a long-needed emotional catharsis that liberated energy. For over forty years, an energetic scar had obstructed his capacity to love and warped his perception of women. Catharsis, though, wasn't enough. In therapy, he had to go beyond this profound insight and apply it to his relationship. It was easier now. The past had less energetic pull, so he did an about-face into his present. Increasingly, he could see his girlfriend as she was, not as just a version of his mother. As a result, his suspicions gradually waned. A trusting romantic relationship finally became possible.

Breaking the trance. Don't let fears fester. For stubborn ones, it's wise to seek psychotherapy (energy-oriented is best; see the Resources section for referrals) or anger workshops. As you recognize your fears, keep breathing them out of your body. Visualize them exiting from a stuck place—say, the stomach—with each exhalation. Also, consider sessions with a massage therapist. Working with a masseuse who's savvy about subtle energy can unbind energetic blocks in the body. Sometimes we physically armor ourselves to keep painful memories at a distance. A masseuse's goal is literally hands-on: to melt muscular tension. Then repressed emotions can more easily break through. Locating a fear's source in the psyche and body helps dissolve an energetic scar.

Tactic #7. Avoid Absorbing Other People's Fears

Empaths alert! There's no upside to taking on the fears of others. As I train my empath patients, be extravigilant when fear strikes to avoid being emotionally overwhelmed. If you've been around a frightened person, and you leave upset or afraid, it's a good bet you've shouldered some of that angst. For example, when Jan, a medical student, was filled with anxiety after talking to a distraught friend at school who'd flunked anatomy, I intuitively sensed Jan's panic as a superimposed energetic appendage. Jan wasn't afraid of failing a class: the friend's fear had glommed onto her. My job as an energy psychiatrist is to find out who's causing what, then help my patients—and you—detach from assimilated external fears. Otherwise, emotional confusion can erupt from the blurring of energetic boundaries. When agoraphobics and those with panic disorders stop absorbing other people's fear, being in public can become a pleasure again. (Also see techniques for dealing with energy vampires in Chapter 9.)

Breaking the trance. When fear crops up, ask yourself: Is this mine or someone else's? Sometimes, though, it could be both. If the fear is yours, softly confront it. If not, try to pinpoint the obvious generator. However, if you've just watched a comedy film, yet you come home full of fear, you may have absorbed the fear from strangers sitting beside you at the theater; in close proximity, energy fields overlap. Ditto with going to a mall. To detach from fear:

- When possible, distance yourself from the source. Move at least twenty feet away, out of others' energy fields; you'll feel relief. Don't err on the side of not wanting to offend strangers. In a public place I don't hesitate to change seats if I get unsettling vibes.

- For a few minutes, center yourself by concentrating on your breath: keep exhaling fear, inhaling calm; practice the grounding and breathing meditations you've learned. Try visualizing fear as black smoke leaving your body, and calm as white light entering; it can yield quick results.

- Fear frequently lodges in your emotional energy center at the solar plexus. Place your palm there, as you focus on sending that location loving energy to flush fear out. Keep pumping love from your heart into the area to purify the emotional pollution.

BANISHING SELF-LOATHING, ANGER, WORRY, AND SHAME

The preceding seven tactics will help you fend off fear. However, other negative emotions, such as self-loathing, anger, worry, and shame can also drain your energy. Conventional views about how humans process such negative feelings leave me unsatisfied. Yes, it's fascinating that rage has been localized in the brain's hypothalamus, and that neuropsychiatry has pinpointed biochemical imbalances related to depressive self-loathing. Energy Psychiatry embraces these givens, but also lends a spiritual and energetic slant. How we handle difficult emotions—which aren't simply meant to torment us— doesn't make sense without it.

Self-Loathing

You might not know it by appearances, but self-loathing is rampant among us. Sometimes courageously honest people come to me and say, "I loathe myself, but I want to change." Others loathe themselves but don't realize it. Either way, self-loathing stems from a deep wound that forms a scar in our energy field; it requires the utmost compassion to heal.

Drawing on my UCLA medical training, I guide patients to untangle negative messages from their childhood or their present that stop them from seeing how special they are. In truth, all of us are special and worthy: this is a covenant of Energy Psychiatry I don't budge on. One unusually unguarded patient who was acutely sensitive to subtle energy as a child was dubbed by his parents "Poor Davey the space man." For years he believed their putdown, loathed himself. As you can imagine, this touched close to home. I know how diminishing it was to be raised by parents who rejected my intuitions. Growing up, Davey was always "different"; he communed with trees, animals, the sky. At twenty-five, a mailman, he was as timid as they come. A real innocent, he lacked worldly savvy, yet possessed a purity that defied cynicism. Davey needed help in blowing to bits his parents' unkind label. I was pleased to assist.

Energy Psychiatry validated so much of what Davey had always sensed, and allowed him to integrate his intuitions into a stronger identity. As a new world opened, his self-loathing began to abate. In a recent session, Davey told me, "I'm going to seek out people who don't belittle me when I say I see beautiful colors around them. I'm going to start hugging trees. I'm going to talk to the animals and tell them I never stopped loving them." Of course, Davey's pledge moved my heart.

Self-loathing can also have roots beyond this reality, as I discovered personally. Let me explain. Once upon a time, we *all* knew the expansive bliss of the Spirit-place from where we came—even the most hard-line, anti-woo-woo rationalists among us. Free of physical limits, our energy-bodies were boundless and soared. (Kids remember this; some need a whole lot of convincing why a gust of wind or a cape isn't sufficient to fly.) The truth is, we've had to compress ourselves to fit a physical form so we can learn the profound lessons of the body. Inwardly, though, we mistakenly link our comparative smallness and lack of bliss with feelings of "not being enough" and self-loathing. I educate my patients about the preciousness of the body and how to adjust from our vastness to a physical form: people hunger to know such details to gain greater perspective on who they are. Though my take on self-loathing is hardly typical, see if it strikes an intuitive chord.

MAKE CHANGES NOW
RELEASE SELF-LOATHING

If you loathe yourself a lot or a little, it's time to minister to your wounded heart. In your Journal of Solutions, survey the people, past and present, who impart(ed) negative messages about you—especially family. List these messages, no matter how painful. Most will be blatantly false. No matter how long you've believed any of them, now's your chance to see the truth. In psychiatry there's a term—folie à deux—for two people who share a similar delusion. Don't be party to this psychosis. It's not egotistical to view yourself in a positive light.

Even if your early criticism had a grain of truth—"You're too fat" is a common slam obese children suffer—the delivery is critical. We can all improve, but use compassion, not disdain, to further the process. In your journal, note what needs work and gently, kindly address it. Also, have mercy on

yourself in this human form. We're constantly faced with so
many physical and emotional challenges. In this program,
view them as a way to love more and fight back darkness.
Never accept some arbitrary negative dictate that someone—
I don't care if it's the pope!—has made about you.

Anger

Anger, an intense sense of displeasure and antagonism, comes from
the Latin *angere,* "to strangle." We get angry at those who've harmed
us, aggravated us, or let us down. We get angry at ourselves. At God.
Growing up, I was angry about being stuck on Earth; I felt like an
alien, just longed to go "home." Sometimes anger becomes a mask
for fear or hurt; it also leads to resentments, which I'll discuss later.
Anger is human; we all have it. In this program you'll learn to identify and healthily release it, then keep moving on. Anger is a toxic
subtle energy. Seething in your system, it can eat you alive, or else
dangerously erupt. Keep in mind: Those painfully polite churchgo-
ing housewives turned ax murderers snapped from repressing anger,
not from consciously expressing it.

Anger can also be physically destructive when it's channeled into
psychokinetic energy, the power of emotions to affect matter. Listen
to what happened to Kate. A competent, down-to-earth mother of a
young son, she'd come to my energy workshop terrified of her anger.
Overcoming her reluctance, voice quavering, she finally told the
group: "I was having a screaming match about money with my husband on the cell phone. Suddenly the huge picture window right
next to me shattered. I was the only one there. God, it freaked me
out!" Kate added that she'd previously cracked glasses and stopped
clocks with her anger, yet had tried to dismiss these "just too weird"
incidents. But a window?

As I explained to Kate, I've seen the energetic pandemonium anger
can cause. It can wreak horrible stress on the body and the environ-

ment. When I worked at a UCLA parapsychology lab, part of my job was to investigate "ghosts." It's always amused me how many people in Los Angeles suspect their houses are haunted. They'd describe electronic equipment turning on and off uncontrollably and dishes flying across the room. Far-out stuff! We researchers mostly concluded, though, that even if this phenomenon was authentic, it was misinterpreted. Generally it seemed to be an extension of anger in the family; as tempers flared, episodes increased. When the family moved, these bizarre incidents accompanied them—exemplifying how psychokinetic emotional energy literally alters its surroundings.

What I advised Kate, and suggest to you: Don't let anger get this far—use the following recommendations to defuse it. When I'm really irked, I know to first cool down. I do lots of journaling, praying, and deep breathing, so I'm not a loose cannon when I approach anyone else. You don't want your anger to damage yourself or anything else. In a way, Kate was lucky—she received instant physical feedback if her anger was over the top. You may too. When you get angry, remember Kate; anger can damage in numerous ways. Sometimes anger can be dealt with effectively in the moment—you clearly state the grievance, listen undefensively to the other person's perspective, and mutually work the issue through. Unfortunately, we're not always so cool and calm. To catch anger quickly and minimize the mayhem, here's an exercise to practice.

MAKE CHANGES NOW

DEFUSE ANGER THAT THROWS YOU OFF BY FOLLOWING THE 48-HOUR RULE

1. *Quickly identify your source of anger.* Impulsive, unconscious anger is the dangerous kind—it can hurt us, others, even break windows. To avoid unhappy repercussions, when anger hits,

slow down your reaction. Immediately identify the cause, but
don't go on the attack.

2. *Give yourself permission to rant for 48 hours max.* The worst
thing you can do is squash anger: trying to contain this energy
bomb will only explode your insides or cause you to passive-
aggressively act it out. But now is not the time to confront the
offender. For 48 hours, let loose and rail about the object of
your anger by yourself, or with a therapist or friend. Doing so
begins your healing by diffusing negative energy.

3. *After 48 hours, start letting anger go.* This means getting out of
your ego (even if you're "right") and into self-preservation.
Releasing anger is a process, but you can start now. I
recommend writing in your journal to vent *all* the venom. Or
keep praying to have it removed. Breathe your anger out of the
emotional energy center in the solar plexus; make sure it
doesn't congeal. Take a few moments periodically to breathe
calm in, and expel the toxicity of anger.

4. *Express your anger to the offender.* First, take a measure of the
situation. If the person is nonreceptive, vindictive, or there's no
positive gain (say with a tyrant boss), it may not be appropriate
to express your anger directly. Instead use the above steps or
minimize contact. If you think the person may be receptive,
remember the goal is not to eviscerate him or her, but to get
your point across and be heard. Keep your calm and firmly say,
"It makes me angry that . . ." The offender may want to resolve
differences or apologize. If not, don't fuel antagonism or engage
in a power struggle. Stay firm and centered in the knowledge
that you've expressed your truth. You might say, "I respect your
feelings, but we have to agree to disagree. I'm sorry we can't
resolve this right now."

Worry

Worry, the mental stress that comes from anticipating the negative, is derived from the Latin, "to constrict": nothing about it expands energy. Worry is a symptom of spiritual disengagement; it's obsessive, repetitive, often inconsolable. When we connect with a Higher Power, when we realize that even excruciatingly painful events can help our Spirit grow, worry makes less sense. Of course, I don't mean to minimize how hard-won such a perspective may be. It's appropriate, say, for a mother to be totally concerned about her sick child, but worry takes concern into the realm of suffering. Of course, I would help that mother fight for her child's well-being. But I'd also urge her to be kinder to herself, soften the worry state. Instrumental action is one thing; acceptance, another; fear, still something else. Though sometimes it seems nearly impossible, we must strive to accept life on its own terms, rather than succumb to worry. Even dreadful events can open our hearts.

My patient Nora, a likable woman with a razor-sharp intellect, just won't relinquish the conviction that she has bad luck. Nora says, "My mother told me this. All my boyfriends have seen it." She believes her singing career is failing because of it. "I'm always in the wrong place at the wrong time," is her mantra. Nora worries about bad luck, projects it onto any career opportunity. Nothing I or anyone can say will convince her otherwise. From an energetic view, Nora is pulling the worry noose tighter and tighter. So much so that I believe she generates a negative force field around herself, perpetuating a self-fulfilling prophecy.

If you're a worrier, I advise starting with a deceptively simple meditation. This gentle approach has begun to offer Nora relief. Like her, you can worry, but it won't do anyone any good. It'll tie your energy in knots. In this program, worry is something to transcend. Rest assured: Not worrying won't take your creative edge away, or make you less compassionate or discerning. Releasing yourself from worry simply stops suffering, an energy-saver and magnificent gift.

MAKE CHANGES NOW
LIFT WORRY WITH A LOVINGKINDNESS
MEDITATION

Worry makes us feel alone and unsafe, with no one to help us.
This meditation, from a 2,500-year-old Buddhist practice,
builds lovingkindness in yourself. Begin by finding a relaxed
position; take a few deep breaths. Once you're calm, repeat
inwardly the following phrases to lift worry. As you do,
picture yourself as a precious child, or as your current self
cradled in the arms of love.

> *May I be free of worry*
> *May I be well*
> *May I feel safe and at ease*
> *May I be at peace*

These phrases shift energy from negative to positive. Keep
repeating them silently whenever worry sets in: in the doctor's
office, taking a test, during meetings. In any situation, let
lovingkindness melt worry away. (I also recommend Sharon
Salzberg's book *Lovingkindness,* my bible on this meditation
practice—see the Selected Readings at the end of the book.)

Shame

Shame is a negative emotion that comes from feeling defective. It's a
sense of worthlessness, inner torment, and failure that makes our
Spirit cower and drains our vitality. John Bradshaw describes shame
as "a deep cut felt primarily from the inside." I read shame as a subtle wound branded on our energy field. We feel shame because our
parents felt ashamed of themselves—just as ducklings imprint their

mother's behavior, we emotionally emulate our early role models. Shame also comes from being abandoned, neglected, or abused. Society can inflict shame on us. Shame about being too fat, not pretty enough, too old. We each carry secret shames, some more weighty than others. One friend, who's pure counterculture, was ashamed of "selling out" by watching *Entertainment Tonight.* To feel our best, our shames need to be surfaced, spoken, healed.

MAKE CHANGES NOW

RELINQUISH SHAME WITH THE FLOWER CURE

Don't let renegade negative vibes from shame (or any negative emotion) undermine your energetic progress. To know what you're dealing with, write a complete "Shame List" in your journal. Then read the list to someone you trust. Hidden shames begin to lose their grip once spoken.

Then try a trip to the florist. For every shame, choose a flower. Perhaps a daffodil if you're ashamed of your body; a lilac for being an outsider; an orchid for being "overly sensitive"; a sunflower for deception. Make a lovely bouquet; take it home. In the future, whenever shame arises, let the associated flower remind you of your capacity to lift shame, forgive yourself, and appreciate your own beauty.

Flowers are our friends. They have healing power. These joyous and generous life forms can remind us of our light.

The emotions I've discussed in this section, and across the board, require regular housecleaning. You know what a victory it is when you clear out your closets and donate bulging trashbags of old stuff to Goodwill? Discarding negativity is just as rewarding. Negativity is prone to accumulate, but it's up to you for how long. By the time bone-deadening exhaustion sets in, it may take months on your back to recover. Facing negative emotions regularly will prevent emotional baggage from dragging you under.

PURGING NEGATIVE ENERGY LEFTOVERS: RELEASING RESENTMENTS AND MAKING AMENDS

At fourteen I fell in love for the first time. Andy's eyes were cobalt blue. I'll never forget how they sparkled when he surfed Malibu. Or the sweet scent of jasmine as we held each other on spring evenings in the botanical gardens by my home. Then one day, after being inseparable for nearly two years, I spotted him kissing the most popular blonde-haired, blue-eyed cheerleader at school. Worse, they saw me, but still kept on making out in her new red Camaro. Crushed, I wept for months, drained of all energy. The hardest part was Andy never called to explain. For twenty years, I harbored hurt and a long list of understandable resentments.

Then one day he called me. We met for lunch in Venice Beach, and I asked him, "Why?" Of course I felt terrific hearing "It was the worst mistake of my life," and "I was selfish. I just wanted to be popular." Teenage priorities: in retrospect they were easier to comprehend. The miracle of the afternoon was that I could begin to forgive him; bitter grievances that I'd held so long started to recede. Perhaps my heart had grown, or people's shortcomings—and my own— seemed more forgivable as I've gotten older. Whatever the reason, I felt energy freed in me that I didn't even know was constricted. From then on, I felt more of my vibrance accessible.

As resentments amass, they're like a film clouding the clarity of your energy. There may seem to be a million "good" reasons to cling to them, but they're a million drains on your energy. You might even get a charge from all that resentment, but in the end it'll asphyxiate you. The better path is to reel your ego in, tenderly sort through lingering hurts, then strive to surrender them. Not for anyone else, but for yourself.

Forgiveness is a state of grace, nothing you can force or feign. In Energy Psychiatry, I guide patients toward the large-heartedness to forgive injuries both caused by others and self-inflicted. Forgiveness penetrates the impenetrable—the obstinacy that stifles love, the tenacious pain that dams our energy reserves. A Stanford research study showed that practicing forgiveness significantly decreases stress, rage, and psychosomatic symptoms. Makes sense, considering all the built-up negative energy that forgiveness expels. I'm not saying that betrayal is ever justified, that you aren't entitled to be upset if someone wrongs you. Or that you shouldn't try to improve or else leave a destructive situation. Practicing forgiveness, though, ensures that resentments don't gorge ravenously on your energy. Finally, remember forgiveness refers to the actor, not the act. You can pardon the woundedness of the offender while acknowledging the harmfulness of the offense.

MAKE CHANGES NOW
LET RESENTMENTS GO

The purpose of relinquishing resentments is to increase *your* positive energy. Select a target: A critical mother. A controlling husband. A cut-throat colleague. Perhaps you've tried to discuss the grievance with no results. (Always attempt to work things out if the person is the slightest-bit receptive.) Or your target may truly be unapproachable. In either case, away from the person, air your resentments without sugarcoating them. Do this in a journal, with a therapist, or friend. For example say, "I despise that double-crossing conniver because . . ." No inhibitions. No shortcuts. Frankly expressing your feelings is a necessary bridge to forgiveness.

But then, in a quiet moment, really reach to find compassion for the person's shortcomings, not the deed itself. Seek to probe. This may be very hard work. What insecurities or fears motivated him? Why is her heart so closed? What caused his moral blindness? Try to discern the context of the person's actions. At this point, you may be able to start to forgive. Perhaps you're not there yet—that's okay. The request itself sets off a stream of positive vibes, a purgative cleansing of your system. Repeat the exercise once a day for at least a week. See if your energy improves. I'll bet you'll feel a burden lift.

Now let's reverse the scenario. What if you're the one who has harmed someone? Inevitably, we all do, even if unintentionally. Admit it, please. It could be a small wrong. A good friend who was nursing a grievance correctly reproached me: "You don't respect my time when you always show up late for dinner." Or it could be a larger wrong. You may embezzle money, cheat on your wife, slander a partner. No matter the offense, to reverse negative energy, you must start by making amends.

Taking responsibility initiates damage control. I knew my friend was right about my lateness, though I must confess I was still tempted to get defensive. Instead, I apologized, promised to show up on time in the future. My friend's resentment lifted. End of story. Sometimes such an admission is all that's needed to clear the slate. Don't let false pride deter you.

Obviously, larger wrongs take more doing to heal. Follow these steps. First, with as much humility as you can muster, admit your wrongdoing. Next, do everything humanly possible to right the situation: repay debts, publicly revoke a slanderous statement, enter couples therapy to mend a betrayal. Ultimately, though, forgiveness is up to the person harmed. In my psychiatric practice, I've seen relationships survive a deep wounding, but only after sincere attempts at forgiveness. However, even if the rift is irreparable, your amends are imperative. They stop the perpetuation of bad energy.

In this regard, I'm moved by a story about Saint Francis. They say that for years he rode from town to town on a donkey. Shortly before he died, one of the last things Saint Francis said was, "Brother donkey, you've been so patient carrying me around day after day. Please forgive me for any inhumane treatment of you." How extraordinary: Saint Francis wanted to get clear with a beast of burden, considered the donkey a sentient being. Surely we can learn from this, at the very least seek a higher ground with our human intimates. I urge you to ask forgiveness for even inadvertent harm. Apart from its benefits to the recipient, such a request will give *you* more exuberance.

A tenet of Energy Psychiatry is that negativity breeds negativity. Stimulus and response: the harm you do others can impede your zest. At this stage in my life I well know that I get zapped by instant karma. If I'm rude, short with someone, or neglectful, it weighs on me. My energy takes a hit. So every night, for a few minutes, I engage in a liberating ritual I suggest to you. In my journal I write a brief inventory of the day: the good things I've done, and amends to be made. There it is, right in front of me. The next stage is to act, the sooner the better. If I quickly correct the wrongs—by e-mail, on the phone, or in person (better for larger amends)—negative energy can't gather steam.

I have a patient, a top entertainment attorney, who struggles with the notion that all behavior has energetic consequences. He asks, "Why then do so many despicable backstabbers only get richer and more influential?" A perennial refrain from Los Angeles patients and friends, especially in show business. Though the laws of physics dictate that every action has an equal and opposite reaction, the disease of deceit isn't always visible. But doctors are privy to concealed truths. As a psychiatrist, having worked with many of these people, I know the terrible price they pay, whether or not they realize the cause. You can't cook up deceit without having it sicken you. Chronic pain, depression, a crippled capacity to love—deceit congeals energetically into toxic pockets. The subtle energy system weakens and springs leaks. Power mongers I've had as patients feel a growing hollowness. In response, they scramble to fill it with more money, fame, acquisitions. The curse is, nothing is ever enough.

With such patients, I've seen how insight into this relentless pattern empowers them to begin to change. Then, when they start feeling better, they recognize the energy pay off. Even so, some may be loathe to admit the connection. A CEO with anxiety attacks declared in a session, "I have to be ruthless to stay on top." Such conviction is tough to alter. Nor as a therapist do I always succeed. The depletion of life force—in him, worsening panic and insomnia—just accelerates. The next time you bemoan a two-faced tycoon who "has it all," remember the energetic interplay behind the scenes.

AS MEMBERS OF THE HUMAN FAMILY, we all have our share of strengths and weaknesses. However, you don't have to take negative energy—yours or anyone else's—lying down. The Positive Energy Program's Fourth Prescription helps you combat darker emotions with awareness and love. Humor also helps. A friend who manages country music bands jokingly personifies the painful pangs of envy he knows too well: "Hey bro'. It's you again. I knew your momma!" Aspire to heal insecurities, but don't give them excess juice.

Constructing and protecting a world of light, inner and outer, requires a resolve to deconstruct negativity. To achieve peace at all levels, there's no way around it. Poet Mary Oliver in *Shadows* reminds us:

Everyone knows that the great energies running amok cast
terrible shadows, that each of the so-called
senseless acts has its thread looping
back through the world and into a human heart.

The energy we project has real repercussions, for ourselves and society. We possess the capacity to become golden, not dark. Practicing this prescription, with mindfulness and mercy, you can overturn emotions that fetter aliveness.

Treat Yourself:

Take an official break from worrying or emotional problem solving to renew your energy. For an hour or more let the pressure off. Call the silliest friend you know and talk about clothes and movies. If you prefer, lie in bed and eat orange slices. Or you could shoot hoops or just stare at the sky. Do nothing, if nothing is all you want to do.

INTERVIEW: IYANLA VANZANT
ON HEALING NEGATIVE EMOTIONS

IYANLA VANZANT IS A NATIONALLY RECOGNIZED
INSPIRATIONAL SPEAKER, BESTSELLING AUTHOR,
AND ORDAINED MINISTER.

✳

For me, positive emotional energy is when your thoughts, words, feelings, and actions are aligned. I can sense this in someone's energy field as a warmth, a brightness. It comes through my intuition. Their aura is peaceful and welcoming. It's tangible. Around a positive person, I can let my guard down. When I generate positive energy in myself, I feel joyful and want to smile at strangers on the street. I consider this energy, also called qi, to be divine—an inner light that radiates through us, the noble essence of every being.

Negative emotional energy, such as fear, anger, and dishonesty, feels totally different. I'm repelled by it, on guard. I'm up against a cold wall. I can see a gray cast over someone—their skin, eyes, and essence are dull. Frequently people are unaware of the vibes they give off.

We all have negative emotional energy to heal. The one thing I tell people: when you set out to pull your life together, expect it to fall apart. Most of our lives have been built on weak foundations. Before I could be in a place to be an author, teacher, and healer, I had to reconcile myself as an angry, abandoned woman of color in a male-dominated racist society. I needed a grander vision of myself. I had to stop being a black woman and just be a feminine expression of the presence of God. Doesn't mean I don't express that as a woman of color. I just needed to rethink the label. To get to a higher realm, I had to really wallow in the belly of the lower realm so I knew what negativity I was releasing. We must examine the emotions restricting us. Otherwise they get stuck in our subtle energy fields, locked in our bodies. We'll carry a heavy energetic weight. Denial causes suffering.

I've worked to transform my negative energy. In my mother's womb I marinated in anger, fear, and disempowerment. That stuff was etched in my DNA. My mother was a poor, single black woman in the 1950s who'd had breast cancer. Nothing came easy. From the start I was a problem. I was born in the back seat of a New York taxi, totally out of place. In my mid-twenties, though, I began to come aware. When people would say, "Why are you so angry?" I finally let down my defenses and asked myself, "Well, why am I?" I've had help from teachers who showed me how the mind can heal. When you go from "This is horrible" to "There's something good I can learn here," your thinking changes. More than an intellectual knowing, it's an energetic shift.

Harboring anger and resentments is unhealthy. I know how important it is to let them go. If they store up, my body reacts. I'm hard-headed. Sometimes I need physical demonstrations to get my attention. My chest constricts. I completely lose my voice. My body holds on to fat more. When I gain four inches on my butt or get shingles under my armpits, this I notice!

To reverse negative energy, my own and in others, I create more positive energy. I try to stay in a place of truth, of gentle compassion. Conscious, deep breathing helps; it slows down my fears and my judgments, returns me to my heart. So does getting a loving massage, a sauna (which removes toxins), or an energy-healing session. Of course, I'm human. Sometimes I feel angry or afraid. But the worst thing I can do is to beat myself up or make another person wrong. There's an old saying, "If you keep pouring water in a glass the dirt will rise to the surface and dissipate." We do this through positive thoughts and actions. Love is the best way to shut negativity down.

Love is the most positive energy we have. I just keep on sending it. Utilizing the strength of our hearts will help heal ourselves and the planet. We've been in denial. To turn negativity around we must acknowledge it exists. Why does recent global terrorism surprise us? Because we haven't made the link between the micro and the macro. As individuals, we don't know our own power. We don't realize that we each walk in an energy field. That these energy fields rise up to create a worldwide environment.

Change starts with us. You know that song: "Let peace begin on earth and let it begin with me." If five thousand of us sat together and prayed to end war tomorrow, it might not happen. It could be that ten people died instead of ten thousand—but we won't necessarily see that. In small and large ways, we can call forth the good, bring love into existence. So, when you're walking down the street and see somebody, smile at them. You're sending a vibration. Maybe she'll smile at the next person. Soon we'll have a whole city of people smiling at each other.

5

THE FIFTH PRESCRIPTION: DEVELOP
A HEART-CENTERED SEXUALITY

HAS SEX BECOME humdrum? Obligatory? Stuck on the back burner? Great news: Your erotic side is about to enter its next incarnation.

Prepare to view sexuality in terms of energy, not from pop culture's warped spin on what this experience is supposed to be. For everyone, a vibrant, true-to-self eroticism is within reach. I'll teach you to birth sexual energy from within—the starting place of claiming this power. Then you can shine it toward your partner. Learning this can make a good sex life better, or rescue a lackluster one from monotony or hibernation. It will also increase your passion for all of life.

We've been brainwashed about what healthy sexuality means. Singer-songwriter Kenny Loggins got it right in our interview on sex and energy when he told me, "In music you hear guys selling themselves like a bad infomercial. The 'I can go all night Baby' refrain serves to mask the hidden geek inside many performers." Maybe being a superlover is your ambition, and you've succeeded: fantastic. But, if you're like me, this goal isn't at all appealing. Sexual styles are unique. I'll help you define your rhythms and needs.

Sexuality is an enigma to many of my patients when they start Energy Psychiatry—more of an on/off phenomenon than an inner connected flow. For some, it's a runaway train that becomes a com-

Judith Orloff, M.D.

pulsion. More often, though, patients come to me with their sexuality long shut down. The exhaustion of raising young children. Passionless marriages. Vast stretches of being without a sexual partner. Past trauma or betrayals that cause emotional retreat. Sexuality can just feel too frightening. Sometimes, however, we're also passive about nurturing this area. It's gone, we figure, it's too much effort to get it back.

Energy Psychiatry makes recovering sexuality easy for you. The focus is on more than physical love between partners—that's glorious, but only a petal of the rose. As I teach it, sexuality is also an energetic entryway to life, spirit, and, most important, yourself. Without this openness, an intimate relationship is difficult. Further, it may seem surprising, but even if you never have a lover again, you can still keep this energy center open. One nun-in-habit attending my workshop who'd felt a sexual surge while meditating was much relieved to hear this! The potential for passion is in each of us. I'll show you how to locate it.

This program's Fifth Prescription is an energy-based guide to blending heart, sex, and soul. Our life force is rainbowlike with distinct radiances—physical, emotional, spiritual, sexual. Yes, we can lead fulfilling lives without being sexually active, but developing this part of yourself—with or without a partner—optimizes your entire energy spectrum. In our energetically insensitive world, sexuality is easily spooked. I hope you'll approach it with special tenderness.

I find it strange that sexuality isn't typically part of wellness programs. From a subtle standpoint, it constitutes a major energy center in the body that increases vitality. As I've said, our energy centers are positioned along the midline from head to toe; each corresponds to different qualities. For instance, the "root" center in the genital area is linked to sexuality and the color red; the heart center in the chest is the storehouse for love; the crown chakra, or halo, is linked to spirituality. Thus, erotic force is a component of a larger continuum. Picture it: sexual force rises upward as it mixes with the energy

160

of the other centers. You'll feel more vital when there's free flow between all channels.

Sexuality recharges everything about you. It releases pent-up emotional and physical angst, which lowers stress. You sleep more peacefully; depression and anxiety lessen. Additionally, as you age, sexual activity balances hormones, increases vaginal blood flow and lubrication; it surely improves your quality of life, may even increase longevity. Nurturing your life force, you can't help but become sexier with age.

When you're erotically awake, your energy field becomes electric. You project vibes others can feel. In *Sexus,* Henry Miller describes his realization that women are powerfully drawn to him right after he's slept with a lover; they sense something compelling. Many of my patients have concurred: "I attract more people if I'm in love myself." Street wisdom says, "Thems that has, gets."

We all hold sexual energy differently. Some of us keep these vibes close to center; others shoot them across the room. Look at celebrities. I, personally, respond to the low-key magnetism of Wesley Snipes. Or the organic sensuality of Susan Sarandon and Sophia Loren. Knowing how you carry your energy is key when relating to others, and also to feeling at home in your own skin. What matters most is the quality of energy we emanate.

Positive sexual energy brings a heart-centered focus to your erotic life—way more sexy than being only genitally focused. It includes how you treat yourself and your partner. These vibes are a stunning mix of feeling warm, cared for, and deliciously aroused. Negative energy is the opposite. Cold, prickly, never really feels safe, though, of course, it can coexist with intense sexual attraction. At worst it's heartless, driven by control, obsession, or abuse.

Historically, women particularly are dogged by attempts to squash their energy. Sad to say, feminine sexual and intuitive power can terrify men. "Witches" burned. Chastity belts. Domestic violence. Clitorectomies. Afghani women—many of whom didn't choose Muslim dress—reduced to asexual bundles in *burkas.* I want to stress: Joy in our sexual selves isn't a self-indulgence or narcissism. It can be a form of political and energetic freedom.

The Fifth Prescription is devoted to how you can mobilize positive sexual energy and purge the negative. Consider it a refurbishing of your energy field. You'll need to do some detective work, be willing to test out possibilities. The intent is to uncover what erotically energizes you. It's a marriage of power and play.

IGNITING YOUR OWN SEXUAL ENERGY

We each have the capacity to activate our passion. Know that it's in you; set out to find it. Erotic numbness is a symptom of energy shutdown—a reaction to everything from exhaustion to old hurts. Igniting positive sexual energy in yourself is an unnumbing process that requires waking up your body and removing the blocks that hinder sensation.

You don't need another person to jump-start your sexuality. How frequently I've heard from patients and friends, "When I'm not attracted to someone, my sexuality goes on hold. It's automatic." Accepting this as a fait accompli is to be exiled to some libidoless limbo. Rest assured, more compelling options exist. *Energy truth #1:* Your sensual self need not be condemned to dormancy or death if you aren't in a relationship. *Energy truth #2:* When you're sensually in love with all of life (this azalea, that Siamese cat, the foam on a cresting wave), you'll feel more passion individually and with a partner. Even without a relationship, your sensual self can be fed. However, if you choose to be with a partner, you won't arrive empty-handed, nor will you expect him or her to kindle a passion you already possess.

As you broaden the range of the erotic, realize that it can arise from unexpected sources. Early in my energy explorations, the force of this took me by surprise. In 1986, I was attending a women's spirituality workshop on the north shore of Kauai. At the start of a period of silence and fasting, I walked through a lush tropical grove to the Pacific at twilight. Soft trade winds rippled through my thin cotton dress as I watched the hula of the palms. Moist air caressing my skin, I was mesmerized by the fluttering leaves of a nearby plumeria; their quivering was arousing me. Astonished, as I leaned against the tree, I felt it sending pulses of heat into me. I glued my back to the trunk, afraid that any movement or critiquing of what was occurring would make the sensation cease. Thank God my mind cooperated. My whole body burst into orgasm.

That evening in Kauai, I was introduced to nature's ecstatic sensuality. My linear physician's mind said, "Impossible!," but my body intuitively testified to the energetic reality I was experiencing. Before this, I'd always depended on a man to trigger my erotic side. Whenever I was single I felt less feminine, almost invisible as a woman. Realizing that sexuality originates in myself and in nature has been transformative.

In the spirit of discovery, the following exercises provide ways for you to invite erotic energy in. Approach each as a loving meditation with a sensual flare—a chance to bring all the heart you've practiced so far to this sphere. Do these exercises alone. The purpose is to feel erotic energy in yourself without a partner.

MAKE CHANGES NOW

AWAKEN YOUR SENSUAL SELF

Set aside quiet time without risk of intrusions to playfully experiment: you'll be lingering in nuances of the erotic. Begin to relax by breathing deeply and slowly. We habitually breathe shallowly to temper sexual and other feelings. Be kind to yourself. As you've done before with negative emotions, keep exhaling any fear or shame about the body.

I want you to sense, not think, to be in your physical self as completely as possible. While practicing the techniques I outline below, the same ones I teach my patients, lightly focus on the sexual energy center in the genital area. From this spot, erotic force—which can feel tingly, electric, or warm—shoots outward a few inches or more. Even if this region feels numb, placing attention there increases your sensitivity.

- *Awakening touch.* Take a fresh flower or a feather and gently, slowly stroke your entire body. (For me, it's a rose in full bloom with petals about to fall.) Start with your cheek, neck, chest, gradually working your way downward. Indulge in the sensations. Then touch specific energy centers with the flower or feather—say, your sexual center or heart. To activate them make repeated, delicate, circular motions over these areas. It'll feel lovely. Energy responds to a barely perceptible touch.

- *Awakening taste.* You're going to taste like you never have before. Pick a few diverse foods, herbs, or spices that have zing. Arrange them on a plate. My favorites are papaya, peppermint, and honey. I have a numbers-barraged accountant patient who perks up her sensuality by savoring a thin, juicy piece of watermelon. To hone your sense of taste, I suggest wearing an eye mask or loose blindfold such as a silk scarf. Then, eyes covered, sample each selection one by one. Don't miss a microsecond of the varying sensations. Taste isn't limited to the mouth; it has energy that spreads throughout the body. Let it stimulate every pore.

- *Awakening smell.* Similarly, experiment with smell, an intimate part of sexuality that can turn you off or on. (Especially in the beginning, a blindfold can accentuate this sense.) One patient, a full-time mom, gets a sensual lift from a few whiffs of lavender or gardenia oil during the day. She keeps them readily available in her desk and car. Test different scents; see how your body responds. Use them as a sensual refresher.

- *Opening to nature.* Draw on the moods of nature to enhance sensuality. Storms, lightning, rainbows, wind in the woods—

> whatever aspect excites you, let it register in your body. Be
> aware of colors, textures, sounds. Absorb it all. Energy is
> communicated from nature to you, a spontaneous osmosis.
> Sometimes, to the low pulse of a distant foghorn, I'll twirl on
> my balcony, overlooking the ocean. It's a magical, sensual
> movement. Dense fog hovers, engulfs muted street lamps, as I
> dance it into me. Focus on a phase of nature that's beautiful to
> you. Let nature's energy infuse you.

These simple, quick exercises catalyze your sensual relationship with yourself. My patients use them as ongoing energy tune-ups. They offer a continued awareness of sensual aesthetics, not just a one-time fix. Seeing life through these eyes, your senses will heighten. Notice goosebumps, tingles, or surges of warmth—how your body feels, all of it, especially belly, genitals, breasts. Never stop reveling in these marvels. You'll experience more pleasure as dormant energy releases.

REMOVING SEXUAL BLOCKS

Sometimes past sexual wounds, forming scars in our energy field, can prevent us from opening. We encounter a numbness that's too daunting to bypass. When I work with patients who have this issue, I begin by interrogating their histories to find the source of negative energy. For instance, male patients who've been raised by chauvinistic fathers have trouble unifying sexuality with heart; female patients with repressed mothers have lacked models for maturing into erotically responsive, heartful adults. Abuse and letdowns also cause an erotic disconnect. Until these crippling patterns are broken—the aim of the traditional psychotherapy I was trained in and use—such intergenerational imprinting prevails. But healing can't stop there. As an energy psychiatrist, I also must act as surgeon to help my patients excise energetic scars. Insight alone isn't sufficient.

Consider how I worked with Kim. At twenty-one, she'd come to me, anxious and erotically shut down. "It happened right after I got married two months ago. Something beyond my control went cold." In our sessions, I began by backtracking. Looking sad and weary, Kim filled me in: "My husband, David, and I fell profoundly in love at eighteen. We had everything in common, and a great sex life. Soon we became engaged. But we were so young. David had an affair. I was heartbroken. I just couldn't bring myself to forgive him, no matter how much he pleaded. Then we separated." But, a year later, missing each other terribly, Kim and David began going out again, though Kim's pain was far from resolved. Before they had a chance to really work things out, however, she became pregnant. They decided to marry. That's when her orgasms stopped. She told me, "David was affectionate and supportive, but when he touched me, I couldn't feel it."

Removing sexual scars requires a multidimensional approach. First, in our sessions I encouraged Kim to howl forth her agony, her rage about being betrayed, so she didn't retain those toxins. Also, to confront a deeper issue of being emotionally abandoned by her father, the energetic scar's origin. All this figured into her capacity to forgive David, and be willing to risk trusting him again. But we didn't just do talk therapy. I had Kim tune in to her sexual energy center, describe sensations there, and breathe the "flat, cold deadness" out. Breath can dislodge remnants of energetic scars. The healing process entails articulating how a trauma feels in an energy center, then expelling those vibes. Kim sobbed endlessly in these sessions. Thank goodness: she was experiencing an emotional and energetic catharsis.

The next few months, Kim's sexuality returned in glimmers. It'd come, then go. But one day there was a breakthrough: "David and I were in the car in front of our favorite Chinese restaurant. He reached out, placed his hand on mine. To my surprise, a warm charge suddenly surged through me. Feeling something, anything, felt wonderful. I started to cry." A threshold had been crossed. Our work enabled her to be primed at the moment she was ready. Energy blossoms when the time is right. From that evening, Kim's sexuality has continued to build. True, David was earning trust by being loyal and loving, plus he'd entered therapy. But without Kim's courageous inner work, saving their marriage would not have been possible.

In this program, I urge you to start healing sexual scars. But, as you do, remember not to let a trauma define you—your spirit is so much larger than any one incident, no matter how extreme. With this in focus, begin by identifying the wound without minimizing its impact. Our minds can too easily rationalize, "That was so long ago. Get over it!" Or "How can you be upset by such a 'small thing?'" These arguments are bogus. A wound is a wound. Case closed. You can try healing it yourself by journaling your feelings, and expressing them to friends. But in this ultravulnerable area, I urge you to seek out a smart psychotherapist with a knowledge of energy. The key is always to unbind a backlog of pain and breathe out emotional residues stuck in the sexual or other energy centers.

READING SEXUAL ENERGY IN OTHERS: IS IT HEARTFELT OR INTRUSIVE?

First, I'm going to show you how to negotiate sexual energy in the world. Then I'll move on to techniques with your partner. In our busy lives we get hit by so much, so fast. Sexual vibes are a major part of that assault (especially relevant if you're an overwhelmed empath). Many of us don't realize we're exposed to them everywhere, are clueless about what we ourselves give off. Some vibes invigorate: a sweet good-night kiss; an acquaintance flashing you a winning smile; a friend admiring how sexy you look. In contrast, negative vibes abrade: a construction worker's intrusive whistle on your way to work; a business associate calling you "Babe"; another passenger on the train ogling you. Signals come in. You're the receiver. Get accustomed to reading them.

As an energy psychiatrist, part of knowing my patients is reading their energy, from emotional to sexual. This doesn't require touching or even talking. Here's what I do: A new patient sits in my waiting room. I open the door. The first few seconds, I quietly notice my body responding as a kind of litmus paper registering the patient's vibes. For instance, in our culture, both men and women are taught to lead with sexual energy, whether they're aware of doing so or not. Pow! In some people it's downright obnoxious, not respectful of boundaries. I think of one patient who, when we first met, sat there with his legs wide open, and looked like he wanted to pounce on me. Then he stood so close, he was right in my face. I was put off by his intrusion, glimpsed how others must react to him. His invasiveness alerted me that our work would be about balance and containing inappropriate vibes. In contrast, I read other patients' sexual energy as anesthetized, mummified, or withheld, particularly with the abused. Here an awakening is called for.

I'd like you to begin to notice the effect of sexual vibes in small and large interactions. The knack is to identify them, especially the dicey ones, so you won't protectively glaze over in the daily hubbub. Sometimes, in the bank line or car wash, you may feel someone's vibes just by being near their energy field. The person need not specifically "do" anything. On the other hand, think about flirting, an erotic energy exchange that is often intentional. A provocative word. A come-hither glance. Your energy meter may register such gestures as positive—a possible prelude to romance—or negative, a smarmy imposition. No right or wrong about your intuitions. What matters is how *you* feel around a person's energy.

For scooping out vibes, here are some trusty indicators:

SIGNS OF POSITIVE SEXUAL ENERGY

- Heart-centered
- Warm
- Balanced
- Respectful of boundaries
- Vitalizing, safe, whole

SIGNS OF NEGATIVE SEXUAL ENERGY

- Smothering, manipulative
- Chilling
- Creepy, crawly, like you've been slimed
- Intrusive
- Draining, unsafe

MAKE CHANGES NOW

READ SEXUAL ENERGY IN DAILY LIFE

Now you're going to put the signs I've described to work. Get used to tuning in to the sexual vibes of others. Pay special attention to sensations in your sexual energy center. I intuitively sense this area as a flower: around some people it opens, around others it tightens up. See what your response is. In addition ask yourself: Am I generally relaxed with how he or she projects sexuality? Repelled? Neutral? Rate the intensity. Is the energy too much? Just right? Not enough? Don't make excuses for the person.

When it comes to intrusive energy, a cigar is usually a cigar. Call it like it is. Practice self-care by moving toward vibes that suit your sexual wavelength.

When others exude a natural, nonintrusive sexuality, it can be an expression of wholeness and energetic health. Balanced vibes may have nothing to do with romantic intentions. Sometimes we get too apprehensive if we simply sense another's sexual self. In truth, that's a sign of our well-roundedness as humans. If we only register a big erotic blank from others, we cease to be alive! In this program, you want to embody sexual energy comfortably, and attract those you're in sync with.

Inevitably, though, you'll also be exposed to negative vibes and must know how avert them. At times it's an easy call. You're out with a guy who won't stop groping you. The solution? End the date—and don't see him again. But how about less obvious cases? A friend's husband keeps gazing in your eyes just a little too long. The car mechanic gives you the sexual willies for no "obvious" reason. You may doubt your read of the situation or try to ignore the energy, yet it won't let up.

Here's my advice: Trust yourself. You don't have to condone unnerving sexual vibes. Or walk around with a reeled-in sensuality because you're afraid. I know how disturbing these vibes can be; I intuitively perceive them as vandals who rob the sanctity of my personal space. As I tell patients, by dealing with such vibes, you're taking responsibility for self-care. However, if you have a constant sense of jeopardy or no partner feels safe, you must explore your barriers to intimacy and mend sexual scars; these can distort perceptions.

FIVE INTERVENTIONS FOR REPELLING NEGATIVE SEXUAL ENERGY

There are some specific actions you can take to protect yourself from negative sexual energy. Try them out in all situations where you feel uncomfortable. This will allow you to claim your power again.

Intervention #1: Eliminate Clear-Cut Predators

If someone is coming on too strong, this unseemly behavior must stop. Treat him or her as you would any skunk who's about to spray you with a foul odor. In a social situation, make a quick escape. No excuses needed. Sexual impropriety at home and in the workplace also must be addressed. Not to say it's easy. Summoning all your strength, you may have to insist that an emotionally or physically abusive spouse get professional help. Or go to employee relations about a boss or coworker. Blatant sexual harassment is more than inappropriate; it's control-obsessed and cruel. Being continually exposed to this negative sexual energy will consume you.

Intervention #2: Speak Up and Set Boundaries

In more ambiguous situations, sensitively surfacing the issue may resolve it. For example, take your friend's husband aside and say in a nonblaming but firm tone, "I might be wrong, but I keep feeling you're flirting with me. It makes me feel awkward. If you are flirting, please stop." This direct approach often does the trick with people who're unconsciously motivated, or who need to have the limits of appropriate behavior defined.

Intervention #3: Recruit Outside Help

If the person still doesn't stop, and if the behavior is really bothering you, you can up the ante. With your friend's husband you might ask a neutral party you both respect to mediate. Or you can tactfully solicit your friend's help directly. The idea is not to disparage her husband, but to couch your vantage point in, "This is how I feel . . . I'd be more at ease if . . ." I realize this is potentially explosive between friends, but a heartfelt tone can often work things out. Always, part of using your intuition is to access whether someone is receptive to this kind of communication.

Intervention #4: Don't Give Negative Behavior Any Juice

This is another option if your direct requests don't stop the person's inappropriate sexual behavior. Be careful not to engage negative sexual vibes. Limit eye contact with the source of difficulty, and avoid handshakes or hugs; this reduces the energy exchange. Keep breathing and centering yourself. Exhale negative vibes so they don't stick in you. Also, don't silently sizzle with irritation or rage; this energetically signals that you're still playing this game. Instead, go about your business. Be loving with your friend, and cordial to her husband. When the problem person doesn't have anything to hook onto energetically, he or she will likely lose interest.

Intervention #5: Respect Your Intuition About the Sexual Willies

If someone doesn't do anything obviously creepy, you can still get the willies. Instinctively, you're picking up something unsafe about this energy. Say, it's a group of teenagers on the street: don't hesitate to maneuver around them. One of my patients couldn't put her finger on why she felt strangely uneasy around an electrician during a remodel of her home. She downplayed the intuition until one day he took it upon himself to tuck in the label of her blouse. This trespassing of her space pushed her over the edge; she hired a different electrician, an option I'd supported all along. Sometimes it's simply smart to duck out of a situation without making an issue of the vibes.

Inappropriate vibes also can arise with a masseuse or energy healer. It isn't necessarily what they say or do. Knowingly or not, they mix sexual energy into treatments. Many of my patients have tolerated this too long because they've questioned themselves. It's the worst feeling to be stuck in a massage, totally exposed, and have these weird, intrusive vibes coming at you. You may want to get someone different. (Some people are more comfortable with same-sex masseuses.) Or, if you have rapport with the practitioner, mention the issue *once*. If he or she was unaware of sending this energy and is open to change, terrific. However, if the vibes don't stop, the person is not for you.

MY FRIEND ANGELA, a gospel choir director in a church with a congregation of thousands, has had to become the queen of boundary setting. Coming from an abusive home where boundaries didn't exist, it took determination to get good at it. Garbed in brightly colored African robes, Angela likes to greet her congregants after a service. A few words for each, sometimes a hug.

Angela is an expert reader of energy, is clear about staying heart-centered, but not sending sexual vibes. Sometimes, though, people have their own agenda. Angela told me, "Every week this one man kept hugging me too tight. It felt needy and slightly seductive. His energy was gooey, like flypaper. So I had to communicate to him, 'It's nice to see you, but I'd rather we didn't hug. It doesn't feel comfortable.' " You'd think a statement like this might set someone off or offend them. But Angela conveyed it with such sweetness and respect that the congregant took it in the spirit intended. From then on, he respected her boundaries. The upshot was she didn't have to dread seeing him each week or be subjected to energy that felt off.

As a medical student I experienced the horror of having to keep my mouth shut around hotshot surgeons who'd tell disgusting sexist jokes in the operating room. At a time when a patient is exquisitely vulnerable—out cold and being cut open—only positive vibes are called for. Of course, the surgeons didn't acknowledge that words are action, that their talk energetically violated both patient and students present. Perhaps I could've said something to my supervisors—but I lacked confidence, was afraid of retaliation. Today, with increased public scrutiny of workplace indiscretions, I'd counsel medical students to surface these issues with their program chiefs.

We are wising up. Dissatisfied with the Old Boy's Club mentality and cultural stereotypes, we're overdue for a fresh take on sexuality. A more enlightened model integrates the heart—being cognizant of the positive energy you carry, choosing the right time and place. The new model also necessitates a war on victimhood, ridding your life of unhealthy sexual influences. This creates more energy for you. When approaching sexuality, begin with yourself, then evaluate your environment. From here, you'll have a sturdy foundation to cultivate your erotic spunk even further.

IGNITING SEXUAL ENERGY WITH YOUR PARTNER

This part of the Fifth Prescription is a primer for you and your partner to hone a heart-centered sexuality. Such power: merging the lusciousness of the erotic with the ecstasy of the heart. For the most energy gain, sexuality isn't only what you do, but the heart with which you do it.

Passion stagnates because energy backs up. There are some predictable reasons that consistently do us in. Relationships fall prey to them only because we go unconscious. It's essential to lovingly heal any dead-end habits that injure intimacy.

COMMON KILLERS OF SEXUAL ENERGY

- Exhaustion
- Rushing
- Repressed hostilities and anger
- Meannesses that wound
- Not speaking your needs
- Losing interest when newness fades

Sexual responsiveness is a delicate barometer; when communication fails in a relationship, it's the first to go. Intimacy involves self-awareness and the ongoing willingness to remove obstacles. (Parents or the overworked must really be creative to beat the exhaustion factor. I'll offer suggestions in my passion-igniting techniques.) I guarantee: With such an effort, desire won't fade.

Spurred by this conviction, I aim to blow apart some pretty grim scientific assumptions about sexuality. Cornell University recently confirmed what your Aunt Harriet always swore: passion can't last. Their report showed that we're biologically programmed to be in love for about two years. Then desire dribbles away along with the hormones that triggered it. Fortunate for us, however, biochemistry tells only part of the tale. What these well-meaning scientists failed to consider is how energy fields figure in.

Regrettably, most of us aren't trained to sustain passion after the honeymoon phase. For some people it ends after a few months, others a few years. I've worked with a slew of patients in long-term relationships who're resigned to being bored in bed. They all say, "We've known each other too long. It's to be expected." Hogwash. Where many couples go wrong is to misconstrue the inevitable shift out of the honeymoon with a deadening of passion. The solution to this age-old dilemma goes beyond studying up on positions or other mechanics—it's about learning ways to move energy. Keeping in mind lifestyle and time demands, I'll offer a variety of heart-centered exercises. Practicing them regularly, you'll experience more passion.

FIVE TECHNIQUES FOR ENHANCING POSITIVE EROTIC ENERGY

Technique #1: Synchronize Energy Cycles with Your Partner

Let's start with the logistics of lovemaking to factor in timing and energy level. These very significant considerations aren't unromantic. Energy-cycle mismatches can wreak havoc with your sex life if they aren't addressed. My patient Laura, a thirty-five-year-old kindergarten teacher, told me, "My husband Greg and I have always had a strong attraction, but it's a real feat to coordinate timing to make love. It's frustrating. We're both overworked, too often exhausted. Plus, for me, sex is better when I wake up. Greg prefers it at night because he falls sleep afterwards. I've tried lovemaking before bed, but I'm usually so beat I'm a zombie; I can barely move. What can we do?"

Once I met Laura and Greg, it was clear their problem really was mismatched energy cycles, not lack of desire. Although research indicates that couples with compatible cycles spend more time together and have sex more often, a few compromises for Greg and Laura made them much happier. It took some experimenting, but they were willing. During the week, they *planned* at least one interlude in the early evening, a compromise on timing. To conserve energy for that night, Laura and Greg agreed to avoid postwork errands or answering e-mails, and to have dinner delivered. In addition, Laura took a leisurely candlelit bath, and Greg often joined her—a gentle entry to sensuality that more naturally led to intimacy. If they were still too tired for intercourse, cuddling was a tender solution. Weekends were easier; they weren't battling fatigue. They tried making love at different times when they both were energized and found that they were mutually drawn most to twilight. The deep violet transition into night felt extremely romantic to them. By lovingly discussing differences and being willing to creatively modify their needs, Laura and Greg's passion grew.

MAKE CHANGES NOW

SOLVE ENERGY MISMATCHES

If your energy cycle is out of whack with your partner's, talk about it when you're both relaxed. Come from your heart, not desperation or blame. Specifically address: When do you each prefer making love? When is your energy highest? How can you both minimize fatigue from other sources the day of lovemaking? Also discuss pleasurable options if time doesn't permit intercourse. Ten minutes of cuddling can go a long way. Don't force your rhythms on your partner. Instead, brainstorm solutions together, and try them out.

For parents. Making love when the kids sleep is a start. Then you won't always have one ear open or be as afraid they'll walk in. Also try to steal romance whenever you can. Plan date nights when you'll have child care. (The erotic boost you receive makes up for any lack of spontaneity.) If the kids are gone, this interlude can be at home. If not, escape to a lovely hotel room, even for a few hours. Or in a pinch, drive to a beautiful spot and park. It's a huge challenge to be parents and lovers. Consistently incorporating minor strategic accommodations yields impressive results.

Technique #2: Keep Passion Alive by Communicating

In relationships, open, loving communication facilitates the free flow of erotic energy. Passion is built on an interchange, not guessing games. The extraordinary range of emotions that surface with a partner, including aesthetic likes and dislikes, must be aired. In our interview, Kenny Loggins, father of five, shared how he and soulmate Julia maintain the magic in their thirteen-year marriage: "When you first meet someone, the sex is very hot, but after months it inevitably changes tone. To keep passion alive Julia and I have to be willing to tell the truth about our feelings in a heartfelt way. Anything we withhold emotionally creates a wall between us physically. It's harder to be passionate if we're angry at each other or keeping a secret."

Negative vibes can wedge an erotic distance between couples. Mistakenly, this waning of passion is often written off as the unavoidable fallout of familiarity. So instead of doing the emotional heavy work to remove obstructions, couples who stop communicating may give up on passion or else seek affairs. Here's the seduction: With a new lover, sex suddenly becomes exciting again because there's no emotional baggage. The lover is a blank slate. I've had patients who've gotten snared in the trap of chasing newness. The story is always the same. They're wild about someone in the beginning, but the minute that person shows any real emotional need, the infatuation's over. They're off to the next affair. The desire for newness can turn into addiction, breaking up marriages and keeping people single. Ultimately, it sabotages the sustainable positive energy relationships can offer. To avoid this dead-end scenario, use the following exercise to improve communication with your partner.

MAKE CHANGES NOW

USE HEART TALK TO AWAKEN PASSION

It's hard to have passion in an ongoing relationship if you and your partner don't communicate—about sex, and also about emotions. The key is in the delivery. To protect the erotic, get into the habit of lovingly sharing the joys and sore points. (Consulting a therapist is also useful when you're stuck or afraid to broach an issue without a mediator.) Here are three strategies I advise.

OPEN UP COMMUNICATION

- *Pave the way.* If you're a couple who hasn't really talked for a while, I advise sneaking up on the subject of your relationship. No formal time for Heart Talk yet. Instead, in everyday conversation, start by mentioning what's attractive about your partner. For instance, say, "You look beautiful today," or "You smell so good." Don't overdo it, but, over time, keep these comments of appreciation coming. Regularly expressing the positives slowly introduces intimacy back into the conversation.

- *Gently bring up your need to communicate.* Make your first foray into direct communication. Express to your partner that you'd like for the two of you to talk more. Always frame your request in love—not criticism or anger—and avoid coming on too strong. A light touch will get you further. For instance, say, "You mean so much to me. I'd like us to get closer. We're both so busy. Let's make a half hour just to talk." Putting your need to communicate in a nonthreatening way enables your partner to feel at ease.

- *Create a safe time and place for Heart Talk.* Choose a relaxed, mutually agreeable time—say, once weekly for a half hour— when you won't be interrupted. Begin by sharing the positive points of your relationship without a sexual focus. Discuss ideas about how you can feel closer and connected. For instance, having more fun together or going on dates. In subsequent discussions, bring up what's working about your sex life. Perhaps the feel of her skin, the way he strokes your hair. Find something positive and express it. Get good vibes going between you to lay the initial groundwork.

GO DEEPER

- *Express your needs without blame.* Now's the time to explore more difficult territory using Heart Talk. The most passionate couples I know take regular stock of their emotional and sexual needs—what's working or not in the relationship—then impart their feelings from a heart-centered stance. The mutual agreement must be that you won't lambaste each other, but aim to strengthen connection. The purpose is to address issues and remove barriers—not to keep talking something to death.

  To set the tone, take a few quiet moments to breathe together, and focus on your heart center, as you've done before. Then pick one issue (either yours or your partner's) to focus on in each Heart Talk discussion. Always speak in "I statements," and try to offer a solution. For instance, one patient told her boyfriend, "I feel you push me away when I cry. It would be wonderful if you could just hold me." Another patient conveyed to her partner, "I need a little more foreplay. I'd love it if we could make the time." Also, don't shy away from aesthetic preferences, but be gentle. After one of my patients asked his gardener wife to shower after a day in the dirt—before they made love—he felt more turned on again. The idea is to hear each other out, and explore the remedy. Such framing of your needs yields very different results than accusations.

- *Address grievances.* If you or your partner has an emotional or sexual grievance list, space the issues out. Present each other with the easiest first. The more heart-centered you are, the better you'll be heard. Test the waters with a small gripe. For instance, say, "It'd mean a lot to me if we could trade off washing the dishes" rather than, "I'm sick and tired of you not doing your share of the housework." See how this approach does. Then next time, up the ante. For instance, "I feel neglected, hurt, or angry when . . ." Also, to balance things out, remember what's extraordinary about your partner, and let him or her know it. After the first issue is dealt with, allow some breathing room—at least a week. Then proceed to issue two. Gradually work up to the most intense concerns. Minute or monumental, every irritant you conceal energetically gnaws at passion.

COMMUNICATE DURING LOVEMAKING

- *Speak your needs in the moment.* Sometimes a formal discussion isn't required. It may feel more natural to address your needs during lovemaking itself. If so, always reinforce how your partner is already pleasing you. "It makes me feel so good when you . . ." Then, over a longer period, one by one, describe other ways to excite you. For example, "It would be wonderful if you touched me there with this much pressure." Then show him or her how. Creative lovers must keep educating each other to avoid ruts. It's not a failing, but a tribute to heartfelt communication.

Technique #3: Make Love with Heart

Learning to consciously exchange heart energy during sex puts the oomph of love back into lovemaking. Being genitally fixated feels like being stuck in first gear when you could travel at warp speed. The math alone is irrefutable: two revved-up energy centers (the heart and root) are more potent than one, for you and for your partner. This entails more than a natural caring for each other—it's a directed energetic synergy that heightens arousal and connection. All it takes is a shift in awareness: use erotic experience as a vehicle to open your heart. I promise: no hard work. Once you catch on, this mutually positive energy exchange will stop sex from feeling mundane. It's unrealistic to assume that purely genital excitement will stay high-pitched in a long-term relationship. From an energetic standpoint that's impossible. Sexuality isn't static; it's an evolution. The most stunning part of bringing heart into sexuality is that such ecstasy has no endpoint. With practice, it just keeps intensifying through the years.

MAKE CHANGES NOW

EXPERIENCE HEART-CENTERED PASSION

You two lovers are going to shower each other with pleasure and love. During foreplay set the heart tone. Take a few moments in each other's arms to exchange love through your eyes. Feel that energy sparkle between you. Also, slowly breathe together, synchronizing in-breath and out-breath, becoming intuitively attuned. Then, chests touching, lightly focus on your heart center. I experience it as a kind of purring, a warm vibration, not necessarily a sound. Felines purr when deeply content. Humans can do it too. It's a transmission of heart energy. Then, during foreplay and intercourse, let this feeling build and extend to your partner. It'll naturally combine with erotic vibes ascending from the genitals. Relax. This energy has its own momentum; let it envelop you.

To further increase sexual intensity you can visualize what turns your heart on. I don't mean the warm fuzzies you get from your kids or dogs, which can be a turn-off here. Rather, the sensuousness of a waterfall, an ecstatic love poem, a sexy scene in a film. Anything with an erotic tinge that opens the heart will do. This chemistry of energy and images can propel you into a sizzling sexual place. Don't worry if you've been married thirty years. Be prepared to purr.

Technique #4: Blend Sex, Heart, and Spirit

Now let's add spiritual energy to stoke the passion mix. Philosopher Alan Watts wrote, "When you're in love with someone, you see them as a divine being"—a realization that can raise sexuality from mechanical to transcendent. Let there be no confusion. That divine being is the very same person who forgot to send in the mortgage payment last month, and who sometimes neglects to pick up his underwear. The capacity to see the divinity in your mate—while making love and always—has everything to do with your perception of energy. And with acknowledging the miraculous in the ordinary.

This is the concept: A relationship is never just about two people. Each of you has a direct line to the divine that you bring to one another. Learning to invite Spirit into lovemaking keeps passion high by infusing celestial vibes. This, in turn, amplifies your body's neurochemical pleasure response. You may think of Spirit as God, Goddess, or love. But to keep things simple, let's just talk energy. Note the dynamics: The energy centers, from head to foot, are all joined by a common channel. During lovemaking, spiritual energy enters through the crown and filters downward; sexuality rises up from the genitals; the heart energy starts central and travels all over. When they all meet, whammo! Feeling our lusty, heartful, and heavenly parts fuse is utter bliss.

MAKE CHANGES NOW
SURRENDER TO BLISS

If you've never had this experience, you have a lot to look forward to. Here's what to do. As preparation, create a sacred space that's sensually and spiritually uplifting. Gardenias. Incense. Candles flickering. Phones and pagers turned off. Your environment induces passion.

Also, to avoid the same old ways of seeing your partner, remind yourself that he or she is a spiritual being who's ripe with all kinds of subtle ecstatic energies he or she is going to share with you. See your partner's physical form, and picture the surrounding light too.

Then while making love, each of you inwardly ask, "May the divine flow through me," a sacred, not sacrilegious request. Visualize your bodies as conduits. When you let go sexually, ordinary boundaries dissolve. Consciousness expands. Bit by bit, as you open together, permit a greater force to pass through you. Don't think it; feel it. Then notice your erotic reaction. You may feel ecstasy shoot through your spine or fingers, even see colors—a fantastic show of sensation and light that often peaks at orgasm. Let these new feelings grow. Go with them. Pleasure is a positive energy. Let it seep into every pore. Make sexual union sacred.

Technique #5: If You're in a Time Crunch or
Too Tired for Sex: "Chakraline"

As awesome as energetically conscious lovemaking can be, sometimes it's not possible. Reality is notorious for elbowing in on even the most well-plotted romantic plans. In your private moments, especially the short-lived ones, you must be expert at guarding passion. To assist you, this technique is what I term "chakralining," a quick way to connect by lining up midline energy centers. With your partner, the aim is to blend your sexual center and heart as your energy fields overlap.

Chakralining is the Rolls-Royce of all hugs—a playful sharing of energy that doesn't involve intercourse or excessive effort. As poet Alden Nowlan writes,

> *It's what we want, in the end*
> *to be held, merely to be held,*
> *to be kissed (not necessarily with the lips,*
> *for every touc hing is a kind of kiss).*

You may be busy. Your partner may be busy. But for a few minutes, just hold each other in this erotically packed snuggle.

I offer my technique to anyone under duress or exhausted, especially heroically stressed-out parents with young children. Chakralining is time-efficient and adaptable. You can do it anywhere—in bed, your Land Rover, a walk-in closet—an undisclosed location beyond your kid's radar. This can feel very sexy.

MAKE CHANGES NOW

CHAKRALINE WITH YOUR PARTNER

Lovingly assume the position: Wrap your arms around each other in a sensual embrace. You can do this standing, sitting and straddling, or lying down. Make sure you're facing heart-to-heart with crotches touching. Let your bodies meld like two seals on a rock. Forget making an effort! Your erotic energy wakes up on its own. Then, as it does, let it rip. Zap, zap, zap: recharge! Trust me, results are fast. One minute minimum, five minutes max. Afterward, eyes twinkling, you can return to the kids, your job, the world. Sneak in as many chakralines each day as you like.

After practicing this prescription's five passion-igniting techniques, you may find that some have special appeal. For example, my patient Kim, whose journey of healing sexual scars I described, has made chakralining a staple in her erotic life. If she notices her sexuality going numb, she lies on top of her husband to reconnect with his energy, both heart and sexual. It makes Kim feel safe and warm, and rekindles feeling in her body. Another patient who'd sworn off men after two soul-squelching marriages can't get enough of Technique 4, "Blend Sex, Heart, and Spirit." Coming from the macho-idolizing Dallas country-club set, she'd never been with a mate who'd honored her sense of Spirit. It took her years to risk opening to a new lover. Now, she's with a man who honors her spiritual life; nothing pleases him more than to bring that energy into the sexual arena. Alternatively, Technique 3, "Make Love with Heart," has been especially soothing for numerous patients, men and women, who've suffered wrenching losses, including the early death of parents. (The closeness of lovemaking often triggers abandonment fears, which causes reactions from withholding sex to impotency.) The extra sweetness of partners consciously joining the heart with the erotic makes intimacy feel more stable.

To awaken sexuality, use the exercises I've presented or design your own. Remember to keep the heart paramount. Combining heart energy with lovemaking will introduce you to sensual capacities you never knew you had. You'll feel what arouses, what falls flat. Knowing how your body responds helps you function at peak energy potential.

THE POWER OF LOVE, PAST AND PRESENT

In Energy Psychiatry I also stress to patients that the past has a role in securing erotic verve. Sexuality is a potent connector. Achieving closure with previous intimates gives you more energy now. In the words of Sigmund Freud, "We are carriers of all the relationships we have," the happy ones and the disasters. Though Freud was referring to how people we've been close to dwell in our psyche, they remain in our energy field too. This may be good news, or bad. How I see it: The more love that surrounds us the better, but ghosts of less-than-loving relationships drag us down. To banish scoundrels or move on after disappointments, you must unfasten the energetic hook an ex has on you. This means saying good-bye completely, both emotionally and energetically. Don't stuff anger, hurt, or grief. Journal about them; talk to a therapist or friend. Then, keep at this program's fear-releasing tactics. In addition, when you're in a quiet state, visualize an invisible energetic cord binding your heart to your ex's. Then picture gently cutting it with a scissors. Let yourself feel the separation. It may be painful, but it's how to be free. The motto I stand by: Healing is always possible.

Because the past lingers, a word of caution: In the energy realm there's no such thing as casual sex. When someone touches you, even once, vibes are communicated. Infinitely more so during sex. With a lover your energy fields merge, even during one-night stands. Whatever its qualities, the energy imprints itself. You'll be subtly changed. It comes down to economics. You must gauge what's to lose or gain.

The superb upside to such imprinting, however, is having a relationship based on mutual respect and love. Such bolstering of your energy field is profound, sustaining—even if two people eventually part. When someone loves you, that energy never goes away. Your paths may diverge. Circumstances change. But, throughout a lifetime, what you've shared will illuminate your personal force.

Love is the great survivor. One recent December, two former long-term boyfriends of mine (their birthdays a day apart) died. A heart attack; a cancer. I had no reason to expect these untimely deaths. We'd been in contact over the years, but had no sense of having to say farewell. With each death I wept, brokenhearted, surprised by the extent of my loss. I've come to realize that for decades both men had lived within me, not simply as memories, but as the finest energy etched on mine, contributors to my soul. Each taught me to love more, helped me to become who I am.

Love wants to propagate itself. I swear, deep down, I could feel the men I've loved rooting for me when I was about to start one of the most significant relationships of my life. This new man and I finally met face-to-face at the millennium. Because we lived on different coasts, it was no ordinary first date. No quick cup of coffee. He'd invited me for a long weekend at his four-room cabin in the North Georgia mountains. Our conversation, and, it seemed, courtship, had begun by e-mail and phone. Though I was already smitten, and he'd been vouched for by mutual friends—good Buddhists all!—I'm shy and quite private. Plus, a girlfriend of mine who knew the ropes sensibly pointed out, "A cabin? What if you don't like him? You need an escape plan!" I never did make one, just trusted my feelings, got on the plane.

That December 29, 1999, transitions in the stars, this man and I found each other. From the Atlanta airport, we drove in his pickup to snowy woods, a rushing creek outside the window, the roaring fire casting shadows on the walls. Fairy tales: it was awfully cold; we soon discovered the water pipes had frozen. That toilet we were to share wouldn't flush. Believe me, weighing the options wasn't a discussion I'd planned on. But, together, we worked it out, and the plumber came in the morning. Laughter, passion, and the real. The start of our love, and of the years we would spend together.

In your erotic life, let the overriding constant be the energy of the heart. Then you can't go wrong, no matter what ensues, rugged or sublime. Trusting the heart is a gutsy, vitality-raising stance that evolves when applied. The Positive Energy Program's Fifth Prescription—developing a heart-centered sexuality—will get you there. Like other forms of energy, sexuality is most pristine when love is present. Little by little, keep refining this alchemy.

Treat Yourself:

Take a few carefree moments to feel sexy, either on your own or with a partner. No expectations or overthinking. Just do whatever sensually energizes you. Rub lavender oil all over your body. Roll naked on freshly cut grass. Get a belly-button jewel and work it! Let out a purr in your lover's arms. Whatever you choose, make it fun!

INTERVIEW: EVE ENSLER ON SEXUALITY

EVE ENSLER IS CREATOR OF THE OBIE AWARD-WINNING PLAY *THE VAGINA MONOLOGUES*. SHE INITIATED V-DAY, A GLOBAL MOVEMENT TO STOP VIOLENCE AGAINST WOMEN AND GIRLS.

✳

I believe sexuality is the greatest gift we've been given. Its energy is the basis of creativity, love, ambition, desire, life. Sexuality has gotten all these bad raps because it's so powerful. Everybody wants to squash it, control it, define it, judge it—as opposed to just rejoicing in it, following where it goes.

What's sexy to me? Being fully who you are. Complete presence. Inhabiting your own body and not being afraid of what comes from that. It's not physical perfection. What turns me on is the undeniable force of self that has great emotion and manifests the soul. That's sexual charisma, a positive energy your intuition can sense. For me, these vibes feel right, like a "Yes!"—like a "Go!" Sometimes they're magnetic. They're definitely warm. Often hot. You want to bask in them.

Jane Fonda, a good friend and supporter, is one of the sexiest women I've ever met. She's sexy because she's totally alive in the present tense. When she does anything, all her attention in that moment is on what she's doing. When Jane speaks, she often cries. Tears can be a great expression of sexuality. If your full self is coming through, sometimes you can't help but cry. Similarly, I find men sexy who throw themselves into something— firemen, cameramen, those who stop violence. Not gorgeous men with flawless bodies. I like someone with a little belly who's human. I have no interest in a man who spends all this energy on looking beautiful. I'm attracted to people who stand up against injustice and fight for the truth. I find Nelson Mandela incredibly sexy.

Sexiness means not canceling out our fullness. Sometimes, though, people get locked into a certain visual—like men who only go for model types. That's so limited. It's an adolescent sexuality they've been indoctrinated to believe. Looks are just the first level. If you really start getting into a person's energy, taste, and touch (skin and smell are crucial) . . . if you go to a place where sexuality beckons, where you get lost, wet, and dank, body type becomes completely irrelevant.

Erotic moments can be small or large. Subtle things can be very sexy—like walking down the street in Manhattan on a fresh spring day with just a slight whiff of lilacs. That could do me in. Or while in the middle of traffic realizing, "Oh my God, I have a vagina! How good is that?" It's really sexy to see your body as beautiful and strong. I find the sexier moments to be when my heart and vagina are in the same place. For example, that beautiful day we opened a safe house in Kenya. The hot African sun. Hundreds of Masai girls dressed in bright red, singing. It was victory, and it was unity, and it was community. We'd achieved something and had beaten the dark back. It was like, "Wow! It doesn't get much sexier than this."

What's not sexy to me? Negative energy—the willies coming from someone that warn, "Hurt!" or "Stop!" It's any time you're forced to be anything other than yourself. Or when you're out of your own body, doing something for someone that doesn't suit you or make you feel safe. When I was younger, I was drawn to damaged men who needed to dominate or hurt. The pattern was familiar. I had this fantasy of fixing it. Now when I pick up damaged vibes I feel compassion and sorrow, but I'm not attracted to it at all. Women must walk away from negative energy. Our sexuality has been so censored, annihilated, tampered with, that our power has completely short-fused.

One of the greatest experiences of my life has been touring the world with *The Vagina Monologues*. It was part of V-Day, a global movement I initiated to end violence against women and girls, and to celebrate female sexuality. I went to cities from Macedonia to the Philippines. (This year there have been 800 productions of *The Vagina Monologues* internationally.) When the play is performed, in whatever language or culture, you can feel blocked energy get released. Desire. Fear. Bad stories. Great experiences. A hunger to be in one's vagina. The love of one's vagina that's been kept hidden. The play allows people to be who they really are. To let go of shame that distorts sexuality. Though the play hasn't been to Kabul yet, a lot of Afghani women have read it and are talking about doing it in their refugee camp in Pakistan.

I think *The Vagina Monologues* struck such a huge chord because it talks about things that need to be talked about—things that haven't been said before. At first, people walk into the play nervous, fearful, and excited. Men and women are really excited about vaginas. Women are excited to have them. Men are excited to get to think about them differently. Afterwards, there's a giant energy shift in the room. It feels open, happy, clean, delicious. Often, though, big issues get stirred up. I know of three people who've had heart attacks after seeing it, and fifteen incidents of fainting! A guy fainted in Seattle who suddenly remembered being abused. The body is powerful. It will tell us what needs healing.

I'm working on a theater piece called *The Good Body* that addresses plastic surgery. For every woman I've interviewed who's had liposuction or breast implants, I've seen someone who's really trying to defend against her messy, explosive, anarchic, sexual self. Look at what it is. You're implanting something that's replacing your own beastly, fabulous nature. When someone holds your breasts, they're not going to be holding flesh anymore, only an idea of flesh, a complete dissociation. For years I didn't have much faith in the body because I was disconnected from my own. Now I know how vital it is to trust what lives inside you. The body is the center of our energy.

Recently I had an incredible dream. There was this wall, and I was telling a group of people from V-Day how to walk through it. They were saying, "You can't." I was saying, "Oh God, you absolutely can!" It has to do with having faith in your sexuality and your relationship to particles and energy. A wall is just a mass of energy. I've been walking through walls for years! You just have to go with the energy of the wall, become it. I woke up realizing that if we were really in our sexuality, we'd have the wisdom to walk through walls. There's a sexual energy and knowledge we haven't plugged into yet. We need to untap and unburden it so our beings can thrive.

6

THE SIXTH PRESCRIPTION: OPEN YOURSELF TO THE FLOW OF INSPIRATION AND CREATIVITY

CREATIVITY IS THE MOTHER of all ener-
gies, nurturer of your most alive self. It charges up every part of you.
When you're plugged in, a spontaneous combustion occurs that
"artists" don't have a monopoly on. This energy rises from your own
life force and from a larger spiritual flow. It's a sublime feeling that
comes from being a conduit, not a controller. To liberate creativity,
you must think out of the box. Reject conformity; choose something
you're passionate about. Even if you feel creatively dead, I'll direct
you to passion. Whether you're writing the great American novel,
laying bricks, or sprinkling rose petals on a salad, your delight and
surrender to the impulse is what catalyzes energy.

I have to admit that I'm a creativity fanatic. Living an uninspired
life has always felt like a fate worse than death to me. That explains
why with my patients I'm a bloodhound when it comes to the creative. I sniff it out in every nuance of what they say or do. As an
energy psychiatrist, my mission is to hunt down and reinforce what
creatively jibes for them, from jobs to finger painting. I also forbid
them to settle for the uninspired. The way I see it, life's just too
short. I want my patients to be vibrant and strong, not lapse into a
glazed acceptance of how they think life has to be. So when one

patient in advertising said, "My job sucks my energy. I'm bored. I hate it," I took that cue to help her move toward more creative work. This turned out to be opening a now hugely popular pet spa. (Ah, L.A.!) From morning till night these lucky creatures are pampered, perfumed, and petted to within an inch of their lives while their owners are out. Alternatively, when another patient, a retired colonel, as regimented as you can get, declared, "I'm not creative. Never have been. Never will be," I didn't buy into that for a moment. This person is now a passionate gardener. One thing I'm sure of: Such energy is waiting to be aroused in each of us.

My program's definition of creativity is energy-based and broad. It means opening to the blended intuitive rhythm of imagination, heart, and intellect. It entails feeling inwardly moved before you act—not merely being seduced by surface glitter, but feeling inspired. It means hearing, feeling, trusting an instinct that transcends the linear. Creativity sets positive vibes in motion. Unlike sexuality or spirituality, which originate in specific energy centers, creativity has no one base. A free agent that travels where needed in the body, creativity restores energy to all chakras, including our emotional center. But creativity is most bound to intuition; creativity and intuition act as sister energies that stoke one another. Both operate primarily through flow, getting out of your own way to allow a brilliance the intellect alone can't conjure.

I'm pleased to report that creative energy can be an antidepressant. My writing has rescued me countless times. At forty, when I yearned to have a child, but no romantic relationship was working out, a grief crept into me, my body mourning what I was never to have. That oceanic melancholy felt irreparable. During this period, I began to write. First, yellow pads. Next, a weekly writing group. Then I began my memoir, *Second Sight*. A torrent of energy ensued; a voice became unstiffled. I wrote about hidden feelings, intuitions that were squashed as a child by my dear and difficult parents. At my father's deathbed I sat next to him with my yellow pad, recording every detail. I will never forget that hospital room. I needed to remember. Words on a page: that magic continues to inch me closer to my soul. A deep need was being satisfied, a different kind of birthing. Incredibly, my desire for pregnancy waned. Life is compassionate, adaptable. One type of energy had been replaced by another, the loveliest gift.

Creativity is not just escape; it's an invitation to a positive force that alters negative feeling and focus. My mind can be reeling with worst-case scenarios or painful letdowns, but after writing I feel larger than they are. Creative energy is the opposite of a sphincter tightening. To me it feels like a warm, sometimes ecstatic flow, a balm for the rawness within. I walk away from writing feeling better, with a more solid sense of self and purpose.

Creative energy heals, flows into those hollow places in us that cry out to be filled. It may not give you a baby, a boyfriend, or a million bucks, but it's expert at turning inner emptiness into home. Creativity is your home. Finding it will take the ache away, make you more whole. It will awaken your potential. It will give latent passions beneath your surface more breath and light.

You can't feel the energy of creativity if you don't tell the truth: the truth about what vitalizes, intrigues, or possesses you—and also what doesn't. Creativity isn't about pretend. Rather, it's knowing what gets you going and following it. To your intuition, creative energy may feel intense or muted; you may sense it as a clicking into gear, a kinked spot loosening, an immersion, an excitement, a simple pleasure, a propulsion into timeless freefall. Though creativity often requires discipline, it isn't coerced or tailored to please anyone but you.

Creativity frees energy by:

- Connecting you with joy
- Getting stagnant life force moving
- Bettering health and mood
- Providing a break from problems

- Counteracting fatigue
- Shaking you out of ruts

In this program I'd like you to approach creativity as a devotional, a hallowed inner quest. Being motivated solely by habit or duty is a drag on your life force. I'll show you how even short creative breaks reverse this. Also, while exploring the Sixth Prescription, make it about personal delight, not about garnering a *New York Times* review or a popularity contest. With regard to creativity I'm an energy purist: what you're after is to reverse numbness in your being. Let me underscore that no creative act is insignificant. All stirrings, quiet or dramatic, are a victory.

Creative energy has infinite facets. It's not restricted to art; it involves politics, biology, cooking, tree climbing, anything you cherish. It helps you solve problems, make synaptic leaps, crack your soul open. I like the image of going to the center of your being until you hear something sing. All this brings a healthy energy rush you'll want more of. Here's the way to begin.

RE-REMEMBER YOUR CREATIVE SELF

Re-remembering your creative self begins with a longing. For four-year-old Tuck, a friend's grandson, it came in a flash. Eyes electric, he bounded into his parents' room in the middle of the night. Standing there, blonde cowlick boinging upward, Tuck firmly announced, "I'm going to be an artist!" These words from the doorway woke his parents up. Tuck's career choice was news to them. They couldn't believe it. There their little boy was, so utterly gleeful, so certain, a pint-sized seer in baseball pajamas. All they could do was hug him, giggle, and say, "We know you'll be an artist. That's wonderful, dear." Tuck's sudden vision seemed clear. But knowing our passion is not so easy for most of us.

Ethan, a young Yale physician attending my energy workshop, had eons ago lost touch with his creative self. He said about the perils of left-brain education: "I feel like I've been in a strange episode of the *Twilight Zone* for a decade, and have to re-remember what's real. I miss it like an old pillow." What was most real to him, he explained, was a dream he'd repeatedly had as a boy. He said: "It always took place in the same poor village in India. Male monks in orange robes were teaching me to meditate. I was the student; they were my guides. I felt so close to them, known by them. It all seemed completely natural. Afterwards, I woke up energized." Listening to Ethan tell it, my goose-bump-ometer registered off the scale. Shivers rippled from head to toe, announcing we were on the right trail.

Clearly, this was a pretty far-out dream for any child, let alone the only son of a sheriff in a 1970s redneck fundamentalist southern town. Although Ethan's mystically interested mother was supportive, and tried to help him see these dream figures as spiritual guides, he didn't dare tell anyone else about them. Time passed. His dreams faded. The rigors of medical school slammed Ethan's creative dreamside down even more. Then, after ten years of fixating on science, Ethan's longing to remember welled up, and he contacted me.

When I hear such a story, there's no ambiguity about where to start: Ethan's dreams were a fertile energy source. (By age seventy, we've dreamed 50,000 hours or 5.5 years—a huge portion of our life is lived in this abundant repository of creativity.) My intuitive read on him was that his life force had been partially severed. It was more than being tired from overwork—his eyes had become dull; I sensed they could be luminous. His body's energy looked overcast, in need of brightness. So, to illuminate a creative dormancy in Ethan, I showed him how to remember his dreams: to get a dream journal, to pose a question to a dream before sleep, to jot the dream down immediately in the morning and note the answer—a technique that revs up dream circuits, past and present. The path of creative reclamation is rarely straight. I walked Ethan through nausea, sweaty hands, fear of a breakthrough despite his excitement. It's all touchingly human; I've seen it many times before.

People frequently come to me to reconnect with what's been split off. As an intuitive, I visualize their process of integrating energies as a kind of Humpty Dumpty in reverse where our broken parts rematerialize into a whole. The truth is: All the king's horses and all the king's men are creative forces within that can put us back together again. Watching Ethan tentatively inch forward—then remember, then remember—I was happy to watch him embrace what had been his all along. I knew this wasn't just a weekend-workshop high. In future correspondence, he wrote of taking classes on dreams and intuition, wanting to weave what he was learning into medicine—music to my ears. Plus, he planned to go to India to track down the village in his dreams. Creativity gave Ethan his sparkle back; it was his new beginning, an energy possessing momentum for a lifetime.

Like Ethan, sometimes we give up too much as adults. We walk around with hollow places throbbing. We feel oppressively civilized; we don't have nearly enough fun. Thank goodness our spirits long for something more. Longing is energy. It'll lead you to an essence that feels most alive.

Now I want you to expand your mind, to allow a wildness to enter you. There's no way to be creative and be bored. You'll feel it: the energy can be smooth, unruly, irreverent, or driven by a move-through-the-birth-canal velocity. Whatever your perceptions—and they can morph by the second—something innovative takes form.

MAKE CHANGES NOW

RECOVER WONDER

Go on an archaeological energy probe. Wonder is a type of creative energy that remains latent in the body as a sense-memory. To activate it, let your mind roam. Remember a time, place, or activity that brought you a sense of wonder. Sometimes returning to childhood helps. For me, it was lazy summer afternoons at the Santa Monica beach with my father. We'd walk under the cool, dark fishing pier watching surf pound the ragged pilings, which I pretended were a sea of ocean trees. My imagination did creative somersaults there.

To recover wonder, remember the simplest things. Watching a full moon rise. Planting spring bulbs with your grandmother. Playing jacks. Fixing a fender. Ponies at a watering hole. Allen Ginsberg reading "Howl." Or if the past seems like a big wonderless blank, search out wonder in the here-and-now. A sea gull soaring in the wind. A walk in the woods. Our Earth, a mere speck in billions of galaxies. Or breathe, just breathe.

Dissect the dimensions of wonder: smells, tastes, textures, sounds—not for seconds, but minutes. You may react by feeling happy, melancholic, wistful: whatever the emotion, this is the energetic switch to your creative current. You want to absorb wonder's full-thrust poignancy and go from there. This will trigger further creative energy.

LOCATE YOUR INSPIRATION

Inspiration epitomizes positive energy: it's seminal to being joyous and rambunctiously alive. You can't be creative without inspiration. It's the whispering muse, the sparks that lead to flame, the incentive for any Big Bang. When you're inspired you can't wait to get up in the morning. You're not fighting the flow—you're digging it.

In this program you'll see how inspiration raises energy on many levels. Physically, it improves health: your body knows you're happy and functions better. Emotionally, it triggers optimism, dreams, enthusiasm. Inspiration is also a subtle energy you generate and exude. Others can sense these vibes; they affect how you're perceived and who you attract. Inspired people radiate an undeniable glow. When I watch a journalist risking her welfare to report from war-torn Israel, a poet, or a mother—to my intuition they feel like a bright sun. Their energy is contagious, intoxicating. I respond to a glimmer in their eyes, a confidence from living close to their truth. Talk about a way to magnetize people, whether friends, lovers, or in your career. Inspiration draws positive energy.

My patient Pam, a thirty-five-year-old physical therapist, couldn't find a mate. She'd searched high and low: dating services, singles bars, parties, but no luck. In a session she broke down sobbing: "What am I doing wrong?" I empathized with her heartache. Some roadblocks, though, aren't amenable to logic. As I've seen with many patients, the cause is often energy-based. Lovely and good-hearted as Pam was, I read her energy as dull, sleepy. For years, she'd functioned on automatic: home, work, chores, sleep. In a session she admitted, "Nothing much inspires me." It seemed so.

Energywise I could feel Pam's batteries were dead, aching for a jump start. So, our thrust became helping Pam intuitively identify her passion. That is, finding new signs of life in her being, listening for what moved her. Penetrating the bland was slogging work, but we stuck with it. She tried needlepoint and bridge, activities her mother would've approved of, but alas, no real inspiration there. Then one day, on a whim, she went sailing with a friend. That spring afternoon, inspiration hit. Out at sea, her boat became surrounded by a pod of hunchback whales. Their massive grace and mysterious songs tapped an electricity in Pam. Those first moments, seeing their migration up close, she loved those beautiful, jeopardized creatures. From then on Pam's inspiration became saving the whales. The blandness in her persona began to be replaced with joy. I could see it; others could too. No coincidence, soon after she met a man with whom she fell in love.

Inspiration brightens the light around you. People instinctively respond. Without inspiration that light grows dim, as if you're invisible. It's the strangest thing: you're intelligent, attractive, kind, but it seems that no one notices you. Inspiration is a way of switching your light on again.

I know well how the absence of inspiration can feel deadly. One winter I attended an academic conference in Turkey on Rumi, the thirteenth-century Sufi, famous for his ecstatic love poetry. My companion had been invited to speak. You'd think such a gathering would emanate positive energy. Instead, we witnessed how academics, in droning monotones and timed fifteen-minute talks, bled dry the highest passion. At the break, when I commiserated about this calamity with Marcel Derkse, a therapist from the Netherlands, he described his work: "At our medical clinic, we consider lack of inspiration a sickness. I run a month-long, live-in program covered by medical insurance, devoted to helping patients reinspire themselves. We teach them how to reconnect with the creative energy of life. We recognize the reality of suffering, but also that we can be an instrument of love. We emphasis poetry, music, and art as ways to creatively celebrate existence."

Astonishing: in that instant, Marcel clarified for me a crucial element of positive energy. True emotional, physical, and spiritual well-being is contingent on inspiration; without it we're in a chronic state of dis-ease. To maximize energy, we must search for inspiration until we find it.

All of us are entitled to an inspired life: passionate work and relationships, playful downtime to refuel. Do what tickles you, large or small; don't act just because you think you should. Artists rely on inspiration: it's how they live. Similarly, we can make every day a living art, a perspective I'll train you in. Sadly, our society doesn't educate us about the value of inspiration. (Starting in kindergarten this should be part of Living 101.) So, as adults, many of us need to recapture it. Since inspiration hasn't been a priority for most of us, this can be a marvelous experiment. Whether you're ninety or nineteen, there's not a moment to waste.

Take an Inspiration Inventory to Find Passionate Work, Hobbies, and the Miracle of Small Moments

Now's your chance to investigate what does or doesn't inspire you by taking an inspiration inventory. The purpose: to honestly assess where your energy goes so you can constructively reroute it. To remember all inspiring inklings, I suggest you keep a journal and review it. Don't be discouraged if you're stuck in a rut or feel far from inspired right now. This inventory will turn all that around. Reinspiring your life takes courage. It's a solution-oriented process of uncovering, then commencing change.

My focus will be helping you find work you truly love, or show you how to reinspire your current job, even tiny bits of it—there's always a way. Also to find a hobby, an inspired pursuit that isn't your day job. A hobby that excites is a life-force rejuvenator, not just something to keep you busy. Then we'll explore how to invest the mundane with inspiration. In each area, aim for a reverence and feeling a creative energy surge. Throughout this inventory, the poet Rumi's words will be our mantra:

> *Let the beauty you love be what you do.*
> *There are hundreds of ways to kneel and kiss the ground.*

But how do we get there? These are the steps. Let's start with a closer look at your job.

Inventory Step #1: In a Journal Define the Conflict About Your Job

For instance, "I'm exhausted after eight hours, and I hate my work." Or "I'm bored and need a change." Or "I feel taken for granted."

Inventory Step #2: Ask Yourself the Following Questions

Why doesn't my job inspire me? Pinpoint the cause:

- Is it the particular circumstances—your boss, office politics, or irritating coworkers?

- Do I dwell on all the negatives, rather than looking for a piece of my work that could give me more juice?

- The most basic issue: Am I following my heart's desire or mired in a career that doesn't feel on center for me?

- Can I work within the system for change? Or do I need to seek another job?

Inventory Step #3: Modify Your Current Work Situation

Re-inspire your job:

- Sometimes lack of inspiration comes from difficult relationships, not the work itself. If there's bad energy between you and a coworker, try to correct the situation instead of aggravating it. Be the bigger person. Start being pleasant instead of prickly. My patient Pat works for a company with a nasty office manager. After weeks of dreading conversations with this woman Pat decided to forge a better relationship and invited her out to lunch. This simple act of kindness melted the office manager's hostility toward her, making Pat's workplace more pleasant. Nastiness can be a mask for a person's insecurities. Kindness often penetrates that. Offer a difficult person a word of appreciation. Do everything possible to shift antagonism.

- Don't expect your boss to be a mind reader. Instead of stewing in boredom or discontent, express your needs. If you know how you'd like to better your job, explore options. See if they are do-able within the framework of your environment. For years a patient of mine was paralyzed by a fear of rejection. It stopped her from getting what she wanted. When she finally summoned the courage to present a project she loved to her boss, and he agreed to it, her job took on new energy. The point is to risk. You'll never know what's possible until you do.

- Intuitively microanalyze your day. Look for any aspect of your job that has some sparks. Remember what initially attracted you to the job other than money. Also notice what perks your magic up and relieves apathy or fatigue. When you hit upon it, you'll experience a more-alive feeling, an excitement, or simply a gentle interest: these are signs of life force in your work. Spend more time in these areas. Document them in your journal. I have a designer patient who's a social butterfly. Doing this inventory, she realized that having lunches with clients, and giving presentations to the staff stoked her energy, but functioning in isolation was a real downer. Another patient, a librarian who likes to keep to herself, gets inspired doing research amongst quiet canyons of stacked books. Both women were getting burned out in their jobs until they reprioritized aspects of work that fed them.

- Gravitate to coworkers who inspire and energize you. One publisher patient who thrived on her busy job often came home tired. Once she realized what a kick she got from interacting with the art department, she upped her visits there. They had loads of laughs, which tweaked her energy at work and afterward. Fatigue is lethal to inspiration. Avoid anyone who drains you. Go toward energy hot spots in your job—people and activities—so your time is skewed toward inspiration.

- Make your work about service and meaning: how to make a difference in the world. This can entail being kind to others and injecting friendliness into your milieu, which will nurture you too. Give a coworker a pat on the back; don't lay into a delivery guy when he's late; turn people on to ideas to better the environment and the world. One of my patients is a producer for national news. Though deadlines are brutal, he's in an ideal position to get positive messages across. Framing his work in service keeps him aligned with inspiration. Whatever your job, the ethics and love with which you conduct yourself, and the positive messages you share, can be of service and spread inspiration.

Inventory Step 4: Consider Changing Jobs and/or Embrace a Passionate Hobby

Make a move:

- If you've tried to reinspire your job, but the situation is unredeemable, you may want to look for another. It doesn't have to be an upward move; a lateral move that reenergizes you is progress. One of my patients who felt battered by her Napoleonic boss's mood swings found her blood pressure normalized and her inspiration returned when she quit that job and began working with another boss she enjoyed. In these cases, a change of place is just what's needed.

If your career isn't your passion, you may be ripe for a larger change:

- Many patients come to me on the edge of transition. Most have had a career, but yearn for something more inspiring. I've never agreed with the assumption that we must have only one career in a lifetime. It's counterintuitive to human nature. When we mature, our interests may evolve, and we deserve to do work we love. As an energy psychiatrist and an intuitive, I testify to the wonder of having found my life's work, a passion that keeps unraveling. Being impelled by such direction is a blessing, but it also results from investigation, following your intuition, the willingness to take risks. If you're considering switching careers but lack a map, here's an intuitive game plan to follow.

MAKE CHANGES NOW

FIND OUT WHAT CAREER INSPIRES YOU (AN
ENERGY PSYCHIATRY ESSENTIAL)

1. Put aside at least ten minutes to sit quietly in an uninterrupted meditative state. Take a few deep breaths, quiet your mind, center your awareness in your body.

2. Begin by asking yourself, "If I could do anything, what would it be?" Forget about political correctness or pleasing your mother. Just see what comes. List the candidates in your journal.

3. Next ask, "If I didn't care what people thought I would . . ." List these too. Maybe you'll remember a college course you loved. Business? Journalism? Fashion design? Or something you've fantasized about but never tried?

4. You can also look through magazines, the classifieds, the Internet, or books to get new ideas. Wait for a zing to happen. You can't talk yourself into inspiration. It's an intuited, spontaneous energy—a gut-centered *Hurrah!* affirming, "This will nourish my soul!"

5. Once you pinpoint a possible job, stay on the lookout for related synchronicities: people talking about it, articles, opportunities. Keep your eyes and ears open. Then follow the bread-crumb path. It can take you to your passion.

6. During meditation or quiet walks, notice any intuitions that come to you about a potential career. A flash of delight or curiosity. A draw toward a certain school. A person in the know to contact. These can confirm your choice. Record them in your journal.

7. Look to your night dreams for answers. Before you go to sleep, pose a question to a dream: "What kind of work will inspire me?" Also add, "I need a clear response I'll understand." Then

the next morning, write the answer down. Try this for a week. See how it clarifies a direction.

Keep repeating the above techniques until inspiration strikes. Be patient; I assure you, it will. Then, move ahead toward a better future.

Marge, a seventy-five-year-old retired social worker who attended one of my energy workshops, is my inspiration guru. She used Step 4 of this inventory to find a new job and regain control of her life.

Marge told me: "I've been extremely independent—raised four kids and adopted one as a single parent. I've fought conforming. When my kids met to decide 'what to do about Mom' and settled on a cozy rent-free condo, I raced to check out jobs." Terrified of being put out to pasture, she answered a newspaper ad for a counselor's position in Kotzebue.

Something drew me. I had no idea where Kotzebue was, but I called to ask. The gal told me it was thirty miles north of the Arctic Circle! Strange: I'd always wanted to travel to Alaska. They sent me a brochure describing the traditional values of the indigenous people. Their belief that humanity was all one family really resonated with me. I know that Kotzebue chose me rather than my choosing it. Before taking the job I had a vision: I was walking down a long hallway with many doors. None of them opened. Then I noticed a fire escape. I went through it and came to Kotzebue. It felt fated. So I moved there, though my kids thought I was crazy. It's been six years now. I married a wonderful man, nine years younger. I've devoted myself to developing a community organization as a voice for the unheard. Kotzebue has become my home.

I urge everyone who's able to try a new career to follow Marge's lead. This may entail sacrifice, but I guarantee it'll be transformative.

I've never had a patient fail who's made such a move. For instance, a French teacher who'd come home angry from a less-than-inspiring job decided to get a Spiritual Psychology degree. This man was willing to brave the student loans and temporary income lag to pursue his true calling: a gift to himself and his future patients. Or the insurance administrator who followed her dream of becoming a real estate broker after a bout of breast cancer. Using this program's tools, go for your dreams too.

Embrace a Passionate Hobby.

Of course, not everyone is in an unencumbered position allows for a career change. If this is you, vigorously try to reinspire your day job, but also pursue an energizing hobby. Use the Make Changes Now exercise on pages 205–6 for finding a career to find a hobby that inspires you, too. A hobby is not a dabbling, but a source of deep satisfaction that must never be trivialized. It could be gardening, animal rescue, volunteering at the soup kitchen. Or discover what kinds of music, dance, or art set you ablaze. (Later, we'll go into detail on finding artistic outlets.) New hobbies activate a quiescent part of your brain, shake you out of inertia; although you're doing more, you'll feel more energized. Nothing is too "silly" or "meaningless." My dentist patient who spends all day looking into decayed mouths feels inspired by dancing flamenco on the weekends. He needs a hobby that gets his body moving. The point is to experience passion, whatever the source.

Inventory Step 5: Savor the Miracle of Small Moments

Remember: All we have is the moment. As a physician, I know the quick turns that life can take: health crises, losses. To realize our vulnerability isn't to be morose—it can incite us to celebrate every moment here. Reminding yourself daily to feel life force in everything you do reveals the numinous in the mundane. Pay particular attention to the following activities.

Doing chores. This is where many of us lose energy because of negative mindsets. Instead of viewing chores as drudgery, try the Zen approach—ecstasy, then the laundry. Self-realization isn't found only in remote Himalayan monasteries. It resides in the here-and-now. Inspiration brought to any task enlivens it. I've watched my friend, poet Mary Oliver, treat going to the supermarket as a holy rite. Every Cape Cod morning, snowy or warm, she shows up at the A&P just as it opens, ecstatic to get her food for the day. Mary approaches her poetry with the same inspiration. When we can capture this sense in one area, it can teach us how to be in others. The next time you go to the bank, wash the car, or walk the dog, consider it a revered task. Do it knowing that if this moment is your last, you'll get everything from it.

Nature, weather, and animals. If ever you're low on inspiration, take a good look at a daffodil or a turbulent sea. Watch the wind making love to scraggly oaks. Feel thunder rumble. Or get a contact joy from animals. All this transports you out of yourself. Instead of motoring around in an insulated mind-bubble, you can be invigorated by nature's energy. One of my patients revels in the oh-so-noble ducks waddling down sunflower-lined paths along the Venice Beach canals. Often, between patients, I spend a few minutes gazing out my eighteenth-story window at passing clouds, shifting hues of light, or at ravens riding updrafts. Observing nature's beauty rekindles inspiration.

TAKE OFF THE BLINDFOLD: TUNE IN TO CREATIVE VIBES

Human life is a testament to creative energy; it's everywhere if you know how to look.

For instance, some people ooze creativity; they're potent energy-conductors. You want what they have. Listen to them. Watch them. Talk to them. Let their energy wear off on you. When seeking creative models, though, don't just go for the glitz. Your local restaurateur could be just as psyched about his work as a political luminary. Notice who makes you gyrate: artists, musicians, gardeners. Their energy fields tell all: someone who is electrified transmits electricity.

Don't worry if your creativity seems lost. Often we need a power infusion from outside.

One event that did it for me was hearing former poet laureate Stanley Kunitz. At ninety-five, he gave a talk the caliber of the Gettysburg Address in a hushed tent at the Dodge Poetry Festival in New Jersey. He spoke of "an innerness that's more mysterious than the events of the day," about how poetry is "living in the layers," and then declared, "I am not done with my changes yet." I nearly fell to my knees, wowed by Kunitz's quiet charisma. I bow with respect for this man, grateful for the gift he bestowed that day.

Certain places are also energy hubs. A hole-in-the-wall jazz club. A library (books exude energy too). A butterfly conservatory where thousands of species fly free all around you. A symphony hall.

Creative vibes build in various venues over the years. When Aretha Franklin sings, she's pumping the place full of them. Such strong energy doesn't dissipate; it forms a field with its own life. While you're in these spaces, during a performance or not, the vibes are palpable. Even unknowingly, you'll assimilate them, become more creative. I'll never forget taking a day tour of the Grand Old Opry in Nashville. One look at that stage, I felt Willie Nelson and Johnny Cash there with me. I had tingles galore. Within the walls of the Opry, the energy imprint of country greats remains. I just drank it in. Visiting such spots can instigate your creativity too.

MAKE CHANGES NOW

SET OUT ON A CREATIVE SEARCH

Pick a person or place that creatively intrigues you; spend time basking in that energy. Don't intellectualize—feel it! Then see what's stimulated in you. Fresh ideas. Flashes. Dreams. Record them in your journal so they don't evaporate. Next, try an insight out. This is how creativity is born.

COMBAT KILLERS OF CREATIVITY

Negative voices stalk any creative territory. If you succumb to these doom-and-gloomers, inner or outer, kiss creativity good-bye. We all have them. We must override these voices before they stifle us. You know the ones.

- The fear-monger in us who says, "It's too late. I don't have talent or imagination. Who cares what I have to say?"
- The conformist in us who's addicted to approval and says, "I'd just make a fool of myself. People would laugh at me. Better stick to the status quo and not make waves."
- The controller who won't loosen that death grip long enough to feel the flow.
- The perfectionist for whom nothing is ever good enough.
- Any person (parents included), a group, or government that seeks to squelch creative freedom.

Let's not mince words. To our imagination these voices are the Antichrist. So, we must stay on alert. However, in this program our intent isn't simply to shut these voices up but to quench them with compassion. Use the following exercise to repel negative voices and protect fledgling creative impulses. Some of us aren't taught we have a creative side; it seems alien or impossible. Never believe you aren't creative. My work with countless patients and in workshops proves that each of us has a unique creativity waiting to be awakened. We must protect its initial, most tender manifestations.

MAKE CHANGES NOW

DON'T GIVE NEGATIVE VOICES THE LAST WORD

Here, treat yourself with the same sensitivity you'd give an unsure child who's discovering her gifts. First, list your negative voices in a journal; recognize them so they can't creatively interfere. Next, use a dialoging process to turn each one around. For instance, fear. When it says, "I can't," you say, "If I didn't listen to fear, I would . . ." Then record the affirmation and act on it. Or when your internal censor or your mother says, "Your painting is too far-out," you say, "I know you're afraid of what people think, but I won't squelch my art to appease you." Or "If I didn't have to be perfect, I would . . ."

One of my patients in a high-tech field was yearning for a more creative outlet. She started throwing pots, and said, "It's one of the most fulfilling activities I've ever done." Yet, still, she was afraid of "wasting time" and "being unproductive," the same words her mother used to describe anything artistic. Now, instead of buying into this voice, she realizes the source, says "thank you for sharing," and continues her joyful art.

Dialoging with your negative voices or vetoing another's is an ongoing strategy that gives the power back to you. (Apply Chapter 4's antifear tactics too.) All along, keep breathing yourself bigger than the voices. Realize they're coming from a scared, insecure place. No amount of convincing will change them. What works is to be compassionately consoling, set limits, then take charge. The negative energy these voices concoct will prevent you from trying anything new. You're entitled to more adventure.

DIVING INTO CREATIVITY

In this part of the program I want you to experience creative energy firsthand. Whether you assimilate it from a film or develop your own creative outlet, what matters is that you're exposed to these vibes. Your subtle energy system will metabolize them. No pressure. Nothing to prove. What appeals to you is entirely personal. Try the following actions and see which ones fit.

Action #1: Experience Creative Energy from the Arts

Art is not just for "artists." It's for anyone who loves life and beauty. There is energy inside beauty—in the visual world, words, sounds, dance. That energy isn't static. It emits a field that you can absorb. When I look at Van Gogh's *Sunflowers* I see the brilliance of the two-dimensional painting, yet I'm also pulled in by a mass of vibrating energy. Those sunflowers are never still. They're breathing, moving, screaming out wildness to whoever will see. The Impressionists were masters at recording subtle energy (though they probably never articulated it this way)—their brush tips making the tiniest pinpoint-specks of undulating color. They were depicting what mystics see: the primary matter of all things. That energy imparts energy to you. For me, this defines great artistry.

You can glean energy from observing art, but don't misconstrue this as a passive act. It's self-defeating to bring your body to a Michaelangelo sculpture and stand there like a lump. Instead, get ready to receive. Breathe deep. Feel yourself open. Prepare to be nourished. Art that's cooking emits a feast of creative vibes.

Some art will stir you, some won't. Experiment. Attend a poetry slam. A Warhol retrospective. The Bolshoi Ballet. I sometimes visit the dinosaurs at the Museum of Science and Industry in L.A. I stand in wonder of these megacreatures, the raptors and *T. rexes*, natural art forms. They make my creativity think big. I can't not be happy. See how art registers on your energy meter. Feel where the voltage is; keep returning there. Make a regular shot of creative energy part of your routine.

I don't know how I'd exist without film. I'm shamelessly addicted to this medium to rejuvenate me. I see at least a film a week. My favorites range from *Wings of Desire,* a masterpiece chronicling the interface between angels and humans in Berlin, to *The Matrix,* a technothriller about outfoxing mind-controlling aliens. In films that compel me, I'm like mush sitting in my seat, crying, laughing, rooting for goodness and booing oppression. I'm activated. I'm vibrating. It's awesome.

Film, when riveting, is a phenomenal energizer. Here's why. We're instantly and without resistance inducted into an expanded consciousness similar to the state of hypnosis. For hours we stop thinking about ourselves and, incredibly, let our problems go. We stop talking and go into intuitive mode. All this adds up to more receptivity. (A hint for intuitive empaths—as I do, sit on the theater's edges, rather than smack in the center. It'll reduce the vibes you absorb from people nearby.) The miracle of the mind relaxing is that your body experiences accelerated subtle energy flow. A clamp loosens. There's added access to life force within. And without: the power of film is that it transmits vibes. When we're moved, it's energy that moves us. An actor with Anthony Hopkins' force can juggle our electrons with just a glance. He's generating so much life force it jumps off the screen into us. The same goes for ravishing visuals and sound. There's nothing passive about movie-going.

The next time you're watching a film, notice these subtle energetics, a usually below-consciousness experience. Now you know. Have fun observing your energy move. It could be an emotional release. Spinal chills. Your chest rushes with heat. You may even feel God's presence. Whatever solidifies your soul—a tear jerker, heroic odyssey, or hilarious hoot—is energy direct from the creator channeled through the human form.

In Energy Psychiatry, sometimes I prescribe movies as medicine. I did for my patient Leah, a cancer researcher with a Sisyphean workload. Leah was so detail-oriented she drove herself nuts. To achieve the life-saving advances she aspires to, Leah had to learn to quiet her mile-a-minute mind. She's tried meditating but still fights it. For now, until meditation clicks in, Leah says, "I sneak away to late-afternoon art-house films to turn off my head. I forget about deadlines and staff meetings. I just sit there in peace with my popcorn." This movie cure gives Leah more breathing room in her being and restores clarity to her work.

Realize also that some films convey negative vibes. There's the *Dumb and Dumber* genre. You may get a few good laughs, but overall your subtle energy is dulled. More malignant are the serial-killer bloodlettings. No matter how masterfully done, they emit shock waves and fear. Some people get a charge from this, but, as an intuitive empath, I'm convinced such negative vibes can make us sick. When I stayed to the bitter end of *Frailty,* a cruel film about young boys brainwashed into becoming murderers by their father, I immediately came down with a violent flu. During the film I'd felt a wave of stinging rays penetrate my abdomen (the emotional energy center), so I wasn't surprised. Like a bad drug trip, we remain under the influence of a film, ingesting negativity that projects into our energy field. Especially if you're an empathic sponge, don't subject yourself to unneeded suffering.

That said, I've also seen how violence in film can be therapeutic in supervised settings. Once, during a two-week women's retreat in the California desert, the leader, Brugh Joy, would show us the most brutalizing films about figures from Hitler to Caligula. The purpose was to use them to dredge up unconscious emotional material (negative energy congealed in our fields) that needed to heal. This rugged nightly ritual got the job done. Intrusive parents, childhood abuse, pent-up rage: all the devils arose as memories and in nightmarish dreams for us women to clear in the group. It was difficult, but ultimately we all felt energized and lighter.

Music can also be replenishing or harmful. Sound is energy. It vibrates though your blood, organs, bones, and also your subtle energies. (Think of the intrusive booming bass from the car next to you at a red light.) Just as a certain frequency can shatter glass or inflict cellular damage, the right sounds can balance our energy and heal.

Listen to these research findings: in monasteries where monks play Mozart to animals, the cows give more milk; with critical-care patients, classical music has proved just as relaxing as Valium; fetuses have preferences, too—they settle down hearing Vivaldi, but rock music agitates, causing violent kicking. (My high-frequency hearing was permanently blown out at a concert in the sixties when The Who demolished their guitars in a theatrical epiphany.)

We humans are vulnerable to sound. Some everyday sounds can grate on our energy. Recently I interviewed Bruce Odland, a "sound artist" who's conceived a clever antidote to noise pollution. Commissioned by the city of West Hollywood, he installed a "tuning tube" on the sheriff's station, which, he explained, "makes a beautiful harmonic out of chaotic traffic noise." The result? A humming, chanting, and a soothing *wah-wah* that reminds me of an Australian didjerido. Along that stretch of sidewalk, this human-friendly sound helps nullify squealing brakes and honking horns. I hear from the locals that pedestrians practically rejoice in relief. They report feeling happier, get along better; some have even broken into dance and song.

MAKE CHANGES NOW

FEEL ENERGY FROM ART

Sample different art forms. Painting, music, film, dance. Just get yourself there; observe your energetic experience. Are you mellow? Amped? Tired? Inspired? Perhaps it's not what you expect. For instance, "high-energy music" may not be high energy for you. Hip-hop gets one young actor patient going, whereas it's bombastic for another who unwinds to Bach. If you're looking for an energy lift or a break from stress, match the art form with your needs.

Action #2: Explore Your Own Artistic Outlet

Now I'd like you to engage your own creativity. You may be longing for this, or be tentative but curious. Even if "artist" is a new persona for you, stay open. An artistic outlet is an imagination-amping activity meant to satisfy an unmet inner urge. It may be your day job, but more commonly it's an extracurricular pursuit that counteracts the daily grind. Embark on it just for fun; see where it wants to take you. In this program, an outlet will intensify your energy gain because you'll be directly aligning with the creative force of the universe. Instead of energy being relayed through an intermediary artist, it goes straight to you.

MAKE CHANGES NOW

FIND AN ARTISTIC OUTLET

- *Ask the right questions.* Investigate your interests, latent and known. Begin by considering:

    What art did I love as a child?

    What has always pulled me, but I've never pursued?

    What feels compelling? Listen for that faint whisper.

    Can a passionate hobby become a deeper artistic pursuit?

    If I didn't care about people's opinions, what would I try?

    One patient used these questions to merge her interests in writing and gardening: her first article was aptly entitled, "The Pleasure of Pulling Weeds." A doctor colleague formed "The Physician's Poetry Association" to blend the healing properties of poetry in patient care through writing, reading, and conversation—birth, death, illness, and suffering are rightly framed as the poetry of human experience. Keep a log

of similar creative flashes in your journal, far-out or familiar.
(I also recommend Julia Cameron's *The Artist's Way* to
stimulate ideas.)

- *Listen to your body's intuitive answer.* Now tune in to the
  possibilities. Close your eyes. Take a few deep, slow breaths. As
  you've done before, shift out of mental mode and focus on body-
  instinct. Tune in to each creative prospect and watch for: Extra
  energy. Feeling younger or more awake. Tension dissolving. An
  unknotted gut. A fog or boredom lifting. Rushes of heat,
  buzzing, or pulsations in particular physical locations. One
  patient, when considering ceramics, felt a hunger in her hands
  for the feel of slippery wet clay. Since becoming a potter, a
  sensual lacking in her hands has been satisfied. Another
  patient's feet just needed to tap; it couldn't be denied. Tap
  dancing gave him the action his tootsies craved. See what art
  your body answers to, whether oiling up a skillet or arranging
  flowers. Your body knows in instinctual ways. It can be drawn
  to a creative outlet either subtly or like a heat-seeking missile.
  Use your intuitive responses (along with the earlier exercise on
  identifying inspiration) to locate your muse.
- *Let adversity inspire you.* A creative outlet can be born in spite
  of or even because of harrowing circumstances. A survival
  instinct, creative energy fights to transcend hardship. I see
  examples all the time. A woman at my workshop donated a
  kidney to her brother. She then started making stunning
  necklaces in the shape of tiny organs (she wore a gold kidney),
  and distributes them to transplant donors and recipients.
  Several years ago I met the publisher of a homeless people's
  newspaper "empowering the poor and unhoused with an
  income and a voice, inviting art from homeless artists and
  activists." Also I'm touched by the performance art of Lynn

Manning, who at twenty-three was shot in the face and blinded when attacked in a Los Angeles bar. (He foresaw his blindness as a boy, even covered his eyes purposely to prepare for the loss.) Courageously, Lynn went on to perform an acclaimed one-man play about his life, and serves as artistic mentor for the visually handicapped. Look to your own triumph over adversity to find a soul-resonant artistic outlet too.

- *Make time for the art you enjoy.* At least once a week, pursue your outlet. Being consistently creative keeps energy moving. The intent is not to become a virtuoso or compete; it's to be nourished (though your outlet may evolve into an intense artistic pursuit). You'll forge a new connection with yourself and the world, a sense of being more you that staves off creative malnutrition.

Action #3: Get Out of Your Own Way: Let Creative Energy Flow Through You

The *I Ching* states, "The beginning of all things lies still in the Beyond as ideas that are yet to become real. The creative has power to lend form to these ideas. Its energy is unrestricted by any fixed conditions." In this program, you're going to entice the creative from the Beyond into yourself, not such a tall order if you have instructions. I'll describe how to enlarge your energy field to hold a greater flow, a central precept of Energy Psychiatry. All my patients learn it; you will too.

I treasure hearing how artists experience this expansive creative state. Always, I listen with an ear for energy. Isadora Duncan talked about "channels of my body filling with vibrating light." Emily Dickinson said that great poetry "makes my body so cold no fire can warm me." Poet Coleman Barks calls it "a dissolving that's felt as a tenderness towards existence, and a laughter." These artists aren't logically dissecting creativity. They're intuiting its subtle energetics, which can verge on natural psychedelia. Sound fun? This exercise can get you there.

MAKE CHANGES NOW

BE A VESSEL FOR CREATIVE ENERGY

The following apply to all creative endeavors, from writing to baking bread:

- *Leave your ego at the door.* Creativity is never just about you doing it. You're a conduit for a vaster energy, a humbling, magnificent partnership that makes you large. Your ego is a puny facsimile. Creativity driven by self-will can feel like trying to squeeze blood from a stone. Rather, let creative energy act upon you; worlds spontaneously open.

- *Let go of control.* Your creative switch flips "on" when you become a true receiver, not a controller—a method every actor knows. Our creative circuits are pressure-sensitive. When you let go, pressure is relieved; more energy gets through. When you bear down, pressure increases; less energy passes through. Our literal mind misinterprets such letting go as "getting nowhere." But to our creativity it means making room for life force to dance.

- *Shift out of ordinary consciousness.* Before a creative endeavor, meditate for a few minutes. In a quiet place, close your eyes, breathe deeply, and still mundane thoughts. Try to be fully present in the moment. With each inhalation and exhalation feel your energy expand.

- *Invite creative energy in.* Silently request that creativity flow through your entire body. Picture it as a radiant sun. Watch the sun moving toward you until it's so close you see it everywhere. Feel its light entering the top of your head and going down to your toes. Warm. Nourishing. Exhilarating. You are the vessel. Allow yourself to be saturated.

- *Melt into the creative trance.* This sweet abandon can feel like a blurring of the time-space continuum, a "being-taken" by imagination's velocity, or just plain peace. You may lose track of the clock and everyday concerns—perhaps some of most sublime moments you'll ever know.

The above exercise formalizes your transition from the humdrum into the creative. It puts your awareness on notice that it's about to change from the small to the large self—which preps you to receive more energy. Creativity is just waiting for a chink in your mental armor to make its move. Invite it in.

Action #4: Defend Your Creative Space

It's crucial to have a safe place to explore creative urges, a self-anointed haven protected from kids, noise, and phones. Ideally it'll be a spot in your home where you can close the door. You'll need to educate your mate or family about the sacredness of your creative space. At first, they may keep impinging upon it, but set firm boundaries until they get used to the change. I hang a "Keep Out" sign on my office so others know not to come in. I disappear for many hours when I write. I don't want intrusions, nor do I want to feel someone's energy lurking nearby, checking on me. One of my most significant relationships was with a poet who understood my need for creative isolation, and defended his own right to this too. Realizing that I can set these parameters with a man makes having a relationship possible for me.

If a creative space at home isn't feasible, stake one out in the world. Enroll in a class. Take an easel to the park. Write in a restaurant. What's great about public places is the anonymity: strangers won't bother you like family members might. You can construct your very own creative cocoon and go wild in it.

MAKE CHANGES NOW
TAKE THIS CREATIVITY OATH

- I deserve to have a time and place to create.
- I deserve to have privacy.
- I deserve to have the energy that creativity can bring.
- I deserve to be loving to myself in these areas.

IN THE *I CHING,* the image for the creative is heaven. Drawing this oracle means that "success will come from the primal depths of the universe." The Positive Energy Program's Sixth Prescription—open yourself to the flow of inspiration and creativity—grooms you to be increasingly agile in flowing with creative forces. An important constant to remember: When your energy goes up, you're onto something; creative successes are always energetic successes too.

Creativity can also reflect a profound vision in us, sometimes even a foreshadowing. I'm moved by the haunting *New York Times* story of Michael Richards, an Afro-American artist killed in his ninety-first-floor studio during the World Trade Towers attack. He'd cast a sculpture from his own body; it paid homage to the Tuskegee Airmen, a segregated unit of heroic World War II Afro-American pilots. The bronze figure, in sleek flight uniform, was pierced in the torso by a dozen fighter planes that appeared to both wound and levitate him. Michael's art was his death premonition. He was sculpting with subliminal awareness his terrible 9-11 future. Such mystery: Michael's heartbreaking clarity remains ineffable.

Our depths are penetrated by creativity. Keep conjuring it. I vouch for the trustworthiness of its direction. Following it cultivates physical energy and a luminous Spirit. Allow imagination's impulses to gestate in you. This is our Creator's music.

Treat Yourself:

Close your eyes. Visualize a scene of perfect peace. Perhaps a sunlit meadow overlooking the sea. Stretch your body out completely at ease. Feel the soft, warm breeze caressing you. Inhale its freshness. Then, inwardly ask the creative energy of nature and the universe to flow through you. Simply open and receive.

INTERVIEW: SHIRLEY MACLAINE
ON CREATIVE ENERGY

SHIRLEY MACLAINE IS AN ACADEMY AWARD-WINNING ACTRESS,
BESTSELLING AUTHOR, DANCER, AND MYSTIC.

When you talk about creativity, energy is everything. For me, it's tapping straight into the divine, an invisible energy that composes life and contains all of our souls' experiences. If I love what I'm doing creatively I surrender to the flow, allow it to go in whatever direction it wants to take. Creative energy gives me physical energy. But because I often end up with a blurred sense of time and place, the trick is to keep my center.

As an actor, I don't totally lose myself in a character. I've never worked like DeNiro or Meryl Streep, who're unbelievable geniuses—they carry a character with them twenty-four hours a day. I won't do that. I shut it off at lunch and in between takes. But during a take, I'm completely in character; my creative energy is sculpted by my internal sense of being centered.

I channel my characters. It's a fantastic feeling. In the film *Madame Sousatzka,* I told my director, John Schlesinger, who didn't believe in any of this stuff, that I was going to create this character, a piano teacher, with him—what she wears, how she walks, how she thinks—then throw it up to the universe, get out of my own way, and let her channel back into me. The character was with me whenever we worked. On the last day of filming, when John said "Cut!" Madame Sousatzka left and I was without her vibrations. I got the flu immediately. My temperature shot up to 102. I don't want that to happen again, but I got a feel for what the experience of channeling was like.

I was originally trained as a ballet dancer. The one thing they teach you is never to think. But there is freedom in not thinking, even though you have all the conditioned technique. Once Isadora Duncan and Anna Pavlova took untrained dancers to Jacob's Pillow, the famed performing center in the Berkshires. Pavlova would teach them in a disciplined way. Isadora Duncan would say, "Here is the music. Let it take you." After three months the kids returned to New York City and went into ballet, but the Duncan dancers excelled faster because they were feeling the music. While I was living with the Masai in East Africa, they'd do these pulsating movements that were dance to me. Without booze or drugs they'd achieved a kind of ecstasy through moving with the drums, and through chanting. Dancing which is simply technique is not art.

Art is about energy, positive and negative. All art has the power to heal because it helps us see who we are, and what we resist. If I respond violently—say, to Mapplethorpes's photo of someone pissing on Christ—I can see the violent part of myself. If I respond to the transcendental in art, it reflects my own transcendence.

Creativity stimulates passion, whether you're acting or gardening. It may seem that there aren't enough hours in the day to be creative, but I find these portions of my life make time bend; I do more than I expect in a short period. I spend a lot of time writing and thinking. I love it. I'm very disciplined, but the idea of getting up and not knowing what's going to happen that day is amazing too. The creativity simply of that. Of letting time do what it wants with you!

One of the most important relationships in my life is with my little rat terrier, Terry. I was walking in Malibu and she called to me from a pet shop. She was six weeks old. I went in and bought her. I needed a dog like a hole in the head, but I've rarely been without Terry since. I love observing her relationship with sounds, smells, leaves, birds, ants, poop, the mountains. She's allowed me to feel unconditional love and she makes me laugh. I sit under the stars with her and my other animals for hours. It's as entertaining to me as the creativity of a good movie or book. It's an expansive expression of God, and much deeper.

I also feel tremendous creative energy in nature. It can be quite calming— a serene flow, a kind of serum. I'm very attuned to the weather; it affects my moods. When the wind blows, it's a cleansing. I feel the wind's energy in me; I become it. It'd be interesting to feel the creative life force of a violent hurricane. All of nature, including wild winds, brings me joy because it's so real. I hear nature speak—especially through the images in clouds. Sitting in my hot tub I watch them all the time. I see faces; some are scary, some are kind, some are gods or angels; I have circular clouds that I swear are huge motherships hovering over my ranch. Nature is as much a part of me as blood flowing through my veins. It's an aspect of creation.

So is spontaneity. Sometimes in the middle of the night, an inner voice wakes me up with various creative instructions. It may say, "Write," or "Dance," or "Go outside." I believe intuitions like these are messages from the divine in myself, so I always follow them. Intuitive talent is creative energy from God. Since time doesn't exist, we can tune in to past, present, and future. But to contact intuition, we must still our minds. I remember Krishnamurti telling me that once he walked for four hours and could honestly say he never had a thought. That hasn't happened to me yet, but I hope it will.

7

THE SEVENTH PRESCRIPTION: CELEBRATE THE SACREDNESS OF LAUGHTER, PAMPERING, AND THE REPLENISHMENT OF RETREAT

BEING SMART ABOUT OUR ENERGY means overthrowing the crazy fallacy that we deserve anything less than luxurious self-care.

This program's Seventh Prescription hails ways for us to invigorate by winding down, offers a welcome tune-up for our bedraggled energy centers. I'm an enthusiast for taking regular respites from the figuring-out mind, of becoming just plain silly; also of escaping the material world periodically to rescue yourself. Your life force needs protection—for me, a practice-what-you-preach deal breaker of Energy Psychiatry. To live it, I've had to recognize that tipping point when doing one more thing or even talking to one more person can cause lethal drain. (This is when my energy field intuitively feels so overstuffed it could burst like a balloon; a single pinprick, then nothing but fizzle.) It's cost me, but I've learned not to play it so close to that edge. Instead, I stop for mini-time-outs or longer retreats.

There are no superpeople who can go nonstop without burning out. If you mistake yourself for one, you're headed for the doomed fall both my achieve-or-bust patients and I have experienced. Maybe you're bull-headed like I was; you'll need to crash to learn. But if you can accept another way, I'll offer it to you: this chapter presents many strategies for increasing vitality. When replenishing yourself, spontaneous fix-its are a last resort. You need to nourish yourself to prevent burnout.

It seems natural that we'd all be clamoring for such relief, but it's often last on the list. Like some of my patients, you may feel undeserving, self-indulgent, or that you're wasting time when you stop to take care of yourself. If so, memorize this in neon: Preventing burnout does more for positive energy than trying to backpedal after you get sick. You have an inalienable right to self-care, an outgrowth of compassion. You don't have to be shy about loving yourself. If you learn to balance your energy, you won't always be grunting against exhaustion.

Not having to be constantly "on" or dead-serious is a cause for rejoicing. Your psyche and energy field relax when assured of ongoing breaks. Most important, you gain credibility with your beleaguered inner child. You're saying to him or her, "Sweetheart, I'm going to take care of you from now on."

REVEL IN LAUGHTER, PLAY, AND ALL-OUT SILLINESS

Recently my patient Wes, an acting coach and jokester, was stuck in a long supermarket line. He was in a rush, but the pace was glacial. Everything that could go wrong did: the harried checker dropped a carton of eggs; a woman with a stockpile of supplies forgot her credit card; an irritating man disputed prices. Wes recalled thinking, "I've had it with all this." The next thing he knew, the coach in him had claimed command. With a booming centurion voice, he announced to the checker and people in line, "Everyone listen. Take a deep breath and focus!" "At first they just stared at me, stunned," Wes said. "Then they all started laughing. I must have looked ridiculous.

My outburst even shocked me; I immediately apologized for completely losing it." Quite a moment. What most fascinated me was that amidst the ruckus, he'd inadvertently succeeded in unjinxing the line. It sped up and kept moving. Getting people laughing made them more efficient, woke them out of their energetic paralysis.

Clearly, laughter liberates. Physically, muscular tension loosens, clearing the wreckage of exhaustion; emotionally, laughter raises your spirits and softens rigid defenses. In terms of subtle energy, laughter bathes your system with positive vibes that ease all that ails you. Studies abound lauding how laughter heals: it elevates immune response and endorphins (our body's natural painkillers); relieves stress, anxiety, and depression; prevents heart disease. Imagine: Allergic welts shrank after patients watched Charlie Chaplin's *Modern Times.* Physician Norman Cousins, beloved father of laugh therapy, treated his own pain from a life-threatening joint disease with a ten-minute daily dose of laughter. With the same strategy, the American Association for Therapeutic Humor advocates "hee-hee healing." In the film *Patch Adams,* a doctor-clown played by Robin Williams similarly taught the necessary magic of incorporating humor into our health care system.

I'm a big prescriber of laughter in Energy Psychiatry. Not the contrived or canned kind, but laughter from the soul. Just as I guide patients, I'd like you to sense when your funny bone is legitimately hit, an energetic place that resonates. True laughter is a surrender to hilarity; a sound, a smile, a heart opening. You feel it in your chest, or your whole body may shake. Also, notice that prior to a punchline, you'll enjoy an air of expectation, a subtle shift in consciousness and attention, the promise of mood transformation. But faking laughter is like faking orgasm: no positive energy to be had there. Since I've never gotten most conventional jokes, I know the awkward position of having to fake a smile because I was afraid to offend or seem clueless. Now I just make a joke out of my not getting it: that feels more authentic and relieves me of the negative fallout of pretending to be something I'm not.

Energy comes from humor. Each of us must locate our sense of what's funny, raucous, or wry. Although jokes often elude me, I really respond to the spontaneous comedy of life itself. I get a huge kick out of quirky little things. Children squealing as they pop bubble wrap. The time a friend's grandmother with Alzheimer's ate the tulips on the table instead of the food, and out of a mix of respect and the utter goofiness of the moment, the friend began eating tulips too. Or looking back at the night I took a sleeping pill, then hallucinated that my mattress was trying to communicate with me! As for those jokes I do get, I love the Middle Eastern Nasruddin stories. He's the legendary mystic trickster-sage (to whom numerous websites are devoted). It was once told that when Nasruddin left home he'd carry the front door with him. When asked why, Naruddin replied, "It's a security measure. This door is the only way someone can get into my house so I keep a close eye on it." Of course, now the place is wide open! I'm always tickled by such gentle, victimless satire of our human fears.

Intuitively I can read from a patient's energy field if they've been regularly laughing. Jillian, a free-spirit florist who often chuckles, has a light quality to her energy with lots of space between the molecules that surround her. I can sense this levity from many feet away. Fred, a thoughtful but emotionally repressed scientist, wants to laugh more but has yet to learn how. His energy field gives off a tautness, conveys a ponderous thud. I also sense an invisible skullcap compressing his head, especially the intuitive center. When patients laugh in sessions, it feels like joy-as-energy showering me and my office; these vibes linger for hours. And unlike traditional Freudian analysts who temper their responses, perhaps too fastidiously, I don't hesitate to laugh *with* my patients. Humor can be a doctor's psalm—the ability to see our weaknesses, bear them, even smile at them. Of course, I never undermine the serious issues at stake. But a humorless therapist is dead weight in the healing process, hinders upliftment. You can't intellectualize someone into the value of humor. We therapists must model what we teach.

I consider loss of laughter a crime against psyche and Spirit. With my patients, laughter's absence never gets by me; I make it my business to notice when it's missing, and help them recoup it. Otherwise, they're unknowingly living in energetic poverty. We don't ordinarily equate lack of laughter with deprivation, but from an energy perspective it is.

Why don't we laugh more? The crux is always that somewhere, somehow our inner child's energy got squelched (an implosion of life force I'll train you to reverse). I've repeatedly seen this dynamic play out in patients and myself. Unhappy childhoods, early losses, or overly serious parents can jam up our laughter. Excessive work and no escape from current problems do it too. We may not even know when our sense of humor wanes, or perhaps we never had one. The secret is recovering our inner child who has silently slipped underground for refuge.

To begin, review your past. See where laughter was left behind. To retrieve it, seek to consciously identify and disengage from any somber view on reality your family or the world communicated. Realize this block doesn't have to dictate your joy today. For instance, when I think about growing up, I can't recall the sound of my very outspoken mother's laugh. She'd smile, make the motions of laughing, but not a peep ever emanated. This might've come from some Emily Post rule for "ladylike" response, a horrifying style she also urged in me. But it felt strange for such a dynamo to be so muted. My father laughed some, but humor wasn't our family's strong suit. At meals my physician parents would discuss patients' cancer surgeries, diarrhea, dementia. No detail was taboo. In retrospect, I find an absurd humor in our deadpan dinner discussions of medical mayhem. At the time I was part mesmerized, part revolted. I needed to hear my mother's laugh more. It would've made me feel safer, that the world wasn't so fraught with intensity. She would've been modeling a lighter side for me, something I've had to strive to develop as an adult.

In my recent life, for some very important years, I had a romantic companion who was born funny. Being silly was a big part of how we were together, a form of intimacy. We sang in the car—he did the melody; I did the background doo-wops. We chased each other around the house, a kind of hide-and-seek. We howled on the roof with a chorus of neighborhood dogs. Once he brought a caterpillar home to roam, and made a sign saying, "Place every foot carefully. Do not walk on dark places on rug!" Happily, my inner child had room to play; the sound of laughter, his or mine, need not be gagged. Of course relationships are complex; they survive or don't survive for many reasons. But from this one, I learned how vital laughter is, a sweet lesson I'll carry with me into the future.

Reactivating laughter will bring the greatest possible happiness. When Bill, a bespeckled, goateed man about forty, came to my weekend workshop, he said: "Everything is peacefully settled in my life. I'm married to the lovely woman sitting beside me." (I "saw" the finest jewel-like twinkle interlacing their energy fields.) "Being a professor of English is gratifying. But I don't seem to experience great awe or laughter as I used to."

I replied, "When was the last time you felt them?"

Bill thought about it, then smiled. He told the group: "You know, I'm amazed to hear myself say this, but I think it was when I was eleven years old." He looked rueful. "I used to have absolute-freedom dreams where I'd soar over hills, valleys, and rivers. I had a crystalline sense of who I was and where I was going. The flying was effortless and blissful."

I was right with him. I sensed the ecstasy of his flight in my body, also recognized the archetypal phenomenon. Flying dreams, I explained, represent the hugeness of our spirit and capacity for delight. This is what many children possess innately, what so many adults have lost. Bill had hit the inner child motherlode, but needed to know how to laugh again. That night, I suggested he request an explanatory dream. The next day, excited, he told our workshop he'd had one: "I'm in a crowded place, some chaotic government office like Social Security. There was a long wait. We were supposed to take numbers, but some other man had mine. I tried to convince him to give it back, but he acted like I didn't exist. The situation was maddening. I knew the number belonged to me, but I couldn't get it."

Listening carefully to Bill, I realized this number held the answer to regaining joy. I didn't foresee his solution's specifics, but sometimes my role involves posing the right questions. One came immediately. I asked, "If you had a number that was just yours, what would it be?" There was a long pause. Then suddenly his whole being lit up.

"It's 46," Bill announced with sudden certainty, and began laughing. "Forty-six was my number when I played football at school. When I was eleven."

Male initiations: eleven-year-olds playing football—a real life's adventure. As we learned, though, soon after Bill stopped playing football, his flying dreams also stopped. Over thirty years later, he was ready to regain his inner child's pleasure in discovery. To be whole, I emphasized, he needed #46, and #46 needed him. As Bill heard this, his face softened, and he began to laugh again. I know how much we can miss this part of ourselves, how stark the adult world seems without it. After the workshop, Bill pledged to find #46 wherever he could—from sports and all kinds of play. He'd make his inner child a priority. In one of the tender closings of a circle that often ensue from a workshop, I later received an e-mail from his wife saying that they'd found a photo of Bill in his #46 jersey striped uniform. As a reminder of who he was and who he can be, they put it on their bedroom dresser. She also wrote that between them now, his nickname is 46, an outcome that continues to make me laugh.

MAKE CHANGES NOW

NURTURE YOUR INNER CHILD: LAUGH MORE

Here are some pointers I give patients to get them laughing. When you do this exercise, be authentic, have fun, and feel the positive energy.

- *Reclaim your inner child's life force.* Every grown-up has an inner child. Both are distinct energetic aspects of our life force. For full vigor, each must be accounted for. Your inner child may need urging to come out and play, but it wants to be embraced. (Having kids often naturally spurs this reconnecting process in parents who otherwise might never get there.)

  For starters, bring out your baby or childhood photos. Really look at them. The photos can rematerialize shelved energy. Next, with photo in hand, promise to honor that child's needs. For example, I promised mine: "You'll never have to smile for a camera again unless you want to"—an expectation I despised when growing up. Recall ordeals you had to endure; vow no repeats.

  Also, begin to recognize when your inner child is in jeopardy. Perhaps you're laughing less, feeling overtired or overworked. Once, during a crazily hectic book tour, I dreamed I saw an infant in a crib turning blue whom I couldn't care for because I had a magazine interview! From hard knocks I've learned to nurture my inner child, particularly during periods when I'm overburdened. Small things like giggling with a friend or renting a funny video go a long way. Reclaiming your inner child will safeguard laughter and restore dormant life force.

  Find activities your inner child loves. Explore what your inner child genuinely finds fun or funny. First, recall activities from your youth that made you smile. Miniature golf. Bugs Bunny. Elmer Fudd. The fast-forward chipmunk voice you get from inhaling a helium balloon. Memories can lubricate rusty laughter synapses.

  Second, see what sorts of fun your inner child responds to now. Peruse the newspaper's leisure section, ask friends what's funny, check out genres of comedy from standup to radio. I get dependable laughs from the homespun satire of Garrison

Keillor's *A Prairie Home Companion* on National Public Radio.
As an adult, I've also become enamored with magic. Not a slick
David Copperfield show, but the wily eccentricity of Ricky Jay.
My inner child is rapt watching him pierce a watermelon with
the ace of spades thrown at a hundred miles an hour. Or
hearing tales of daredevils and singing mice in his book *Learned
Pigs and Fireproof Women.*

How do you know when something's really funny to you?
The subtle energetic signs are spontaneous laughter; a
surrendering; a lightening of your load; a shot of vitality. One
thing you can depend on—your inner child is an expert energy
reader, can tell humor that's hot from a mechanical *shtick.*

- *Seek out people who laugh.* We absorb funniness by osmosis.
Hearty laughers spread those positive vibes to us. What counts
most, though, is the energy behind the laugh, not just sound or
facial expression. Take the Dalai Lama's infectious giggle, which
comes from a place of love and wonder—its healing energy goes
straight to our hearts. At the other extreme are people who have
grins on their faces, but whose laughter often stems from malice
or psychic pain. So confusing. They're laughing, yet you're
being slimed with negative vibes. There's no joy coming your
way. Don't be fooled; trust your energetic assessment.

- *Play with children.* Children have Ph.D.s in play; their lack of
inhibition is contagious. Spend time with them. If you're lucky
enough to be around infants, watch how they grin at six weeks,
then laugh at four months, a natural instinct. Or observe
children at play; they haven't learned to guard their emotions or
hold in squeals and giggles. They're just beaming. Try to open
your heart, and absorb these vibes.

If you're a parent, remember to play with your children. This
can be easy to forget in the whirlwind of goal-oriented activities
from homework to computer camp. (Like us, kids can become

overly scheduled.) So, learn to laugh again from children, and enjoy yourself.

- *Set your intention to laugh as much as possible.* From the moment you wake up in the morning, look for things to laugh about. Regularly laughing buoys our energy field, reverses learned seriousness. If our parents had said at breakfast, "Be sure not to miss out on any laughs today," it'd be a lot easier. But most didn't, so we have to teach ourselves.

At Santa Monica's Wellness Community, cancer survivors have laugh-a-thons. They share jokes, crack up at just about everything including medical misadventures, and know that this will help healing. Real wisdom we all can benefit from, but let's not wait for a health challenge to catch on. So, be amused by whatever you can, especially your own foibles. Laughter is a way of cherishing your energy.

In this program, also keep an eye out for cosmic humor, a wink from on high. Cosmic humor can be mind-bogglingly synchronistic, implying there's something larger than this reality, and gets you lovingly laughing at the human condition. For example, at a luncheon where I was guest speaker, a woman told me that when her husband was dying she dreamed he left her for a woman named Lucille. Hearing this, he said, flabbergasted: "Leave you? Are you nuts?" A few months passed. Her husband died. Bringing flowers to his grave one day, she glanced at the inscription on the adjoining stone. Guess who? Lucille. What cosmic comedian could've orchestrated that scenario? In this woman's despair, laughter consoled. She felt watched over, and in the grand scheme, that all was well. Cosmic humor is percolating everywhere. Be hip to it. Its positive perspective is a blessing.

MAKE PAMPERING PART OF YOUR ROUTINE

I looked up *pampering* on the Internet and there were over a million references! Certainly ample opportunity to partake luxuriously. The difficulty is, both sexes often consider pampering an excess of our consumer culture or only worthy of a rare "indulgence." Men may get itchy around the term, consider it a pejorative, erroneously equate it with being effeminate or for women only. (As one male friend said, "Try going into the Dallas Cowboys locker room and telling those guys to pamper themselves. See how they'd react!") In the Positive Energy Program, however, pampering is a portal to larger energetic dimensions. I define it as a sensual, energy-restorative pleasure other than sex, self-care that can include both manicures and watching Wimbledon. In this state, you don't give to anybody else; you only take energy in. Pampering is the opposite of stress and sensual stinginess. The purpose is to relax, enjoy, and relieve exhaustion. This rich surrendering can, at times, put you in an altered state that triggers the visionary. It also penetrates the recesses of your being, and irons out energy blockages.

I'd like you to choose a regular type of pampering that fits your schedule, and more special treats for occasions when you need more. I'll present four categories to choose from, and describe how each increases your subtle energy. As you practice them, remember that it's not selfish to let go; it's being good to yourself, compassion made real. Let yourself experiment with pampering by trying each option I present.

Soak in Hot Water in Bathtubs, Jacuzzis, or Natural Springs

Throughout history, across cultures, water has been linked with magic and healing. In 4000 B.C., the therapeutic value of mineral baths was mentioned in Sanskrit. Babylonians, Egyptians, and Tibetans used water therapy even before the famous Roman baths. Hippocrates, the Greek father of medicine, prescribed the sea's healing properties for patients, and also recommended boiling water before drinking, purifying advice way before its time. Edgar Cayce, renowned for his medical intuitive readings from the early 1900s until his death in 1945, recommended immersion in mineral waters. This hydrotherapy cured Robert Frost's back pain and the ailments of many others. Franklin Roosevelt, crippled with polio, used hydrotherapy, and founded a rehab center for the physically handicapped in Warm Springs, Georgia. Further, miraculous healings have long been attributed to the "divinely blessed" spring in Lourdes, France, to which the disabled and ill make pilgrimages.

In my Energy Psychiatry practice, I urge patients to soak in baths or Jacuzzis, a treat often taken for granted. (Mineral springs, though less accessible, offer a more direct connection to the earth's elements.) Water is very giving. It comforts, infuses our weariness with life force, cleanses the body, and flushes negative vibes from our energy fields, especially useful for intuitive empaths.

Every evening I can't wait to take a bath. At the first sound of water gushing from the spigot, relief sets in. (After even a good day I need some respite.) When the tub is full, I light a few jasmine candles, then inch into the steaming water. My muscles and brain quickly relax, but the pleasure is more than that. I feel lifted to a dreamy womblike awareness. What bliss, this letting go. At times I just zone out, or observe as intuitions flash by. Water amplifies intuition; ancient seers were utilized by kings to read the future in a pond's reflective surface. Some of my most accurate insights have come when I'm submerged in or near water. (You can imagine my thrill visiting the Pythian springs in Delphi where the oracle bathed before her readings in the amphitheater!) A bath washes away the coating of energetic gook I've absorbed during the day. Plus it puts me happily back in my body, a connection daily stress is notorious for precluding.

Make a ritual of the act of bathing. Some of my patients burn incense and light candles. Others love bubbles, an inner child's heaven. You can also use bath salts. Or add essential oils; these constitute the immune system of plants—lavender is a traditional relaxer.

Also, keep in mind: Bathing is one of the rare times you're naked, a beautifully vulnerable state (clothes distance our chakras from the natural world). Skin touches air touches water. The energies of the elements and our bodies intermix. Soaping up your chakras feels sumptuous, will awaken them. Also, scrubbing with a loofa sponge stimulates circulation. I prefer tubs to showers because you're cradled and surrendered, hands and feet buoyant, weightless; you don't have to do anything. During showers you have to stand, though they can be beneficial too. While in water, try touching your intuitive center between the eyebrows. Then just lie back; see what visions come. Such deep relaxation and opening to instinctual forces fortifies energy.

Get Regular Body Work or Beauty Services

One afternoon during a winter storm many years ago, I was having a massage in my home. Covered by a white sheet, I could hear the wind howling above the breaking surf just outside. I was carried by its untamed power as the masseuse's fingers gently stroked my forehead, my neck. *Ahhh.* Then, in a split second, a vision came. I saw myself in a circle of forty people teaching intuition. I was happier than I'd ever been. This was a totally surprising scenario considering that at the time I was a traditional psychiatrist in private practice. Later, though, it became clear how the vision was a preview into my future.

A good massage calms the mind, drains tension from the body, can even transport you to an altered state. The object is to get energy flowing though your subtle system. A massage opens chakras; it also may prompt visions and memories or release pockets of blocked emotion. Healing proceeds by letting it all come through. The wonder of massage is that, eyes shut, you're under a covering but exposed, more open and less armored, poised to yield to pleasure. This dramatic consciousness shift is particularly relevant for my hypercerebral patients. Like them, you might find a massage gets you out of your head, into your body. It's also a succor for those not in a romantic relationship, an opportunity to be touched by caring hands.

The types of massages range from the gentle Swedish variety to Rolfing's deep tissue work to the specific point stimulation of acupressure. There's also the heavenly face and scalp massage of a facial; it activates intuitive and spiritual centers in your forehead and crown. Sample different massages, see which one attracts. Get referrals from friends who've had good results. Also ask your physician, contact massage therapy schools, or the American Massage Therapy Association, a national organization.

It's best to find a practitioner who works with subtle energy, though some do so naturally without knowing it. How do you find out? Inquire about a masseuse's training. Many take courses on Energy Medicine and chakras during massage school and afterward. Or, if you're booking an appointment at a spa, read the brochure: acupressure, shiatsu, and Reiki, for instance, deal with energy flow, whereas a sports massage more likely focuses on muscle release and injuries. When practitioners lack a feel for energy, massage can become mechanical; their hands move, but they don't transmit healing vibes. For me, this takes most of the fun out of it.

My patient Jane, a record producer, learned what she needed from a masseuse by experiencing one who was all wrong for her. Jane's the type who's turned off by small talk, and this guy got chatty right away. Then he started working on her. She said, "It was bizarre. He was a preprogrammed automaton. His hands were massaging both shoulders with the same motion at the same time. They felt like rubber gloves; no human energy came from them. Finally, following the massage he handed me a long list of relaxing remedies I had to go out and buy. Ugh. More to do." After this debacle, Jane went on to find an energy practitioner whose touch and manner wasn't robotic or overwhelming, a better match for her.

When seeking a bodyworker, always evaluate:

- Do I prefer a man or woman?
- Does he or she work with subtle energy?
- Do I like deep or light pressure?

- How long a massage do I want? A half hour? An hour? More?
- Do I prefer silence? Or calming music, and/or some talking?
- Do I want to socialize before and after? Or have only a minimal exchange?

As I tell my patients, a massage is just for you. It's not about pleasing the practitioner, or putting up with unnerving vibes, including sexual ones. It is about conveying to the practitioner the amount of pressure you like, and other terms that make you most comfortable. For a seasoned masseuse, this is expected. I've had many patients who've stuck with a practitioner because they're afraid to offend or aren't good at ending relationships. One assertion-phobic patient had a New Age masseuse who continuously "channeled" messages from the Pleiades, which amounted to her talking the whole time. My patient just wanted peace and quiet, but couldn't say so for months. Finally she did, but her masseuse just couldn't adjust. At last, my patient found another woman who felt at home working in silence. Surrendering to a massage is an exercise in trust; you must feel at ease.

Regular massage is most effective. A weekly session is ideal, but monthly ones can still improve your energy. Designate this as sacred time, an appointment not to be canceled except for emergency. I prefer a masseuse to come to my home in the evening. Then I don't have to go out, and I can savor the energy. Afterward, I take a bath, go to sleep, then drift into dreams, cocooned in this stress-free state. In contrast, some young mothers I treat look forward to escaping to a salon for an appointment while their mate or babysitter watches the kids. Never forget: Putting yourself first for a few hours *is* good mothering. The better shape moms are in, the better shape kids will be in too. Plus children learn to model such enlightened self-care, and will later give it to themselves.

Along with massage, I'm also a proponent of pampering yourself with a range of beauty services: manicures, pedicures, body wraps, aromatherapy, mud baths! They all feel divine, feed your body and energy field. When you approach beauty services as a form of healing, not narcissism, the energy gain for you is huge. Because vibes are sent whenever you're touched, be sure the service-giver is heart-centered and doesn't burden you with his or her problems. This isn't too much to ask. If the referral came from a friend, get the lowdown on the person's style; if it sounds compatible try him or her out. Or if you're going in cold to a spa, you may need to do a few test runs. See if you like someone's energy and manner. Also, at the reservation desk, feel free to request the kind of person you want, quiet or outgoing. There are many caring, skilled people around.

Allow Yourself to Veg Out or Pursue Non-Mind-Stressing Activities

Vegging out means turning off your mind and becoming as vegetable-like as possible. Vegetables are colorful, shapely, and nourishing, but they're not known for their brains. Thank God, we have the ability to emulate them. To me, the occasional veg-out is a spiritual state because it restores energy. I might watch trashy television instead of CNN. Or stay hunkered in bed all afternoon with the phone unplugged, doing absolutely nothing "constructive."

See what kinds of vegging out you prefer. Perhaps it's snuggling in with the *New York Times* crossword puzzle. Or watching televised sports events—but don't let them steal all your free time or become an addiction distancing you from family or life. (My mother used to have to pry my father away from the TV, a perennial struggle between them.) You may like leafing through beauty breakthroughs in women's magazines. Or reading *People*. Nothing to feel guilty about. It's healthy to temporarily forget about the world's woes and your own. Sometimes when I've had it with everything and everybody, I veg out for a while. Even a few hours is freeing, quickly renewing. I highly recommend this no-brainer form of pampering.

Splurge on Treats

Webster's Dictionary defines a splurge as "an ostentatious extravagance." It implies some grandiose depravity only for spoiled princesses.

Not true in this program. I define splurging as an expansion of energy, a generosity of spirit and attitude wherein you periodically lavish yourself with something special. It's not emptying out your children's college funds to buy a Ferrari or yielding to the compulsion of shopaholism. But it does mean spending more on energy-boosting extras that won't bleed you dry. For instance, one patient, a tennis lover, splurged on a top-of-the-line racquet, a source of great pleasure for him. Another paid for prime seats at a Tina Turner concert. You may opt to go to a new restaurant. Or buy a pair of pricey shoes. Adding to your wardrobe isn't just a materialistic concern. It can spice up the vibes you project. Everything you wear gives off subtle energy. As attached as I get to my holey jeans or frayed sweaters, there comes a time when they're energetically kaput. It's hard to say good-bye, but they must go. Splurging on an item or two with fresh oomph can give you a lift.

I'm all for being practical and keeping within your budget. But constantly skimping holds energy too tight, a kind of constipation. Splurging enlarges your universe and aura, gets life force moving.

EXPERIENCE THE REPLENISHMENT OF RETREAT

After my mother died, I went through a cardboard box she'd kept for me with everything from my first baby hair to my grammar school memorabilia. I was stunned to see my teacher's comment on my third-grade report card: "Judi [my childhood nickname] is an excellent student but puts too much pressure on herself." Wow, I thought. I was that pressured even then! Because of my lifelong tendency to push so hard, I've learned the necessity of planning regular retreats from the status quo to resuscitate my peace of mind and energy.

Finding your own right rhythm of worldly involvement and withdrawal is crucial. What constitutes a retreat? It's a stepping away from phones, paperwork, and small talk to seek a stillness in your being; a reconnecting with Spirit and/or nature; a conscious nourishing of your energy so you can reenter life reanimated. Retreats differ from social vacations—say, a Caribbean cruise or a trip to Paris—which are exciting and outer-oriented; these replenish in a different way, fulfill more gregarious needs. You can take retreats at home for hours, days, or longer, or plan extended stays around the world. Though traditional medicine would typically deem this topic more appropriate for a travel agent than a doctor, in Energy Psychiatry I see it as central to a patient's total health. I educate each of my patients about this energy-relevant issue.

Age-old spiritual traditions revere the energetic restoration of retreat. In Judaism, there's Sabbath, from Friday sunset to Saturday sunset, devoted to introspection; the Sabbath is welcomed as a bride; candles are lit and families join in prayer. Christianity has Sunday as a day of rest, a mirror for God's rest on the Seventh Day. Sufis are asked to make a monthly *halwa,* a reflective time alone. Before the Buddha's enlightenment, he withdrew for six years of ascetic practice; retreat has always been at the core of Buddhism. Regardless of the tradition, retreat is a returning to the heart and the Eternal.

Retreats aren't only for monks or renunciates. We, in the world, desperately need them too. Perhaps your spiritual tradition offers retreats you'd like to participate in. If not, I'll describe how to design one that's practical for you. What matters to me is that you take this opportunity to bask in the replenishment that only going inward brings. I promise: it's easier than you think.

Take Retreats at Home

Home can be a place of retreat, not merely a pit stop where we plop ourselves on the bed after work, stare at the TV, inhale a fast-food dinner and crash, only to stagger up and out the door again the next morning. We're not obliged to keep reenacting this bleak, energy-numbing sentence. You can make your home a haven. Happily, it doesn't take much.

Start by creating a sacred space, a self-fashioned altar, away from intruders. Find a specific location in your home, a refuge where you can kick off your shoes, breathe deeply again, meditate, and rejoin yourself and Spirit. Your sacred space may be in a separate bedroom, nook, or alcove, or it can be part of an office in your home. My patients who have young children and limited square footage often assemble one out of reach in their closets. Explain to your kids that this is Mommy or Daddy's special place; if they want to touch the objects there, they can do so only with you. Soon they'll get used to respecting this area. Wherever you choose, it's ideal to be able to shut the door. Pick a site where guests don't go, one you can designate "off limits" to your kids or mate, at least for blocks of time. A sacred space isn't supposed to be a conversation piece, but rather a refueling sanctuary.

My sacred space, a corner of my second bedroom/office, is very simple. It consists of a small wooden table that I used years ago in my Venice Beach apartment. I like that the table has part of me in it, reflects my history. As a covering, I selected a material with Asian women on it dressed in blue kimonos. On top are two candles, a clay incense holder, a bowl of fruit, which I replenish often, a photo of me with my parents, and a porcelain statue of Quan Yin, the Far Eastern Goddess of Compassion—all symbols of sacredness, of what's important to me, and who I am. I try to meditate in this space daily. When my mother was dying, many nights I'd sleep there for the consolation offered. Beholding the luminous Quan Yin, often through my grief, enabled me to stand fast to truths I'd long worked to make my own, and to begin the next day energized.

My friend Laurie Sue Brockway, formerly an editor of *Playgirl,* is now an interfaith minister. The single mother of a son with a physical disability, she built an extraordinary sacred space. She said, "I made my entire one-room Manhattan apartment into a temple with my goddess statues—Athena the huntress; Aphrodite, goddess of love; Quan Yin. My tiny overcrowded apartment went from a place I wanted to escape from to a tiny overcrowded haven that energized me. There was just a wall between us and busy Forty-fourth Street near the United Nations. But regardless of what was happening in the world or down the block, my home had a peaceful vibe." (Her book, *A Goddess Is a Girl's Best Friend,* was born there.) Whenever I visited Laurie Sue's apartment/temple, it felt like entering the omnipresent embrace of Goddess arms, a loving lift for the weary. Laurie Sue and her son lived in that apartment for the first ten years of his life. Alex, now eleven, told me, "I liked being around the goddesses. They helped us stay safe, listened to our prayers, then helped us get a new place." These days Laurie Sue, her mate, and Alex share a home in Queens, where the living room has become the goddesses' domain.

When your life gets busy or you need an energy refresher, go to your sacred space. Think of it as a vacation spot. No matter how stressed you are or how your mind is reeling, sitting in this atmosphere of stillness will help slow everything down and center you.

MAKE CHANGES NOW
CONSTRUCT YOUR OWN SACRED SPACE

Scout your home for a location for which you feel an affinity. Your choice may be obvious, or require some imagination. If you're not sure, audition locations for privacy and comfort. See how they feel. You don't have to make this a big production: start with a candle; light it; close your eyes. Then sit quietly focusing on your breath. Or, as you've learned, actively meditate on opening your heart. Even five minutes can lessen frustration or fatigue, but you can stay longer.

After you meditate in the same spot, a vortex of positive energy builds. All that heart percolating in one locale. Some of my patients also use this space to think out decisions, mull over the day, or write in their journals. You can try that too. Gradually bring items there that uplift you spiritually, beautify, or contain meaning: flowers, shells, a photo of your dog or other intimates, or holy talismans and symbols (conventionally religious or not). Your sacred space will remind you of the sublime, and honor the great Mystery.

You might find that your sacred space spurs you to make the rest of your home more energy-conscious. I've come to see my physical environment as an expression of energy, a calming inner sanctum. The ocean sunlight filters through bay windows in every room. I have two pieces of "rainbow art" sculpture that reflect an unbelievably brilliant spectrum of colors dancing on my walls. A pitcher of roses rests on the living room table, radiating lushness. Potted plants of all sizes and shapes enliven my space. Check out the vibes in your vicinity. Ask yourself, "Are my choices in sync with what gives me energy? Have I decorated my space to impress or conform, or does it truly nurture me? A small, warm touch here or there makes a big difference: A flash of color, a striking wall hanging, or soft lighting can transform. Plants literally bring you a breath of fresh air. Select what's pleasing to your eye, what feeds you after a long day. To create such a positive energy environment, you don't need a palace. Any space will do if the desire to transform it is there.

You can use your home for longer retreats. I was intrigued by religious scholar and mystic Huston Smith's account of such a time. When he was a professor at Syracuse University, he took a seven-month sabbatical. At first, he and his wife planned to go away to avoid interruptions. Instead, they decided to turn off the phones and notify family, colleagues, and friends that they were on a home retreat. Such a clever idea! They put a message on their answering machine, saying, "The Smiths have 'dispersed' for seven months. For emergencies contact . . ." They announced that if they saw people they knew when going for groceries or running other errands, they'd smile, but would observe their vow to speak only to each other.

Incredibly, during their retreat, there was just one intrusion: the chairman of Smith's department required a signature. When he came to the door, he simply pointed to the page, and left respectfully without a word. In retrospect, the great joy of this retreat, Smith says, is that everything slowed down, became unpressured. He and his wife spent more time meditating, writing, flowing with life's rhythms without alarm clocks or distractions.

Of course, you don't need seven months to enjoy a home retreat. Try it for an afternoon, a day, a weekend. (I've always had an umbilical pull toward home, so restoring myself there has particular allure.) The point of any retreat is to eliminate external impositions that gnaw at your energy and let life spread itself out before you. Use the open-ended time to meditate, contemplate, listen to beautiful music, read poetry, take walks, be silent, fill your well with positive energy.

There are various options for home retreats:

- If you live alone, simply pick a time, get coverage for business or other concerns, turn off the phones, and dive into whatever replenishes.

- With a mate, you can plan a joint retreat, a deep and quiet intimacy. Together determine the length, preferred activities, and flow. With a mate, I love meditating, writing, or reading in different parts of the house for many tranquil hours without conversing. You can spend your retreat separately or with one another.

- If you're comfortable with your mate being at home but not participating, agree on parameters: How long will your retreat be? Are you going to interact? Be silent? Would you prefer the TV off? The phone unplugged in specified rooms? No knocking on your door? Negotiate and observe these terms.

- If your mate can't or doesn't want to take a home retreat, go solo. Choose an agreed-upon period when he or she is out. Say, "This is a time to recharge myself. It means so much to me that you respect this." Then, to avoid intrusions, set a specific point to rendezvous later. Some mates will understand; with others it's a process of gentle education.

• If you have young children, a home retreat is a much bigger challenge. For you to have peace, they must be out of the house, so you'll need to arrange for child care. Otherwise you'll always have an ear open for them. Also, like some of my exhausted parent-patients, you might find you fall asleep during this lull. That's fine too; think of it as a period of hallowed replenishment.

Home retreats take household planning and good communication with family. They provide a geographically desirable strategy to cultivate energy in a frenetic world. The effort is well worth it.

Take Retreats Away

There is also great value to longer, out-of-the-home retreats. Here, the idea is to get far away from the familiar—new places and people lend new perspective, can clear out the cobwebs in your energy field. But not just any places or people. It's important to be around supportive others, such as on meditation or contemplative retreats. Also to travel to locations that reverberate with life force: Utah's rugged red-rock canyons, Maui's seven sacred pools, and the ancient rocks of Stonehenge are a few. In *Travels,* Michael Crichton writes that whenever he feels stagnant, he takes such trips to regain a fresh point of view. You can take these retreats with your partner, with good friends, or alone. It's optimal to schedule at least one a year for a few days minimum, but preferably longer.

I often recommend meditation retreats for patients to relax and recenter themselves, a natural extension of Energy Psychiatry. Some give instruction on technique and arrange time to socialize at breaks and meals; others are silent. Meditation retreats are offered at Buddhist or yoga centers, some New Thought churches, Twelve Step programs, and as a part of Jewish mystical groups. In addition, many spas have a meditation program along with massage and yoga; you might prefer this setting, where meditation is part of the package but not the whole theme. Recently I gave an intuition workshop at the Miraval Center for Well-Being, a gorgeous "mindfulness spa" in Tucson, Arizona, that had a lovely meditation center, sublime hot-rock massages, and Jacuzzis designated as silent. If you've never tried a meditation retreat, start with an evening, a day, or perhaps a weekend. Deep lovers of this practice often continue for a month or more, but it's best to start with a shorter retreat.

I recently visited the Insight Meditation Retreat Center in Barre, Massachusetts. That autumn afternoon we arrived in the midst of a three-month (!) silent retreat with a hundred participants. For this duration they direct their attention inward, don't read, write, or speak. When we first pulled up I nearly tackled my companion, who was still in travel mode, as he began to ask a lone meditator on a walk for directions. We were there to see our friends Sharon Salzberg and Joseph Goldstein, Buddhist teachers who run the center with so much love. On our grand tour, I tuned in to the meditators: many of their energy fields looked golden, less taut than inundated city dwellers. Year round, people attend these retreats, silent or not, weekends and longer; they're a pristine, safe place to become large-hearted and renewed. I was also amused to learn of Joseph's latest project, "Dharma Retirement" (*Dharma* means "the truth of the way things are")—a meditative center for us baby boomers to age together during our later years, perhaps with assisted care and a nursing facility. Since one of my worst fears is ending up drooling and alone in some God-forsaken nursing home, I'm grateful to know that such a live-in "retreat" for elders will exist.

In Energy Psychiatry sometimes retreats are just what the doctor ordered. Take my patient Bruce, a bank executive, who consulted me for anxiety. He told me, "I've been anxious for months. I've thought about asking you for Valium, but taking it doesn't feel right. I'm just so on edge. I used to look forward to work, but lately I feel like a cog in a big conglomerate. I'm just turning forty. Maybe this is a midlife crisis. I don't know what to do."

Certainly Bruce sounded anxious. When I tuned in to him, I also sensed the bone-deep lethargy that had been gaining on him for months. Then, in my mind's-eye, I saw a series of snapshotlike flashes. A Jewish spiritual center I'd known of in New Mexico. Then a star of David. Then a feeling of communion with the Kaballah. I shared these intuitions with Bruce, asked if they made sense. He just smiled and said, "For so long I've been yearning to get away on a retreat, not a vacation. But things just keep coming up. A place I've fantasized of going was the center you mentioned! I've been curious about Jewish mysticism, but I've never pursued it." Over years of medical practice, I've seen how therapeutic such intuitive bull's-eyes can be by affirming a patient's unrequited needs. Their accuracy told me that medication was premature, though I don't hesitate to dispense it in the proper circumstances. In Bruce's case his being was crying out for rest, specifically a retreat. "But will you do it?' I asked. "Will you take off from work?" After a short pause he said, "Yes, I'm ready."

So, to his credit, Bruce planned a few weeks at the location I had seen. He had a tiny room with a view of the mountains. Meals were delivered to his door. Bruce meditated, attended spiritual talks, thought, read, was quiet. For him, a dream come true. Not surprisingly, when this time ended he was revived and his anxiety had markedly subsided.

Like Bruce you can envision your own retreats. They don't have to be associated with a group or conference center, though I suggest natural settings away from the rat race. As the poet William Wordsworth wrote, civilization can be "too much with us." Spending days or weeks in nature, a storehouse of subtle energies, can be the most replenishing of all. It has been for my friend, Dr. Larry Dossey, who has written some of his most compelling material on the healing power of prayer while in the wilderness. He told me:

> For three decades, my wife Barbie and I have taken a one-month trek in August to remote alpine lakes and forests in the Rockies. We hire wranglers to pack us in, and return to fetch us on a specific date. We essentially disappear and become

invisible to all our friends and everyday contacts. We don't take any cell phones or global positioning devices. This is raw primitive living, truly on the edge, in a tent exposed to the vagaries of weather. The experience involves an altered state of consciousness. Exposure to sun, sky, rain, and sleet changes one's awareness. We find the isolation restorative. Nothing else we've discovered returns us to a fresh view of the world. For us, this is a spiritual event on the order of pilgrimage—jour-neying to a sacred space, returning more whole and energized than before. We can't imagine living the rest of the year with-out it.

The kind of sacred travel that Larry describes taps a primal reso-nance in you. Rest assured, you don't need a month off or such iso-lation unless you choose. Personally I'm happier in a secluded, well-heated house in some forest, with all its amenities, especially my hot bath—but we're all different. You might prefer a first-class hotel in Yosemite to camping. Go with it. I'd like you to find retreat spots with living conditions that suit you. The essence of any retreat, though, as compared to a social vacation, is to have contemplative time. Your goal is to become soulfully energized from your destina-tion.

Be aware of spots in the world that intuitively call to you. This can manifest as a simple desire to go somewhere, or the pull can be stronger. One of my patients, who'd been physically abused as a child, had an irresistible attraction to Bali: its music, dance, lush veg-etation. So she saved her money and went, a healing trip to well-tended rice terraces and the presence of women at home in themselves. This helped her recover a stronger sense of her body and the feminine. Not long ago, I dreamed that a mother with auburn hair and cobalt eyes was rocking me in her arms, singing Celtic songs of longing that felt utterly familiar; I've yearned to go to Ireland for months, a trip I plan to take soon.

In daydreams or night dreams, you may keep returning to a locale, but not know where it is. If ever you recognize it in a travel flyer, a book, movie, or in conversation, go there. Something awaits you. Inevitably you'll have a sense of homecoming, completion. Also there are power spots worldwide that contain stupendous spiritual energy: Machu Pichu, the Great Pyramids, the Temple of Delphi. The very soil they're built on and the structures themselves can impart a healing energetic transmission. Even now, thousands of years later, we glean the benefits of these sacred sites.

In this program, I'd like you to embrace the notion of retreat. Schedule at least one a year so you'll have a guaranteed escape hatch. Psychologically, this is freeing. Plus, after a retreat, the positive energy stays with you. Whether you're at a meditation gathering, a cabin in the sequoias, or visiting the enchanter Merlin's cave on Cornwall's rugged coast, what you see, smell, learn, dream will keep seeping into your consciousness, a time-released balm. Allowing such reflection catalyzes stamina for months to come.

THE POSITIVE ENERGY PROGRAM'S Seventh Prescription—celebrate the sacredness of laughter, pampering, and the replenishment of retreat—ensures that your energy program will be balanced. As always, there's a dynamic between being proactive and knowing when to hang back. Even if your strenuous schedule doesn't seem to yield a moment to breathe, you must make time to replenish. Despite the very human tendency to want to scrap everything under duress, don't let negative energy gather such momentum. Along the way chuckle at the humor of it all; occasionally put superachieving on the back burner. Baby steps yield large results, particularly when you're beset.

Living in such balance improves your energy here-and-now, and also softens the aging process. Though aging is inevitable, how we age has much to do with us. Knowing how much energy to dole out or preserve as we mature can help make aging an expansion into brightness, instead of an irredeemable downslide. Aging gracefully thwarts stress, an energetic toxin that withers us prematurely and anesthetizes our hearts. Case in point: high school reunions. Why does one classmate have a timeless radiance, while another seems to have fallen apart? Genetics aside, heart energy is the fountain of youth: it imparts glowing eyes, a light step, a spirit that twinkles. People who live from the heart seem ageless, compared to those ground down by an oppressively adult, humorless life. (The Chinese God of Age has a long white beard and cherubic child's face.) Lack of heart becomes etched on our faces and energy fields as melancholy, even ugliness, visible or sensed. The more heart you personify, the more wonderfully alive you will be. Heart energy instills an ineffable lightness of being that defies chronology.

On the path to heart, be unstintingly accountable for what recharges your total energy. Defend every atom of your resources. I salute everyone who's prepared to make a commitment to counteract pressure and opt for ongoing replenishment. Enact such earthshaking change now. The energy of the moment is the unforeseen gift we've been given. It's up to us to cherish it.

Treat Yourself:

Just for fun, imagine you have total amnesia about anything to do with stress, worries, demands. By some miracle, that data have been completely erased from your memory bank. Instead, all that's left to do is laugh, play, and be silly. Let your happiness rip. Acknowledge today's magnificence.

INTERVIEW: WAVY GRAVY ON LAUGHTER

WAVY GRAVY IS AN INTUITIVE CLOWN AND WAS MASTER OF CEREMONIES
AT BOTH WOODSTOCK FESTIVALS. THE *LOS ANGELES TIMES* CALLS HIM,
"LEGENDARY LOCO-LAUREATE OF THE WOODSTOCK NATION."

✴

Laughter is like the valve on the pressure cooker of life. Either you laugh at stuff or you end up with your brains or your beans on the ceiling. I use laughter a lot. When you laugh at something your defenses go down. Laughter is a painkiller. It also gives you energy. Once you begin to laugh at yourself—especially at yourself—you're able to see your dilemma and perhaps take a break.

My job as an intuitive clown is to take humor right to the very gates of hell. It's important to approach adversity with humor. I've had five spinal fusions. Before surgery I had to be in a body cast. We painted my first cast blue, and put stars all over it, called it the "All-Star Cast." The last cast, which was in '72, we covered with money from all over the world. That of course was the "Cast of Thousands."

Some people are always serious. I just did a convention of psychiatrists. I got them all in a circle. I said, "Okay, let's go around. I'm going to give you my squeaky nose. Just give my nose a squeak, say your name and a funny incident from your life." Only two out of sixty could think of one! I put them on the spot, but it was scary! Even so, by the end, I had them melting into the ground and growing up as flowers, trees, and shrubs. So it was quite worthwhile. People can become so tense they can't deal, or where you're dealing from is not a very centered place.

I didn't set out to be a clown. I started in the fifties reading poetry in New York coffeehouses. It was a big craze. People would line up around the block to look at the beatniks. We'd pass a basket and make tons of money. It was embarrassing. We'd drive around on motorcycles and stick it in bum's pockets who were passed out on the streets. I remember when Bob Dylan came in the Gaslight, where I was poetry director. He was wearing Woody Guthrie's underwear. He had a sign on his guitar that said, "This machine kills fashion." And he said, "Can I go on?" I said, "Grab the mike." I said, "Here he is, a legend in his own time. What's your name?" We ended up sharing a room over the Gaslight, and "Hard Rain Is Gonna Fall" was written on my typewriter.

It became difficult at the Gaslight because the poetry got really short, like haikus. In between poems I'd stall and talk about the weird things that happened to me that day. Finally this guy heard me do that, put me in a suit, and helped me to go around the country. He said, "Skip the poetry. Talk about your weird stuff." The next thing you know I'm doing standup, opening for John Coltrane and Thelonious Monk.

Early on, I learned about humor from Lenny Bruce, who was briefly my manager. He taught me that the truth is really funny. You don't have to make stuff up. There's enough going on in reality; all you have to do is point your finger at it. At Woodstock, when I announced from the stage, "What we have in mind is breakfast in bed for 400,000," I wasn't trying to be clever. But it was picked up by *Entertainment Weekly* as one of the top lines of the twentieth century. We were just trying to get Dixie Cups of granola to hippies in sleeping bags.

Then there's cosmic humor. Popcorn is the Lord. And a coincidence is a miracle God doesn't take credit for. The line from the movie *Georgie Girl* "God always has a custard pie up his sleeve" is true. When the Hog Farm, my extended family, and I arrived at the first Woodstock, we thought we were doing a free kitchen and a fire trail. The press was there with cameras and bright lights. This reporter says to me, "Oh, the Hog Farm. You guys are here to do security." I said, "My God, they made us into cops." I said, "Do you feel secure?" The guy said, "Certainly." Then he said, "C'mon, what are you guys going to use for crowd control?" I said, "Cream pies and seltzer bottles." They all wrote it down!

At Woodstock, the energy propelled us. Sometimes, though, I'd be so busy I didn't notice when the crowd was laughing. I just felt this incredible rush of energy. The Hog Farm and I had plenty to do. But whenever we thought that *we* were doing it, we'd immediately fall on our butts in the mud. If we surrendered to the energy, we could do everything.

Soon after, we were recruited by a Texas pop festival to stop the friction between the hippies and rednecks. At one point, conga drummers took over the stage as far as the eye could see. I laid down in the middle of them, saying, "This is Wavy Gravy on the floor. Don't dance on the Wavy Gravy." A guy grabbed a microphone and yelled, "This is Mumbly Wombly. Come in, Wavy Gravy on the floor." BB King was the next act just arriving. He put his hand on my shoulder and leaned me against his amplifier: "You Wavy Gravy?" I said, "Yes, sir." "Well, Wavy Gravy, I can work around you." That's when the name really slammed home. Then BB took out his guitar, whose name is Lucille. Johnny Winter stepped on stage, and they played until sunrise—celestial jelly, the Lord's own jam. It was incredible.

When I returned to California, I had a grant at Cal State teaching improvisation to physically handicapped kids. My classes were filmed through one-way glass. To a new group, I said, "Hi, I'm Wavy Gravy." The professors ran in after class, and said, "Keep that name. The kids love it." So I stayed Wavy Gravy. On the telephone I usually do Gravy, first initial W. The telephone operators occasionally say, "Are you him?" Then they help me make my phone calls.

Laughter is amazing medicine. I've worked with hundreds of terminal kids. Sometimes they laugh. Sometimes they cry. I usually bring popcorn. I'll catch their tears in the popcorn and we'll eat it together. I don't come to do a show per se. I'll bring games, jokes, bubbles. A few kids are terrified of clowns; my makeup scares them. So at the hospital, I'll put it on in front of the smallest children to kind of de-monster-fy the clown. They need to get that I'm really a person. I find that laughter can also be helpful for grieving parents. "Good grief" are the two words I got from Charles Schulz and *Peanuts*.

My wife and I run Camp Win-A-Rainbow, where kids learn the circus and performing arts. Some scholarships come from my ice cream flavor royalties—Ben and Jerry's named a flavor after me!—and from the Grateful Dead soapboxes and pajamas I endorse. We want to create human beings who can deal with anything with a little grace and panache. Laughter is part of that. Sometimes the kids are so tied up they can't express themselves or laugh, but we work through what's holding them back.

I see laughter as a survival tool. As Emerson says, "God laughs in the flowers." When you laugh at something, everything lightens up. Whatever tightness you have, that particular log jam is broken. The energy of your life force begins to flow again.

part two

CREATING POSITIVE RELATIONSHIPS AND COMBATING ENERGY VAMPIRES

8

THE EIGHTH PRESCRIPTION: ATTRACT POSITIVE PEOPLE AND SITUATIONS

ARE YOU LONGING FOR RELATIONSHIPS that do your heart good and generate stronger connections? Tired of poor choices? Tepid chemistry? Want a more commanding role in who you attract? Knowing about energy can transform your ability to build positive relationships, prevent loneliness, and ward off insidious fatigue.

How you deal with relationships is integral to how much energy you have. The Eighth Prescription offers a massive missing piece of the puzzle. It'll help you grasp the energetic exchange between people—who gives energy, and who drains it—not a passive or haphazard alchemy. Shame on traditional psychiatry for being so enamoured with the biochemistry of behavior that it's blind to how subtle energy can enlighten us here. As a physician and woman I feel cheated without the complete facts. I rail against accepting anything less than invoking our full power in all interactions. To achieve this, I'll show you how to magnetize people and situations who vitalize you instead of painting yourself as victim or simply being resigned to what comes. My prescription goes beyond setting an intention or making wish lists of desirable traits in a lover, friend, or job. It requires perceiving energy clearly and adjusting the homing signal you transmit.

Attraction: that mysterious, seemingly elusive magnetism between people. It masterminds love, friendship, work, and the chemistry of shared ventures. Attraction's opposite is repulsion or aversion, forces that push us away. In Energy Psychiatry, I've been voraciously curious about the forces that bring goodness, love, and vigor into our lives. Though attraction is often paired with appearance, IQ, bank account, or charm, these aren't enough to summon such blessings. You don't just want attention; you want the right kind, this section's premise. The level of attraction I'm referring to has to do with life essences interflowing, a by-product of both karma and smarts. You can't completely control it, but you can modify your vibes to maximize possibilities.

Here I'll explain four energetic laws that govern positive attraction. They'll help you coax or wrestle the wildebeest of relationships back to the province of the heart. Friendships, career, family, romance can all profit. The idea is to find reciprocally nourishing interactions, not to win a popularity contest. I won't propose run-of-the-mill dating strategies. Nor going to a party to see how many men or women you can attract, an overzealous tactic that rarely succeeds. I'm referring to a new way of being and seeing that helps you to attract, be more attractive, and hone a discriminating radar for everyone you contact.

While working at a UCLA parapsychology lab, I was fascinated to discover an invisible anatomy to relationships. We were using Kirlian photography to measure energy fields by putting a finger or other objects on a light-sensitive plate. The energy auras we recorded looked like astonishing rainbows. The first time I saw an aura, I was awed; it shot off the edge of someone's fingertip like a flame of a magnificent white fire. My work focused on measuring the aura of plants and how they interacted with humans. One day an arrogant Ivy League psychiatrist visited the lab. It was immediately evident that his purpose was to put our work down. Thus we wickedly decided to use our research to show him something about himself. First we measured the boundaries of a leaf's energy field on a Kirlian plate. Then, we asked the psychiatrist to place his index finger beside it. Startled, he watched as the corona of the leaf recoiled and shrunk to half its original size. Wow. The leaf's sentiments about this psychiatrist matched our own.

As with leaves, so with human beings. I think you'll enjoy seeing how some talented people I interviewed identify the vibes of people to which they're drawn.

GOLDIE HAWN, ACTOR: Their energy feels expansive, like I'm walking into a field of light. It's an openness of spirit and heart, a fearlessness. I'm elevated, excited. I can be myself and not be harmed.

NORMAN LEAR, PRODUCER: A positive person is someone who's hugging the moment.

JAMIE LEE CURTIS, ACTOR: People emit an energy pulse. You see the positive in a connection of eyes, an expression of compassion. When such a person looks at me and I've connected with that energy port, it's a palpably loving sharing.

QUINCY JONES, MUSICIAN, COMPOSER: A positive person feels good, like the glass is half full, not half empty. I'm attracted to these people. Don't have time for anyone else.

The Eighth Prescription expands on ways to recognize and attract positive people, a monumental influence on health and serenity. (See Chapter 9 for dealing with energy vampires.) Rest assured, you don't have to be a Maharishi to emit positive vibes. We all can. Look for them everywhere: in a cashier, a neighbor, a coworker. There's an interconnecting subtle network between us that's constantly tweaking our energy system. As an intuitive empath, my well-being relies on scrutinizing the quality of these exchanges. Some people can make me sick; others are rejuvenative. The great delight, though, is that such sensitivity to energy synergizes loving feelings, a gift that far outweighs empathy's potentially enervating aspects. In your relationships, these laws enable you to make the most of empathy too. Keep noticing how you respond to all interactions. Positive vibes attract others on the same wavelength, setting up a nurturing feedback loop.

The energy-based people skills you'll learn work in concert with all the program's prescriptions. To prevent unchecked toxic relationships from torpedoing your best efforts at wellness, you must first set the stage for the positive. Then, with these strategies intact, you'll be better prepared to deflect negative input. Assembling a circle of kindred spirits will enable you to thrive.

FOUR LAWS OF ENERGETIC ATTRACTION

The following laws are a call to action, not merely theories to ponder. By making energetic shifts, we really can draw good things to us. Each of us deserves such abundance.

When applying these laws, think of it as tuning an instrument to make its most beautiful music. As you grow more positive, like-minded people will be impelled toward you. Also, your choices become smarter. Test out each law on family, friends, office mates. In your journal, keep a log of cause and effect. Some successes will come more quickly than others, but living these laws will keep radically improving your relationships.

Law of Attraction #1: We Attract Who We Are

A basic dynamic of energy is that we attract who we are—the more positive energy we give off, the more we'll magnetize to us. Ditto for negativity. It works like this: Love attracts love. Grumpiness attracts grumpiness. Passion attracts passion. Rage attracts rage. The explanation: We are all subtle energy transmitters. We're constantly sending out signals that others on similar frequencies pick up on and gravitate toward—an instinctual call we may not be aware of. Why opportunities do or don't show up in our lives is a function of this.

A striking phenomenon known by many a therapist is that we often attract waves of patients who mirror our current struggles and joys. It's as if a communiqué is issued to the universe saying, "I'm here. This is what I'm going through. Come to me." For example, soon after I sold my first book, *Second Sight,* which fulfilled a great dream of mine for creative expression, a series of patients also had beloved projects that came through for them. A few years later, as I helplessly watched my father losing control of mind and body from Parkinson's disease, I received a burst of anguished calls from new patients whose parents with Parkinson's were suffering the same harrowing decline. On a lighter note, when the daughter of a psychologist friend got pregnant, my friend's practice suddenly became a parade of expectant parents.

How can we harness this intriguing alchemy to bring yearned-for prospects to us? The crux is to strive to energetically embody what we want to attract. Take at look at where you're at now. First, define what being positive does and doesn't mean for you in terms of attitude and behavior. Once you're definitive about this, you can strengthen these traits in yourself, and attract the same. Don't worry if you're far from a positive place now. The point of this program is to get you there. It's an evolution. Give thought to what you value most in yourself or others. Keep a running list in your journal. Here's the essence of how I see it.

POSITIVE PERSONS ARE:

- Committed to developing compassion toward themselves and others, and having an open heart
- Courageous about following their dreams
- Authentic; they believe in themselves, even when the world is crumbling around them

- Aware of their dark side and are trying to heal it
- Willing to learn from mistakes

POSITIVE PERSONS AREN'T:

- Obsessed with seeming perfect or positive all the time
- Beating themselves to a pulp over their shortcomings or floundering in a black hole of pessimism
- Constantly mired in fear or tolerant of letting their hearts harden
- Squeaky-clean do-gooders who neglect their own well-being
- Saccharine pleasers who ignore their dark side and unconsciously act it out at the expense of others

Never forget: we're real human beings; we all have our good and bad points. What sets positive people apart, though, is a determination to do their best, and not succumb to what's negative in themselves or around them. Learn to let go of your idealized expectations; everyone has irritating/challenging/disappointing aspects. Earth to humans: we're inhabiting the material plane with all its foibles. Even so, you can legitimately hope to personify and attract others fighting their way out of the muck with an open heart and sense of humor. These are my heroes and friends. In contrast, someone who comes on as "too perfect" feels like fingernails on the blackboard to me. You don't want to be anything like those always-smiling, aiming-to-please women robots in the horror flick *The Stepford Wives*. These are the evil twins of the positive person I'm portraying.

This law of attraction will make doors open. But the root truth of my energy program is that quality of relationships, not quantity, counts. Understanding this demands that we see beyond our culture's obsession with popularity. I appreciate how inbred the desire may be. High school can be hell for anyone "unpopular." I, for one, felt so agonizingly out of it; the "cool" kids hung on the "upper patio" while I snuck cigarettes behind the auditorium with my scraggly hippie friends. Thankfully, as an adult, I realize that popularity is a mixed bag and doesn't always deliver happiness. Yes, opportunities may increase. And, of course, it feels good to be liked. But I've seen this need turn into addiction. I've worked with actors whose self-esteem is inextricably tied to their public's adulation, certain suicide for self-esteem. Mass popularity can lead to confusion and defeat. One patient, a drop-dead-gorgeous model, can't get from the parking garage to my office without a guy coming on to her. This woman has a seeming jackpot of romantic options, but still keeps choosing the most horrifyingly flawed men, a destructive pattern that brought her to see me.

The following exercise isn't intended to summon the hordes, though it could. If you're energized by lots of people, it'll help you attract the right kind. If you like a smaller circle, it'll enable you to distinguish quality.

MAKE CHANGES NOW

BECOME MORE POSITIVE AND ATTRACT POSITIVE PEOPLE AND SITUATIONS

Energy doesn't simply have an on-off switch. Just as a radio has a volume control, you can adjust your vibes. You can amp them up with some people, tone them down with others. Here's how to boost your positive signals.

1. *Identify your best parts and speak from them.* Pinpoint your finest qualities. Perhaps irreverence, sensitivity, compassion, humor— then project them to the world. Don't worry if you've always downplayed these qualities until now. By speaking up and stepping out of your comfort zone you're enlarging your energy

field. Before meeting new people or going to important events, prime yourself. Take a break for an inner pep talk. Think, "I'm not going to focus on my insecurity but on a strength; I'm going to feel and trust the positive energy inside me. I'm going to claim my full power." Such selective attention puts your best parts front and center. Then, perspective shifted, it's easier to confidently move forward.

My patient Dee, a single mother and flight attendant, lost her job. For months she was unemployed with three children to feed, sinking into despair. Dee's way out was to fire up her beloved spunky self again and give it a voice during job interviews. She did this by taking quiet moments each day to focus on that part of her that said, "Go, girl!" She just sat there, eyes closed, inviting that positive energy back in again. Such conjuring spurred Dee to apply for positions in the fashion industry, a gutsy career shift she'd fantasized about, and now made real. Let Dee's struggle and success guide you.

2. *Extend heart energy outward.* Love creates an irresistible charisma, a warm glow that makes us and others happy. You can send it in any situation, a nurturing that won't drain us. How? Focus on your heart center (see Chapter 2's meditation), and envision something you love. A flock of sea gulls. Your son's smile. A blooming rose. Then, during a conversation, inwardly ask, "Let love flow through me." Feel it rise from your chest; notice a sense of heat, serenity, radiance. Beckon these vibes outward. People soften around them, feel safe, want more. The next time you're standing by your boss, start pumping away. Loving energy smoothes the rough edges of any circumstance, facilitates rapport. Try it even if you don't like someone but seek to get along better. Our loving heart can melt the feistiest curmudgeons. It conveys the sense of what Buddhists call the "groundless ground," an ultimate secure

place that stabilizes us from the inside out. Others pick up on this primal draw. Without heart, people are energetically wobbly, despite outer confidence. (For instance, a spiritual teacher who talks a good game but doesn't emit heart energy is an imposter.) The kinder we are to ourselves and others, the more love we communicate.

3. *Meditate regularly.* Happiness can be increased by meditating. Cutting-edge brain research confirms that we all have a certain mood set-point, a range of feelings we usually inhabit. But with regular meditation, it's been shown that we can alter our habitual moods toward the positive. When feelings surface during meditation, monitor them. Focus on what's uplifting, not the swirl of negative emotions. As you've done before, use your breath to center yourself. This inner turnabout transmutes pessimism to something higher. Your vibes will change; others will respond.

4. *Commit to emotional housecleaning.* A fact I'll keep trumpeting: healing negativity prevents toxic buildup in your energy field. As I emphasized in Chapter 4, consistently chipping away at the negative makes room for more light in your being. Self-awareness is our greatest ally against fear and its bullying cohorts. When these brutes appear, it allows you to say, "I know you. Now scram!" Psychotherapy, introspection, meditation, journaling, and/or talking with friends all further healing. As negativity remits, your energy becomes more alluring.

LAW OF ATTRACTION #2: INTUITION CLARIFIES SMART CHOICES

Let's zoom in further on key elements of attraction. There's you: what you give off. There's the other person: what he or she gives off. And there's a situation, such as a project or job, which has its own energy field. Your goal is to cohere all the elements. The fields combine or clash; they explain who you're attracted to and why. Relationships are tricky; they can be a big blur even when your eyes are open. Intuition clears your vision, and steers you to the right target. Here's the formula. First, listen to your body: respect the positive and negative intuitions about relationships and identify those that highlight compatible matches. Second, act on this information, which is often the hardest part. Let me walk you though the process.

Recognize Your Body's Intuitions About Vibes

Most of our parents didn't know how to intuitively read vibes. Thus, they couldn't teach us how to do it. We've learned to draw conclusions from surface data: how nice someone seems, looks, or their education, or how a situation adds up on paper. But attraction goes deeper; to make it work for you other ingredients must be considered. Review the techniques for reading energy in Chapter 1. Now I want you to become even more definite about a positive person's energetic gestalt, and how you react to it.

Here's a general guideline of body-based intuitions. As my patients and I do, use this checklist at a first meeting to troubleshoot problems if you're already involved, or to weigh "opportunities." Feel free to add to it. As an intuitive, I know that a signature energy always accompanies situations or people. Remember the jinxed cartoon character in *Li'l Abner* who always had a black cloud hanging over his head? Not a vibe that bodes well for auspicious outcomes. Learn to gravitate toward brightness, a positive intuition your body's responses will affirm. When tuning into vibes, forget intellectual analysis. Look for the following signs to determine attraction.

POSITIVE INTUITIONS ABOUT RELATIONSHIPS OR SITUATIONS

- You have a feeling of comforting familiarity or brightness; you may sense you've known the person before, as with the experience of déjà vu

- You breathe easier, chest and shoulders are relaxed, gut is calm

- You find yourself leaning forward, not defensively crossing your arms or edging away to keep a distance

- Your heart opens; you feel safe, peaceful, energized, expansive, or alive

- You're at ease with a person's touch whether a handshake, hug, or during intimacy

NEGATIVE INTUITIONS ABOUT RELATIONSHIPS OR SITUATIONS

- You get a sick feeling in the pit of your stomach or increased stomach acid, which may prompt an unpleasant sense of déjà vu

- Your skin starts crawling, you're jumpy, instinctively withdraw if touched

- Your shoulder muscles knot, your chest area or throat constricts; you notice aggravated aches or pains

- The hair on the back of your neck creepily stands on end

- You feel a sense of malaise, darkness, pressure, agitation, or being drained

These criteria provide a no-nonsense appraisal of your body's comfort zone. (The more positive intuitions the better—even one can be definitive—but nagging negatives should put you on guard.) They'll lead you to friends, lovers, and work milieus with copacetic vibes. Plus, you'll know when to cool it or exit in the face of blatant warnings. However, what may obscure the picture is intense sexual attraction. If so, go slow until you get a keener intuitive read. Anxiety can also cause crossed signals. Whenever you can't separate the jitters about first meeting someone from "beware" messages your body sends, give the relationship some time. Meanwhile, breathe and keep centering yourself. Also, when others are nervous their vibes may come off as squirrelly. Typically, though, as you get to know someone, early jitters (yours or theirs) dissipate, but your body's pro or con instincts persist. Before making any conclusive moves you must address these distinctions.

My patient Alison at forty was consistently attracted to the wrong men and wrong jobs. Being deserted by her boyfriend after a miscarriage was "the kick in the head" that brought Alison in. She said, "I've always looked to others for what I 'should' be doing—how I behaved, dressed, who I dated or became friends with. I kept changing careers based on what people deemed right for me. I never asked myself what I wanted."

I taught Alison this program's first law of attraction, which necessitated defining her intuitive needs. To keep Alison on track, I served as a kind of drill sergeant, gentle but firm. When she'd meet a man or interview for a job, I'd ask, "What does your body say about the vibes?" Each time, I'd instruct her to go through the positive and negative intuition checklist. "Write them in your journal; bring it in. We'll review the results together." My job was to help Alison trust her read on vibes. As does everyone at first, she doubted herself, got scattered, forgot to tune in, talked herself out of what she did sense. But, from experience I know there's always a moment of critical mass when intuition creates magnificent outcomes. Once Alison risked acting on her body's signals, her choices became aligned with what she really wanted. Now, she's pursuing a career as a freelance illustrator that delights her and is beginning to spot and attract caring, compatible men.

Alison's intuitive growth involved tuning into people, but you can also calibrate the vibes of a situation or locale. My friend, the Reverend Mary Morrissey, has become a genius at sensing energy, lets its pull guide her in all decisions. She told me:

> Years ago, our young church met in a movie theater. When we learned it was going to be turned into a multiplex we had thirty days to move! In crisis emotions are high, but I wasn't going to let anxiety get me. We found two possible new loca-

tions: an affordable building in an industrial area, which the business people were pushing for, and a more expensive but rundown site in the country. I visited both, tuned in to the energy. At the industrial building my aliveness shut down. I felt constricted, like wearing a suffocatingly tight wetsuit. The country place was different. It was overgrown, smelled bad, animals had been living inside. But when I stood on the deck and got quiet, everything in me became alive, bright, expansive. A veil lifted. I saw a vision of hundreds of children on the lawn having an Easter-egg hunt. The property didn't make financial sense, but I felt drawn there, knew we could make it work. For twelve years, it's been our spiritual home.

In this part of the Eighth Prescription, get to know your body's reactions to vibes, and better gauge where you're drawn. When evaluating the intuitive checklist, pay particular attention to the experience of déjà vu. It's the cellular memory of having known a new person at some other time or place. To meet is not an introduction, but a reunion. (This sense of inexplicable kinship differentiates déjà vu from sizzling physical chemistry, though both have juice.) Déjà vu may be positive or negative, sudden or slow, will be more significant with some people than others. Always, however, it's telling you to "stay aware," perhaps to complete what's not yet finished. Whether instances of déjà vu are explained by a premonition or a past-life recollection, they'll draw you toward mystical alliances.

Many of my closest relationships have begun with déjà vu. In the first few minutes with a person I sense a special attraction. It isn't that I associate them with someone else or that their traits are simply appealing. Rather, my body and soul relate to them not as strangers but as spirits with whom I have an earned trust and shared history. With others, the timelessness of this rapport is missing.

Reflect on your relationships. Have you ever been chatting with a woman you just met at a business meeting and suddenly it strikes you, "Ah-ha. Here's an old friend I feel I've known all my life." It's obvious: You're both just resuming where you left off. Other déjà vus are protective. In dicey situations they caution you to halt, separate friend from foe. The instant a screenwriter patient of mine, who's facile in the tools of Energy Psychiatry, walked into a meeting to sell a project, he cringed. One look at the prospective buyer, whom he'd never even spoken to before, and every cell screamed, "I know him. Get us out of here!" Fortunately, my patient knew to trust his intuition. Soon after, the buyer was indicted for fraud. Either heralding a good omen, or veering you away from harm, déjà vu is your body's way of taking care of you.

The second law of attraction systematizes how your body listens to others. It'll train you to act from instinct, not impulse—a look-before-you-leap wisdom that points you to positive energy. When it comes to whom you love, where you work, or any other important decision, the last thing you want to be is vague. Tuning in keeps you specific. Practice the next exercise to get this down.

MAKE CHANGES NOW
PIN DOWN AND ACT ON YOUR VIBES
ABOUT ATTRACTION

Now you're going to tune in, trust your body, and make choices based on the vibes you sense.

- *Tune in.* Choose a relationship or situation that needs clarification before you can decide to go forward. Perhaps you're confused about a friendship, vacation, or move. Begin with an easier target before you take on higher stakes. Run it by this section's criteria for positive and negative intuitions—or others you find reliable. It's helpful to make a top-five list of your most-killer indicators of positive attraction. For one of my patients it includes feeling energized and safe. Another must register an increased aliveness and peaceful sense. Write your top five in a journal so they don't get hazy. See how they add up here.

- *Act on vibes.* This is where we must be warriors. I know personally and from patients how much easier it is to tune in to than to act on vibes. Insecurity, ego, lust, stubbornness can obscure your better judgment. Sometimes it takes succumbing to them all to realize you won't tolerate such battering again. But if you don't have to take such a bumpy route, try these options. If the vibes feel overall positive, go for it; explore possibilities. If the vibes are mixed or you're unsure, take a pass or at least wait. If all you sense is negative, have the courage to walk away, no matter how tempting the option seems. Then observe how listening to energy in this way leads you to the juiciest opportunities.

Law of Attraction #3: Seeing the Beauty and Goodness in People Magnetizes Them

All human beings contain beauty and goodness. To look at others through such eyes is a gift to them. Turn your perception around: instead of reflexively accentuating the worst in a person or situation, invoke laser vision for the best. Choose to energize positive qualities, not negative ones. The object isn't to flatter, make nice, be politically correct, or ignore intuitive red flags. Nor to deny someone's dark side or placate abusers with whom you have no business staying. Your goal is to mine the gold in positive relationships and elevate the communication in more difficult ones.

When I intuitively read someone's energy, their beauty is something to behold. I see it as crystal-clear light, complete, possessing a feisty intelligence. The most astonishing part, to me, is that it responds when recognized. I don't care how deep goodness is embedded in you, it grows brighter if seen. When I say to a depressed patient, "You have shown incredible courage," a little flame in him starts flickering. "I'm here," courage cries from a distance. "I'm here." Or if I remark, "You look lovely today," to a patient who's insanely stressed, immediately a part in her softens, goes, "Ah." It's really quite simple. When you speak to the positive in someone, that energy begins to awaken in them.

Recently, I got picked up at the airport by a crazed taxi driver. The kind that jerks the brakes, then speeds, then jerks the brakes again. He's in control, needs you to know it. At such trapped moments, I usually quietly seethe, want to kill the guy. My vibes are obvious. In turn, my assailant's silent rage slithers over me. But, as the cabby was pushing sixty past the Balona wetlands (a forty mph zone), it suddenly occurred to me that if I survived the trip I was in fact going to get home faster. That, I had to appreciate. This helped me relax. Pulling up to my condo, the driver looked aggrieved, poised to be criticized. In a way, he read me right; normally I would've been exuding that attitude. Instead, I surprised myself, told him, "You made great time." The change was instantaneous. This cabby looked at me, beaming. "I try so hard. Thank you. Thank you." I nodded supportively. As he pulled away, he was all smiles. Going the speed limit, I noticed.

We are all starving to have the goodness in us acknowledged. If you want to connect with someone, notice his or her assets; mention them. Consider it an experiment. Let's say a coworker whose desk abuts yours is snitty. Realize: happy people don't act this way. So, instead of being snitty back or constantly miffed, redirect the energy by not taking the bait. Comment on what she's doing right—the long hours she puts in, or her dynamite shoes. I'm not saying be phony, but find a way to maneuver around a stumbling block. Use this approach for a week; watch the vibes change.

Larry King is a firm believer that gratitude fosters positive interchanges. In our interview he said, "You sit down in a restaurant, and your toast is burnt. There's two ways to handle this. 'Waitress, my toast is burnt!' She might go in and spit on it. Or, 'Oh miss, I know you work awful hard. This toast is a little dark for me.' Who gets the better toast? It depends on what you give off. You create positive attitude back." The power behind Larry's practical wisdom stems from the energy of the communication, not merely spouting words. Gratitude reflects respect for others. It travels from heart to heart, elicits the goodness in people, makes them flock to you.

Prioritizing the best in people necessitates seeing the worst in them too, but making a choice about your emphasis. Knowing this has saved me when making presentations on intuition at medical school "grand rounds," an academic ritual where physicians debate patient care. My ideas for using intuition to aid clinical decisions are sacrilegious to hard-core scientists who revere technology over instinct, not grasping that the two can be wedded. Thus, I'm prepared for heated, even hostile discussions. A friendly UCLA psychiatric resident I was supervising asked me, "How can you sit there so calmly, not get defensive?" I replied, "My goal is to get through to people, not push them away. Of course, receiving anger feels uncomfortable, but I don't feed into it." To retaliate isn't courageous. It just backfires. Rather, I insistently address the humanitarian in each skeptical physician—I know it's there!—by practically showing how intuition can hasten healing. The sweet reward of such energetic diplomacy is seeing how many minds open. It's gorgeous to witness, well worth the forbearance and effort to get there.

The gist of this law of attraction is to see others as you want to be seen. What results is more heart in your relationships. You admire someone; they're more likely to admire you, and you're in a good groove. Aspire to this place. We all can get there. Deciding what to respond to in people will improve all your relationships. Here's an exercise to excavate the positive in others by putting Law 3 to work.

MAKE CHANGES NOW

ATTRACT PEOPLE BY ACKNOWLEDGING THEIR

BEST POINTS

- Tell at least two people you love what you're grateful for about them.
- Tell at least two people you don't love what you're grateful for about them.
- Spend an afternoon noticing the goodness and beauty of everyone you meet; adjusting your perception of the world liberates old habits.
- Praise other people's abilities. Say to a gas-station attendant, window washer, or cashier, "You're doing a great job," magic words that can make a person's day. Practice this first with people on the periphery of your life, then move on to your mate, coworkers, or friends.
- If you're irritated with someone, try to turn the situation around by first speaking to their admirable parts, not their shortcomings. Be Zen. Keep your center. Take a breath. Don't meet resistance with a clenched fist. Say to yourself, "Okay, this person is being a real bear, but I refuse to get into it on this level. How can I glide around the daggers and soften his or her defenses?" This isn't "giving in" or being inauthentic. It's a sprinkling of positive energy that prepares the path for more effective communication.

Keep improvising on these tips. Notice how your energy mounts, and how others gravitate to you more. It helps to see each person as a human being, just like you, trying to navigate an often-difficult world. With such perspective, it's easier to cut them a break.

Law of Attraction #4: Soulful Giving Generates Abundance

Our style of giving often defines who we attract. In Energy Psychiatry it also tops my list of contributors to wellness. I teach all my patients how to give well, an often life-and-death therapeutic concern. It's a lesson nearly all of us need to be taught. Why? Because giving isn't always a virtue. Believe me: I've seen how unhealthy giving can emotionally maim, even kill people, can invite warring, destructive relationships. We may unconsciously slip into such a pattern, then be unable to extricate ourselves from it. Giving is supposed to feel good; if not, something's wrong. Here, you'll learn how to give from a self-possessed, productive place without giving too much away. Staying open in this fashion, you'll summon other generous spirits in your personal sphere. (I'll address the issue of service to communities and the world in Chapter 10.)

In terms of energy, I've defined two main categories of giving: soulful and codependent. Soulful giving is a way of nurturing yourself, enlarging your capacity to be more caring to people. It means giving unconditionally to others. You give for the joy of it, expecting nothing in return, no strings; it's a restorative sharing from your heart, never forced. In contrast, codependent giving bleeds life force, is driven by obligation, guilt, or a martyr-complex, conscious or not. It leaves the giver feeling sucked dry, unappreciated, put upon.

As a psychiatrist and intuitive, I've not been exempt from having to figure out how to give soulfully. The indicator is always my energy level. Because I'm cursed with the tendency to overextend myself, I must constantly monitor my energy. After lecturing on the road for five years, often presenting daily workshops for months at a time, I utterly overdosed on giving. In fact, I never wanted to give again! I had no choice but to take a deep, year-long rest. Very slowly I came to realize I loved teaching, but absolutely had to do it differently. Now, with a much more moderate schedule including large chunks of quiet time, giving once again feels joyful. Recently, I received a photo someone snapped after one of my workshops. I was talking with a participant, touching her shoulder. As I studied the photo, I was truly delighted to see that I looked elated, glowing, completely present. Of course, this is the space from which I always want to give.

To keep your energy high, I'd like you to recognize your style of giving—codependent, soulful, or a mix. How do you offer personal and charitable gifts, or emotional support, or evaluate large requests such as donating a kidney? You want to give for reasons that energize you, not because of codependency, which means taking inappropriate responsibility for others or giving so much you forget to give to yourself, both symptoms of a do-gooder gone wrong. The old joke is that when a codependent dies, it's your life that flashes before her eyes. Not your goal! You must retire the misguided notion that giving demands losing yourself in someone or crucifying your energy levels. (I recommend Melody Beattie's *Codependent No More.*) To ensure your giving is soulful, I'd like you to understand the following points about this law of attraction.

Compassion Requires Setting Boundaries

To be a soulful giver and attract the same, be canny about what compassion means. This program views it as feeling what it's like to walk in someone else's shoes, offering support, but not shouldering their suffering. We're trained as loving people to equate compassion with giving to others, easing pain. But many of us, especially intuitive empaths who're energy sponges, don't stop there. Inadvertently we imbibe their angst. Suddenly we're the desolate ones. This severe loss of center doesn't serve us. Compassion demands we set boundaries about what energy we take in or tolerate. Buddhist nun Pema Chodron warns against what she brilliantly calls "idiot compassion," using kindness to avoid conflict when a resounding "no" is required. I agree wholeheartedly with her conviction that to stop people from draining our energy, we must know where to draw a line.

My patient Ken, a big-hearted psychologist, wanted to open a clinic for domestic abuse survivors, but feared he'd give himself into the grave. For good reason. Ken admitted, "I can't set boundaries.

I've had so many mini-meltdowns carrying patients and friends through crises. Troubled people have radar for me, as if an invisible arrow points, 'Go here.' But if I say no, I feel like a heel." I taught him to reframe his mode of giving: "Without limits, people often don't know when to stop taking. However, if we convey, 'I care, but this is all that's available,' they'll have better cues." Thus, Ken's mandate became keeping an open heart but asserting limits, a balance in soulful giving for which I'm pleased to be an avid cheerleader. Naturally, it helps to have someone on your side saying, "Take care of yourself. Then when you give, it'll feel good." Ken kept at it. And at it. This effort improved his relationships—the needy masses dwindled—and preserved his energy at work. Now, a year later, Ken feels ready to pursue the clinic, an undertaking that would've eaten him alive without his revamped perspective on healthy giving.

In this phase of the program ask yourself, "Does giving usually sustain or drain me? Do I attract mutually supportive relationships? Or do I fall into the trap of 'idiot compassion' and get walked on by people? Am I ready to say 'enough's enough' by setting limits? How can I give in a way to nourish myself?" Meditate on these questions. Write your insights in a journal. Then enact them. Don't despair about codependent propensities. They're in us all, but with mindfulness, we can turn giving into superabundance.

Giving Is an Energy Exchange

A gift is a transfer of energy from one person to another. Typically the giver chooses an object, wraps it, writes a card, and presents it. Then the receiver reads the card, undoes the wrapping, reacts to the gift, and takes that subtle energy in. These vibes continue to permeate the recipient if he or she uses or displays the gift. Ideally this ritual is an extension of the heart, a sign of respect, appreciation. At worst, though, it's a ploy to manipulate, bribe, blackmail, show off, or incite a give-to-get cycle, all energetic dead ends. In this program, you'll experience how soulful giving draws caring relationships and brings them to fruition.

Gift-giving can be read in many different ways. Freudian psycho-analysts adamantly view a patient's gift to them as "acting out," and never accept it. Rather, they probe the alleged unconscious motives behind the gift, such as the patient wanting to be liked or to appease guilt. But therapeutic modes diverge. In my practice, I don't adhere to this analytic dictum. I adore keeping gifts from patients in my office. They like to see them there; I like to have them. (I got a good laugh from a website that offers "Freud-toys" as gifts, such as blow-up Freud pillows and after-therapy mints.) Despite the Freudian thesis, many cultures would consider rejecting a gift to be an insult. In Japan, modest gifts are traditionally exchanged on first meetings, a sign of respect. However, there are also cultural faux pas such as a present of a clock in China—the word for clock is similar to the word for death, an ominous gift!

Use the following gift-giving strategies to spread positive energy in your world. As with all soulful giving, they're intended to generate bountiful vibes for you and the receiver. If you give from your heart, your vitality will soar.

MAKE CHANGES NOW
PRACTICE SOULFUL GIFT-GIVING

To reorient your giving habits, experiment with each approach and observe how they affect your relationships.

- *Give spontaneous token-gifts for no reason other than you want to.* Don't just wait for designated holidays. Any time is right to offer simple tokens: a candle, rose, small plant, fragrant soap, a funny card. I like to be the "date fairy" by leaving small bags of jumbo dates on a friend's front steps. Similarly, surprise your friend, dentist, office manager, or mate; they'll be thrilled. A token gift lets them know, "I appreciate you." Don't overdo it. Simply understand you're disseminating unexpected sweetness. Though you don't do this to "get something back," you set in motion an energy cycle that inevitably brings sweetness to you.

- *Distinguish "good" from "bad" gifts.* A "good" gift matches the recipient's needs, not just the giver's wants. It represents a commitment to a relationship. A "bad gift" is something you can get anybody. It symbolizes what you want the person to be—say, getting your girlfriend a Thighmaster, or your mate a utilitarian appliance. Hilariously, one study declares, "It's not a romantic gift if it has a cord attached." A "bad gift" is perceived as a bribe or aimed at securing some favor.

- *Choose gifts that resonate with the person.* You may see something you intuit a friend would love. It leaps out at you, gives affirming shivers of "yes!," makes you smile, or whispers to you, "I'm the One. Buy Me!" For example, I remember at eleven, spotting in a gallery window a huge wood carving of two majestic horses, as if in flight. I became all goose bumps. I wanted to give it to my father, though he'd never expressed a particular interest in horses. Somehow, though, I knew it belonged to him. So I used every penny of my saved-up allowance to buy it. The carving was bigger than I was; the store had to deliver it in a station wagon. My father was not only moved by my effort, but always treasured the horses. They hung in his radiology office above his desk for thirty years. Similarly, if you feel strongly about a gift's resonance with someone, just buy it, though it need not be extravagant. You may not know the import the gift will have, but trust the force that's compelling you.

- *Add loving vibes to gifts.* Do this by holding the object or wrapped box in your hands for a minute, closing your eyes, and sending it a blast from your heart center. These vibes will spontaneously expand out from your chest, down your arm, into the gift, which absorbs them. Sometimes I'll keep presents I've bought for others for months before I give them away. It allows my energy to accumulate in their substance so the gifts are more alive and personal.

To receive gifts also requires an energy awareness. The easy part is when they're offered with love. Accept them in that spirit; let the positive vibes infuse you. If you feel there are negative motives behind a gift, you have a few choices: accept, reject, or negotiate. One of my patients had a sleazy business associate send him an expensive set of golf clubs, which he politely refused, not wanting to be indebted. Another patient, a twenty-something punk rocker, had an aunt who'd mail him birthday money, but would criticize his wardrobe purchases, which felt horrible. Finally, he announced he'd decline the money if she kept getting down on him. Impressively, she listened, and let up. Finally, if someone offers a well-intended gift you don't like, it's not emotionally dishonest to graciously accept it. That's what returns are for.

Anonymous Giving Builds Energy

Giving without credit to people you may know or not returns you to your heart, reverses negative thinking. Walk a little old lady across the street; hold open an elevator door; let a car go before you in traffic; or do something nice behind the scenes for someone, but don't get found out. Such good deeds karmically accrue, add light to our energy field, ultimately drawing the same goodness right back at us. (I joke with patients that there must be some *really* big warehouse somewhere in the Bronx housing all our karmic points.) The paradox is that we can most profit from giving anonymously at those times when we may least feel like it. Making the extra effort provides a speedy reversal for the misery of self-obsession. As a fourteen-year-old friend told me, "The best way to cheer yourself up is to cheer up someone else." Be heartened: what goes around comes around, sooner than you think.

THE POSITIVE ENERGY PROGRAM'S Eighth Prescription—attract positive people and situations—is formulated to petition happiness and love. Keep following its directions. Go full throttle in seeking out compatible people and situations. But you must do more than will it. The dance of attraction beguiles because it asks you to go for what you want while detaching from the outcome, a cosmic equation that galvanizes forward motion.

I got my first eyeful of this truth while attending "spoon bending" parties in my early days of investigating energy. These gatherings were led by Jack, an engineer and dear man who exulted in showing ordinary people how to bend metal with their minds. Envision this suburban scene: there we were, twenty apparently reasonable adults, holding our spoons high, yelling, "Bend! Bend! Bend!" Then, in the midst of our fervor, Jack instructed, "Now, let go of any desire to make the metal bend"—a complete about-face of focus. We heard. We attempted. In mere seconds, voilà: a succession of spoons melted. Wow! So: What facilitated this mind-over-matter extravaganza? The win-win combination of intention and release. Without enlisting both, nothing happened, as those who couldn't quite detach were disappointed to discover. Remember that when you set your sights on attracting a target, a tight hold can become a death grip. Instead, be light about your approach; leave some wiggle room for the universe to do its thing. You can't force a response, but if a possibility has energy, you'll feel it.

In your relationships, use this prescription to mobilize excellence and kindness. Emphatically say "no" to anything that doesn't further the heart. Cheer each success. Don't cheat your joy by jumping too quickly onto the next ambition. There's always more to want, to accomplish, the never-ending seduction of the material realm. Resist this gimme-more fixation. Instead, pledge to value even the tiniest of triumphs. That's what the art of living is about.

Treat Yourself:

Scan the friendships you've attracted. Identify a person you really click with. Take a break from the hustle and bustle to get together, or, at minimum, talk on the phone. Make this interlude an unabashed love fest. Really groove on each other; be quick to praise. Appreciate your amazing self, and this amazing person: a miraculous coming together of friends.

INTERVIEW: LARRY KING ON GENERATING
POSITIVE ENERGY

LARRY KING IS EMMY AWARD-WINNING HOST OF CNN'S *LARRY KING
LIVE!*, BESTSELLING AUTHOR, AND RADIO BROADCASTER.

✳

All my career is based on the energy I bring to the broadcast. For over forty years I've been live on the air. I love to think on my feet and be totally in the moment. I enjoy that immediacy. There's nothing about interviewing I don't like. I'm never bored. I listen to my intuition, tracking a person's body movements and everything he or she says. Also I try to create a positive atmosphere by being curious but nonjudgmental. This makes guests more comfortable to express themselves. If topics run on or dry out, I can feel the energy dropping. Then my job is to rev up the interview. I have to raise my energy level by playing the devil's advocate or bringing a fresh slant to old arguments. I hate it if I know what an answer is going to be. I'm never afraid to ask a new question.

I wanted to be a broadcaster at six years old. I didn't have any other ambition. I've always been insatiably inquisitive. I'd go to baseball games at Ebbets Field in Brooklyn and wait outside the clubhouse to talk to the players. I'd ask bus drivers, "Why do you want to drive a bus?" I'd ask plumbers, "What do you get out of plumbing?" If, like some of my guests, you said, "I talk to dead people," I'd ask you how you do it. As an interviewer, I don't have an agenda. But I try to connect with the most positive parts of people, which helps them open up.

Having empathy is important. When asking questions, I come from my brain and my heart. I care about people. I like them. I empathize. Some people call that soft, which is idiotic. I once asked a friend, the greatest lawyer I've ever known, "What do you want from a jury? What's your goal as a lawyer?" Simple, he said: "To put the jury in my client's shoes. Once they're there, I'm home. Even when a guy's head is shot off, if I can get a jury to believe, 'I would've done that in this circumstance,' I've succeeded." On my show, I start with empathy, and go from there. The easiest interviews to conduct are, "You're a rat fink! How could you do that?" This just makes people defensive. Then they build a wall, exactly what you don't want.

But I'm not there to just bring out the positive. I'm there to bring out the person. If someone is negative, that should surface. If you leave saying, "Boy, I hate that guy!" then I've done a good job. If I'm interviewing Hitler, I'm not there to make Hitler a good guy, I'm there to learn about him. That doesn't mean I approve of what you did. It means I'm open to finding out why you did it and listen. My judgment is immaterial.

When I'm interviewing someone, it never works to be hostile. This just escalates negativity. In the past I've gotten hostile. I interviewed George Wallace years ago. He was an angry guy from the beginning. That was when he was really in racist mode. I picked a fight with him, and he won because I lost control of the show. I stopped being the centered me and started being the off-camera argumentative me, so I sank to his level.

I'm also not afraid to be authentic as an interviewer. The first day on the air I learned that. Never been nervous since. I'd always wanted to be in radio. Finally got my chance, got my first big day, but nothing was coming out of my mouth. I looked up and said, "This is a pipe dream. I'm scared." Then the general manager opened up the door to the control room and said, "Hey, this is a communications business. Communicate!" And I swear to God, I turned on the microphone and said, "Good morning. This is my first day ever on air. I prayed for this all my life, and I can't think of anything to say." I told them what happened. I brought them into my shoes. Being vulnerable makes the audience care about you. Any goof I made the rest of the show they'd say, "Hey, it's his first day."

Your energy creates what happens around you. Being positive attracts the positive; being negative attracts negativity. Swami Satchidananda taught me, "In the morning say, 'Thanks for this day.'" I don't care who gave it to me—God, no God. I'm just grateful to be alive. I talk to athletes about this. Here's a great baseball story: An average player went to Stan Musial of the Orioles, a home-run hitter, and said, "Boy, Stan, I feel great today. Breakfast was great. My shower was great. The sun is bright, and I'm consumed with energy. Ever feel that way?" And Musial said, "Every day." Stan brought that positive attitude to what he did. It made him a better hitter because he went in confident. I go on the air confident too. You create positive energy by giving it off. I can do this on my show. But I can't always do it in life—I'm a Type A personality—though I try to turn my attitude around as quickly as possible.

Healers talk about the subtle life-force energy that runs through us. I've never seen it, though around loving people I often feel a warmth. During my heart attack I didn't see any golden light, or have an out-of-body experience. But that doesn't mean I don't believe in subtle energy. The best proof is that right now running through this room are electrical currents. It's possible that we're generating energy fields all the time. But throughout history, progressive people were always laughed at. When Edison said he could light New York City, the vote of the City Council was four to three in favor of financing him. The *New York Times* called those four people idiots. Ben Franklin also must've been laughed at flying his kite in a thunderstorm.

I'm an agnostic. I wish I knew I was going somewhere when I die. I wish I knew someone was watching over me. But I don't. All I can say is, "I don't know." In life, I believe in only one rule. If everyone followed it and raised their children that way, there wouldn't be a problem on this planet: Do unto others as you would have them do unto you. Yeah, that's my philosophy. I believe in the power of being a good human being. You don't need anything but that. It generates positive energy in your life and the world.

<h1 style="text-align:center">9</h1>

THE NINTH PRESCRIPTION: PROTECT YOURSELF FROM ENERGY VAMPIRES

EACH MILLISECOND OF OUR RELATION-
ships is governed by a give and take of energy. Some people make us
more electric or at ease. Others suck the life right out of us. I, a physician board-certified by the American College of Psychiatry and Neu-
rology, want to state formally that energy vampires roam the world
sapping our exuberance, an epidemic that medical texts don't
address. In my practice and workshops, I've seen their fang marks
and the carnage they've strewn. But even my most caring traditional
medical colleagues lack the conceptual framework to see what's all
around them. Thus, alas, the public remains uninformed, and many
of us mope around as unwitting casualties, enduring a preventable
fatigue. If this hits home, not to worry. The Ninth Prescription will
tell you what's going on and offer a cure. As an educator, I'm on a
campaign to install "energy vampire"—a cute term with not-so-cute
repercussions—into the medical lexicon. If you don't get a handle on
how to cope with these life-force leechers, they can become the bane
of your existence.

Everyone has a vampire story. In America and abroad, I've never
met someone who can't relate. My workshops sometimes function as
a self-help forum for "vampire survivors" to vent and find solutions,
a scene *Saturday Night Live* could surely have a field day satirizing.

Though I love to laugh, often at myself, these sessions are serious. The atmosphere gets intense with crying, laughter, anger . . . then empowerment. It's downright liberating to discover why you've been worn out and find the remedy, the magnificence of following this prescription. I'm always moved to hear participants' accounts of intrusive parents who don't know what the word *boundary* means; needy spouses who bleed their partners dry; coworkers with a penchant for exhausting drama; friends whose nonstop whining on the phone leaves you splayed. Unfortunately, I can identify. For decades that seemed like centuries, my Jewish-doctor mother had no qualms about critiquing my boyfriends, my "wild hair," my "inappropriate" clothes, all "for my own good." Always, these zingers took the wind right out of me. Such everyday episodes can be lethal, puncturing our self-esteem and energy field, but many of us feel we can only either grin and bear it or explode. Why? We lack tools to do anything else. The result? Witness the vampire's handiwork: chronic lethargy, anger, depression, or physical symptoms from ulcers to heart attacks.

Be forewarned that vampires can be so self-destructive that they bring you down with them. When I interviewed John Densmore, drummer for the Doors, he gave a touching account of singer Jim Morrison's tragic descent, which took a vast energetic toll on those close to him. John told me:

> At the start of our band, Jim was hopeful, youthful, naive. In a few years, he was morose, alcoholic. I could sense he was getting more and more desperate. By the end, his negativity got so dark, I had to stand back for self-protection, even though I loved him like a brother. Jim would come into a room totally negative. I felt, "I have to get out of here or I'll succumb to something dark and be drained."

This program has zero tolerance for enabling a vampire's behavior, no matter how gifted or endearing the person. We've become far too blasé about forfeiting our energy. The Ninth Prescription will teach you how to identify and combat these drainers in a resolute but sensitive way. You can feel for someone, even have sympathy for the devil, without becoming a target. As a start, get hip to all the vampires' shapes and sizes. They range from the intentionally malicious to those who're oblivious of their effect, including passive-aggressive types. Some are overbearing or loud; others are charming or soft-spoken. Vampires can be neighbors, coworkers, telemarketers, or big shots barking orders to a waiter in a small café. Mates, children, and in-laws may drain us too, even if they don't intend to. Still, what's common to all vampires is that they take our energy and exhaust us. Once you're onto them, you'll achieve more vibrant relationships, even with those with whom you share blood ties!

In Energy Psychiatry, my patients learn the ins and outs of vampire reconnaissance and defense. How do you know if you've encountered a vampire? The tip-off is that even after a brief contact you leave feeling worse, but he or she seems more alive. To make up for the loss of life force, you may want to sleep, overeat, or crawl into some hole and vanish. Always realize that there's a difference between bad chemistry with someone, which simply doesn't feel good, and being drained, when energy is taken from you. You also must distinguish between early anxiety—say, in a new job—which gradually dissipates in positive situations, and the persistence of vampire-induced fatigue. In the same way that I prep my patients, I'd like you to notice early signs of drain by tuning in to your physical reactions. The quicker you locate the leakage, the better you'll be at preventing it or initiating damage control.

Consider:

- Does my chest tighten every time a certain person enters the conversation?
- Do I run for the refrigerator and stuff myself after an interaction?
- Do I need a nap after hanging up the phone with someone?
- Do I have a headache, feel queasy, or slimed when a guest at a party starts talking to me?

- Does my energy bottom-out at family dinners? At staff meetings? Or other social gatherings?

- Do I feel attacked, criticized, or blamed in a relationship?

- Is a person so needy or clinging she seems to stick to me like flypaper?

More than ever, observe how your energy responds to particular people. Each day, log in your journal any significant vampire assaults, particularly from people with whom you interact regularly. Then you'll be less tempted to argue yourself out of why you're suddenly dead on your feet and gorging on ice cream. As I advise patients, name the person and the behavior in question. If you're not sure what trait is the trigger, record that too. As you learn to discern different species of vampires, you won't be fair game.

Everyone is susceptible to vampires, but sometimes we're at higher risk. Look for these problem areas, which can make you vulnerable.

- Not enough sleep

- Poor diet

- Lack of exercise

- No spiritual replenishment

- Excessive work

- Emotional stress

- Illness

- Substance abuse

- Intuitive empathy on overdrive

If you want to protect yourself from vampires, you must be diligent about self-care. For me, skimping on the basics of diet, exercise, and rest quickly makes me feel energetically brittle, less resilient when confronted with drainers. Illnesses, from colds to cancer, also weaken defenses; that's a time we have to be especially loving to ourselves. I know from the decade I worked at inpatient chemical dependency units that substance abusers are at heightened jeopardy for absorbing negative vibes. In Native American lore, alcoholics sitting at a bar are prime targets for possession. They disconnect from their bodies, leaving an undefended vacancy in their energy fields. I help all my patients in recovery to become more body-centered and to master strategies to repel drainers.

Intuitive empaths are acutely sensitive to environmental subtleties—noise, light, odors, emotions, other people's pain. We're particularly easy prey; a vampire's sneak attack can exacerbate our sense of being overwhelmed, test our groundedness, and send us traipsing from doctor to doctor with "unexplainable fatigue." Or it can trigger a vicious cycle of overeating and weight gain in a futile attempt to buffer ourselves. Such Energy-Defensive Eating, discussed in Chapter 3, demands a reevaluation of relationships so you're not continually struck by poison barbs. To be an empath besieged by vampires can spell double trouble. It drove a patient of mine, Mel, a Woody Allen–like playwright, to hole up for days in his Hollywood apartment. Whenever he'd attend a family gathering— "like walking into a den of vampires," he told me—or encounter an arrogant agent, or even a rude receptionist, he'd feel jabbed, deflated, spent. (Contentious family dinners also compounded Mel's "holiday blues.") To cope, he'd inhale whatever sweets he could get his hands on. I said, "Mel, you've turned into a victim, but you're going to have to come out sooner or later." In sessions, we focused on his using the Positive Energy Program's techniques to protect his energy instead of turning to isolation or candy bars to relieve his anxiety. Fortunately, the techniques freed him from the bunker of his apartment. Living as an empath in hiding is pitiful. We need to stand our own ground anytime, anywhere.

I intuitively sense when a patient is a drainer. Within minutes, I get this horrible sluggish feeling, as if I'm sinking into quicksand. I start going down, down . . . Brain mush sets in. Eyelids get heavy. Heavier. Everything is in slow motion. When the eons of our fifty minutes end, I may be done for. Still, I don't get thrown; I know it's a temporary condition that a little meditation afterward can alleviate. On the first few meetings with patients, I purposely stay energetically unguarded to make my initial diagnosis. I need to know if they have vampire tendencies so I can assist them. (I always wait for the proper opening once rapport is established to address this sensitive topic.) It's a good bet that if I'm feeling zapped, other people are too. However, once my intuitive diagnosis is made, I don't hesitate to protect myself.

Why does someone become an energy vampire? Over the years, I've observed that childhood trauma—abuse, loss, neglectful parenting, illness—can damage a person's subtle energy field. A leak occurs that impels vampires to feed on the life force of others to compensate. (Picture an invisible octopus-like tendril extending from their energy field and hermetically sealing onto yours.) Realize, though, that most vampires don't just wake up and decide, "I'm going to take that woman's energy." Usually they're disconcertingly out of touch with the damage they're wreaking.

However, the rare few will come in and say, "I think I drain everyone around me. What can I do?"—a realization of courage and humility for which I have utmost respect. One such self-aware vampire sought my counsel. Sherry, owner of a trendy Malibu restaurant, was chagrined by her unerring capacity to burn employees out. She protested, "We vampires are outta luck. People badmouth us, but nobody explains how we can join the club of positive people." My first task in helping her was to uncover and begin to heal the early wound responsible for the leak. Then her energetic immune system could kick in to patch it up. Always, there's a kind of posttraumatic stress disorder that must be dealt with. In Sherry's case, a drug-addict, deadbeat father skipped town when she was five. Like the demonic people-eating plant in the classic film *Little Shop of Horrors,* Sherry had a subliminal emptiness moaning, "F-e-e-d me, f-e-e-d me." I explained to Sherry that she had an unconscious drive to steal energy whenever she could. Then I helped her identify which behaviors (see vampire types discussed below) were most toxic to others and showed her how to alter them. Constant *kvetching* topped the list. Using these combined approaches, I helped her restore the integrity of her energy field and replace self-defeating styles with savvy interpersonal skills.

Whether you're a drainer or a target, the Ninth Prescription will illuminate your situation. I'll describe common types of vampires so you'll recognize red-flag behaviors in others or yourself. Paired with these will be strategies; some work better with specific drainers, while others can be more generally applied. It's fine to mix and match; see which ones most deftly defang your nemesis. If you're energetically built like a hulk, vampires will seem less threatening. But if, like me, you're more permeable to outer influences, this program's information can give you your life back. Intimate connections will finally seem possible even if they've felt engulfing before, and you won't have to go on permanent shutdown for fear of getting energetically/emotionally demolished.

Prepare for a monster mash with these everyday Draculas where you take the lead. Your goal is to dance them silly with the right moves, not to run scared. For each type of vampire, I've suggested an approach, but it's possible to use more than one. As you proceed, keep a sense of humor. Be confident that no one can drain you if you don't cooperate.

PROTECTING YOURSELF FROM COMMON TYPES OF ENERGY VAMPIRES

To protect yourself from energy vampires, you must first identify what type of vampire someone is. Once you've identified the vampire category, you then can develop energetically appropriate counter-strategies.

Energy Vampire #1: The Sob Sister

Whenever you talk to her, she's whining. She loves a captive audience, casts herself as a victim. The world's always against her, to blame for her unhappiness. This may stem from a childhood feeling of utter helplessness, or from emulating whiner-parents who didn't take responsibility for their lives. When you present a solution, the sob sister says, "Yes . . . but." Her posture may be droopy; so is her energy field. You're starting to droop too as she shamelessly recounts gruesome details of her misadventures, wallowing in each perceived slight. You might find yourself listening for hours, hearing the same complaints over and over. She ends up renewed. You're exhausted.

My patient Denise, mother of three young girls, came face-to-face with such a vampire when she hired a nanny. At first the woman seemed like a godsend, but soon after she started work, the nanny turned into a nightmare. She'd complain about how her boyfriend kept jilting her, how her mother turned her stomach, how her friends constantly failed her. The nanny's negativity was so unrelenting she overwhelmed poor Denise, who was already nearly comatose between household duties and child care. Denise spoke with the nanny about this, but nothing changed. After two weeks Denise had no choice but to let the nanny go.

MAKE CHANGES NOW

PROTECT YOUR ENERGY BY SETTING CLEAR BOUNDARIES

It's crucial to limit the time you spend discussing a sob sister's gripes. (And remember: there are "sob brothers" too!) When approaching her, stay aware: The difference between being a bitch and setting boundaries is attitude. Instead of saying, "You're selfish and self-obsessed, I can't take you anymore," which a part of you likely feels, take a breath and shift to your heart. Let that energy set the tone.

If this is a friend or family member, lovingly say, "I really value our relationship, but when you keep rehashing the same points it wears me out. I can listen for ten minutes; that's my limit. However, when you want to talk solutions, I'm here for you."

With a coworker, I'd take a less direct approach: Keep emphasizing that you have work to do, can only listen a short time. If after five to ten minutes, the sob sister's still kvetching, redirect the conversation or politely end it. Should she continue to ignore your request, reduce contact. You don't have to convince this vampire of your stance. Getting defensive only increases the encounter's negative charge. If she pushes your buttons, you must decide not to react; instead define clear boundaries. An inability to do this sends out a signal, "Take my energy. It's yours!" But when you set consistent limits, the relationship can find equal ground again.

Energy Vampire #2: The Blamer

The blamer has a sneaky way of making you feel guilty for not getting things just right. He berates, doles out endless servings of guilt, or resorts to verbal abuse, an attack posture learned early on. Psychiatric research shows that children who've been blamed often become parents who're blamers. Compared to the self-pitying sob sister, this vampire is more overtly angry, projecting negativity into your energy field. He'll use nasty ploys such as, "If it weren't for you, we wouldn't be in this mess." Or, "It's your fault that I'm on drugs." He uses accusation to drain, leaving no room for discussion. You walk away feeling knifed, that you haven't lived up to expectations, are somehow defective.

My patient Holly's father-in-law Max, a widower, has always been a rabid blamer, though he can be charming too. With age, his blaming has escalated. Now, at seventy, Max is driving Holly's family nuts. He lives in a nearby apartment, comes for dinner twice a week. Holly told me:

Max has a negative comment to make about everything. It's tiring me out. The chicken's overcooked, the new couch is bad for his back, if I were a good mother I'd quit my part-time job counseling teenagers. One night after a really awful visit, I had a nightmare I was in the hospital with kidney failure, hooked up to a dialysis machine. I woke up thinking, "Wow, I guess Max really got to me." The kids are turned off by his bitterness, too, refuse to be left alone with Grandpa. Fortunately, my husband and I have a united front. We're attempting to set limits by saying, "Max, we love you, but your blaming hurts us and must stop," which has mellowed him some, but not nearly enough. What else can I do?

Some blamers can be deleted from your life. Others can't. For those who are fixtures, establishing boundaries of acceptable behavior is an excellent first line of defense, and an approach to continue. But Holly needed something more, and fast. Her dialysis dream was an intuitive SOS indicating a breakdown in her body's defense system against incoming toxins. In Energy Psychiatry I take seriously such foreshadowing of possible illness; it necessitates crisis intervention. So, as part of the Ninth Prescription, I offered Holly the following technique. Try it with vampires who're habitual blamers, and other types too.

MAKE CHANGES NOW

PROTECT YOUR ENERGY BY

VISUALIZING WHITE LIGHT

To deflect a blamer's vibes, you can use your own subtle energy as a shield:

Imagine yourself enveloped in a cocoon of white light.
Picture it as a shield forming a fail-safe barrier around

every inch of you, a covering that stops you from being harmed. It's semipermeable, allowing what's positive in, but keeping negativity out.

Musician Kenny Loggins told me he calls it "putting on my invisibility cloak. Around a blamer I'll ask for white light to surround me. Also I'll use it to prevent intrusions, like when I'm at Disneyland with my kids, and want to be 'just a dad.' It works a lot better than camouflaging myself in dark glasses and a hat."

Shielding isn't meant to make you numb or shut off emotions. You've built a buffer zone where negative vibes can't disable you. You may still hear a blamer ranting, but he won't cut into you viscerally anymore. This is a handy form of protection for intransigent family members or inescapable coworkers, a deliberate defense to insulate your energy and create psychological distance.

Energy Vampire #3: The Drama Queen

She's the Sarah Bernhardt of vampires, has a breathy flair for exaggerating small incidents into off-the-charts dramas. Life is always extreme, either unbearably good or bad. She spends life flitting from crisis to crisis, energized by chaos. Histrionics are her middle name. (Typically, her parents equated trumped-up "disasters" with intimacy.) We dare not ask how she's feeling—she might tell us. I was amused to see that the e-magazine *Salon.com* had a "Drama Queen for a Day Contest." They described their winning contestant as "She came. She puked. She conquered," a stark truism about how this vampire operates on a subtle energetic level. She exhausts our life force with intense emotion; then she goes in for the kill.

If you suspect someone may be a drama queen, take this program's quiz. Answering "yes" to at least two questions is suggestive. Three or more "yeses" indicate a sure thing.

DRAMA QUEEN QUIZ

- Does she frequently start sentences with "Oh my God, you'll never guess what happened?"
- When a brown spot appears on her skin, is she sure she's dying of a fatal disease?
- Is she always making up or breaking up with her boyfriend?
- When her husband forgets to e-mail one night while traveling, does she accuse him of having an affair?
- After a few phone hang-ups, does she call the police, hysterical that thieves are casing her house?
- If her boss doesn't instantly compliment her work, does she frantically tell everyone in earshot she's about to be fired?

The roller-coaster antics of a drama queen put you on overload and wipe you out. My patient Greg felt this after working with Joan, a new employee. The two consulted together on computer projects but because Joan always had a drama brewing in her life, she'd consistently leave Greg hanging. One week, Joan suffered food poisoning, "almost died." Another week her luggage didn't arrive on her flight—the World War III she waged with customer service made her late for work. Then her vintage pink Mustang, "her baby," was towed yet again! By the time Joan left his office, Greg felt tired and used.

With a drama queen, setting limits will rein in her emotional extravaganzas. Greg had to continue telling Joan, "You must be here on time to keep your job. I'm sorry for all your mishaps, but work comes first." By staying calm and also shielding himself, he didn't fuel her hysteria. Understand: This vampire doesn't get mileage out of equanimity; she wins only if she succeeds in jangling you. To keep your calm also practice the next exercise.

MAKE CHANGES NOW

PROTECT YOUR ENERGY BY BREATHING DEEPLY

AND CENTERING YOURSELF

The moment you sense a drama queen revving up, take a slow, deep breath to center yourself. Breathing is a wonderful way to quickly reconnect with your life force so her in-your-face intensity won't sear into your energy field and cause burnout. Keep concentrating on your breath. Tell yourself you know what's happening, and you can handle it.

As I remind my patients: you have power here. I know how easily we can lose it. But, when beset by this overheated drainer, you need to own that moment. Do so by letting your breath release tension and ground you. This will keep you from getting caught up in a drama queen's shtick.

Energy Vampire #4: The Constant Talker or Joke-teller

This chronically perky motor-mouth has no interest in what you're feeling, demands center stage. He's only concerned with himself, his stories, his opinions, his jokes. At first, he may seem entertaining, but when the jokes don't stop, you begin to fade, wonder what's going on. He's addicted to his own voice, overtalks either because he's nervous, a narcissist, a control freak, passive-aggressively hostile, or is unconsciously mimicking gabby parents. Often, constant talking overcompensates for feeling emotionally abandoned or "not heard" as a child, a condition to empathize with but not feed into. Because I worship silence, constant talkers can really irritate me. From banks to beauty salons, there seem to be armies of these shameless noise polluters yakking on their cell phones. They grind our energy field down like a relentlessly yippy Chihuahua who badly needs a walk.

If you meet a constant talker at a party, you might wait for an opening to sneak a word in edgewise, but no such luck. Even worse, lips flapping, he can physically move in so close he's practically doing mouth-to-mouth resuscitation. You step back, he steps closer. You may glaze over, assume your lethargy is from stress or lack of sleep as you gulp your second espresso. But, in fact, this vampire is draining you. Locales where there's no escape are his forte: airplane, car, while you're on the treadmill in the gym. Then he lunges. This kept happening to me with a doctor I'd run into at a monthly hospital staff meeting. He had an unerring knack for cornering me beside the sign-in sheet. When I consistently excused myself, he eventually gave up.

MAKE CHANGES NOW
PROTECT YOUR ENERGY BY STAYING NEUTRAL
AND DEFINING YOUR NEEDS VERBALLY

Some constant talkers can't be averted. The secret to dealing with them is knowing they don't respond to nonverbal cues. You have no choice but to make your needs audible. (If they still ignore you and/or you're stuck somewhere, shielding will repel their barrage.) Tone is especially critical with these vampires. They're hypersensitive to rejection, which provokes them to amp up their verbiage. So, with a constant talker try to be caring—these are wounded people!—but stay definite and neutral. The vibes they pick up from you can determine their reaction. Silently sizzling or snapping back only costs you energy and makes them retaliate.

Around these drainers, inhale deeply and slowly, feel your feet solidly planted in the ground, and don't let exasperation override the calm you're striving for. Then, from a neutral place, set the parameters of your dialogue. Then you won't be left limp, resentful, or forced into rudeness.

Here's how this approach deals with:

- *Strangers.* These are the easiest to fend off, but you have to open your mouth to do it. For example, on airplanes I don't hesitate to say nicely, "I hope you can appreciate this is my time to relax. I'd rather be quiet and read." Still, that probably won't stop my seatmate from gabbing with the person on his other side, but then it's up to me to center, focus my attention, and/or shield to tune out the babble.

- *Neighbors and coworkers.* My patient, a bookish introvert, moved into an apartment complex with chatty neighbors. They tried to rope her into long discussions about everything from terrorism to the toilet breaking. She told me, "Whenever I spot one man, my colon goes into spasm. I need an antacid when he's finished with me." I suggested that instead of simply dodging her neighbors, she smile, listen for a few moments, then politely say, "I'm a very quiet person, so excuse me for not talking a long time,"—a much more constructive tack than, "Shut up, you jerk!" Fortunately, the neighbors recognized her sweetness, saw she wasn't itching for a fight, and increasingly left her alone. With coworkers, use the same low-key approach to keep the peace, but continue emphasizing that you must return to your job. However, if this vampire ends up resenting you for not joining in, so be it. Not your responsibility.

- *Friends and family.* With loved ones we get most flummoxed. Wanting to please, we may lose our neutral center, lapse into victim or child-mode. Should this happen, recognize you've regressed—we all do!—and shift back into your adult self. Do this by preformulating a script. Sometimes intimates will respond to, "I feel left out when you dominate the conversation. I'd really appreciate a few minutes to talk too." The problem is, because the chatter is compulsive, it's hard for the offending person to control.

At family dinners, my friend tried asserting her needs with a motor-mouth sister, who'd only pout and pontificate about how angry and hurt she felt. Such exchanges upset her elderly parents, the last thing my friend wanted. Now, at these dinners (the frequency of which my friend has limited), she's lowered her expectations, keeps focusing on her breath to stay centered, and attempts to be neutral by viewing her sister's blathering with more compassion. Plus, she shields to tune the negative energy out. These efforts conserve her energy.

Energy Vampire #5: The Fixer-Upper

This vampire is like a fixer-upper house that requires endless repairs. There are two types to watch for. The first makes you into her therapist. At all hours she calls desperate to have you fix her problems, unlike the Sob Sister who simply complains. As a friend you want to comply, but her conundrums are endless: "How can I get my boyfriend back? Why am I so fat?" Yada, yada, yada. Her tyrannical neediness lures you in, takes you for all the energy you're worth. No way around it: you're the sucker who gets dumped on. You participate with the intention of "caring," hoping to lessen her pain, not wanting to abandon a friend, a compassionate impulse gone overboard into codependent giving (excessive focusing on others discussed in Chapter 8). As children, these drainers lacked the parental support to develop self-worth that leads to independent problem-solving. Then on cue, you make your entry. *Drumroll!* The valiant rescuer has arrived who knows what's best for her, an exhausting role. Eager to hand over her power, she becomes dependent, infantalized. In this relationship, no one wins.

A second type of fixer-upper is someone who you perceive needs an overhaul, and you take him on as a project. This vampire is so seductive because he doesn't put up enough of a fight to dissuade you from trying to fix him, yet he's not interested in change. Over the years, I've watched bright, sensitive patients get enticed by a fixer-upper's "potential." I know they're on shaky ground when they excitedly emote, "He has so much going for him. I just have to bring it out!" One woman, sure she'd met her soulmate, a perennial playboy, declared, "If I love him enough, he won't be afraid of commitment." Another man had high hopes for his alcoholic sister: "If only I can get her to stop drinking, she'll be part of our family again." Inevitably, both reformers slunk into my office bedraggled and disappointed after their extensive campaigns failed.

With fixer-uppers, a confusing intuitive phenomenon can occur: You have a compelling déjà vu connection with someone, but he doesn't reciprocate. Instead of knowing to read this simply as potential, you assume the relationship is meant to be. So, you set out to convince him (a type of fixing), or put your life on hold until he "comes around," a choice I advise against. Even if you're intuiting an authentic tie, it can still remain unrealized. Maybe the person can't or won't respond. Try to accept what is. To retain your energy and time, don't get lost in the limbo of unrequited longing. Find people who can love you in return. There's more than one soul connection possible in a lifetime.

In all these cases, if you're a fixer, you're genuinely looking for a loving bond, yet refuse to accept people as they are. Your pipe dream is, "If I help _____ change, our relationship will be happy." The outcome of that saga? Years go by. He doesn't budge. You're left tired and brokenhearted.

MAKE CHANGES NOW
PROTECT YOUR ENERGY BY IDENTIFYING
YOUR CODEPENDENCY ISSUES AND DISTANCING
YOURSELF WITH COMPASSION

It takes two to play the fixer-fixee game. To disengage from such codependency, realize these immutable truths.

- Others must take responsibility for their own lives.
- It's none of your business to try to fix anyone.
- As a fixer, you'll *always* end up with your energy drained.
- A mutually loving relationship can't grow unless both people are working on it.

If you're susceptible to fixer-uppers, try to mercifully understand what ropes you in so you don't repeat this going-nowhere pattern. Ask yourself: Am I motivated by the desire to be liked? To feel wanted? To control? By guilt? An inability to say "no"? Perhaps as a child you got kudos for playing the caretaker role, had needy parents. However, to sustain your day-to-day energy level, these patterns must evolve.

When a fixer-upper appears, start by setting the ground rules of how you interact: offer emotional support without compulsively spewing solutions. If you're consistent, many will be dissuaded from calling; others will be spurred to rely more on their inner wisdom and/or an appropriate health care professional. Along with this, here's a visualization to practice.

When obsessing about how to fix someone in any shape or form it's important to compassionately withdraw your energy from him. Put your hand on your heart center and inwardly say to the fixee, "I honor your spirit and wish you well." Then feel your energy receding from him and rematerializing in your own body. Visualize your energy field as completely distinct from that of the problem-plagued person. You're a luminous orb. He is too. But there's no overlap with each other's energy.

Keep your heart open without compulsively intervening, a healthier stance than being a "fixer."

Energy Vampire #6: The Outwardly Nice Socializer

There's nothing obvious to give this drainer away. He may look and sound perfectly fine, isn't necessarily boring. Still, after just minutes of contact your energy dims. He's keeping up the conversation—you can see his mouth moving—but you're fading fast, a little seasick. As usual, you may peg yourself as "neurotic" or figure you're coming down with the flu, but don't put the pieces together that he's a drainer. This vampire's impulses are instinctive, unconscious. Often he was an emotionally starved child who learned to grab subtle energy from any human being nearby when energy fields overlap.

You'll often meet these "nice" types at parties, celebrations, or holiday festivities. You're relaxed and ready for fun, which makes you prime pickings for this vampire. Your encounter may be brief. He closes in for some innocent small talk, then wham! He zaps you, a hit-and-run style of draining that lends itself to social occasions. He might make multiple pounces in an evening or stick with one willing target. The decorums of etiquette work for him. Not wanting to offend, we who were "properly raised" typically stick out the interchange until the bitter end. For years, I needlessly endured these people and suffered, reluctant to hurt a stranger's feelings. How many of us are so loath to appear rude that a raving maniac can be in our face and still we don't cut and run for fear of offending him? No more. Not in this program. Now that you know how these vampires operate, this is what to do.

MAKE CHANGES NOW

PROTECT YOUR ENERGY BY GIVING YOURSELF

PERMISSION TO WALK AWAY

Let's say you're chatting with a man you've just met at a conference, and your energy starts bottoming out. Don't think twice about politely removing yourself from this killing interchange. One of my favorite foolproof lines is, "Excuse me, I really have to go to the bathroom." Even the most intrepid vampire doesn't have a counterargument for that. It's important that you move at least twenty feet from him, beyond his energy field. If you receive immediate relief, there's your answer.

Whenever your well-being feels at risk around certain people, make a tactful and swift exit. In a spot, physically extracting yourself is a sure, quick solution.

Energy Vampire #7: The Go-for-the-Jugular Fiend

The most malevolent of bloodsuckers, she is vindictive and cuts you down with no consideration for your feelings. Driven by envy, competition, or severe insecurity, she deflates your energy with just the right insult. Her jabs can be so hurtful, it's hard to get them out of your head. Whoppers my patients have endured include: "Darling, gray hair is so unattractive"; "Forget him. He's way out of your league"; "Don't be absurd, you're not material for that job!" Some are unapologetically bent on bloodlust; others are more passive-aggressive. This fiend uses her own darkness to maim and insinuates that darkness in you, a maneuver she probably learned from her parents at the dinner table. Energetic fallout from these vampires is nuclear, leaves you sickened by siphoning vital energy. Excessive exposure can cause illnesses from chronic fatigue to depression. In this program, you'll recognize these malicious people to prevent health consequences.

My patient Jessie, a massage therapist, met such a vampire at a friend's baby shower. All went well until Roz appeared, a college roommate (from Hell, it seemed) of the mother-to-be. She wore a stained sweatshirt (could've been blood) and reeked of smoke. In the midst of the gifts being opened, Roz let out a yawn, stood up, and announced. "I'll never get pregnant because I couldn't tolerate getting a fat butt!" Suddenly a joyous occasion went thud. Roz's spiked remark was meant to poison the party's energy. Luckily several women took charge and ushered her out to the balcony where she couldn't insult the pregnant woman again.

The go-for-the-jugular fiend is most damaging when she has you cornered. The place you least want to be is stuck in a car. The noxious vibes from her comments pollute that closed environment. You, the recipient, can practically feel them congealing in your arteries. Research has shown that driving brings out horrific behavior; cars are a setup for road rage, aggression, and family warfare. A common form of spousal abuse is for one partner to verbally incinerate the other in a car and start driving erratically. Heed this warning. If you suspect someone belongs to this vampire species, don't even consider getting into that vehicle!

What to do about this drainer? Move heaven and earth to eliminate her from your life. There's no gain to being exposed to such venom. However, if she must stay, never stoop to her level by countering meanness with meanness. That only inflames her power. Instead, do your best not to take her poison personally—she's an injured person who pitifully can't do any better. In a temporary situation—say, with a pipsqueak despot who's filling in for your boss—feel free to shield to your heart's content and not go for the bait. If we're talking about your mother, who's there to stay, go further by firmly asserting, "Mom, we need to treat each other with respect. Your remark about _____ was unkind. I won't permit you to treat me that way." Don't cave in. Limit contact or enforce other consequences if she persists. A realistic expectation is to gradually modify her behavior. I also suggest the following tactics to further diffuse vindictiveness.

MAKE CHANGES NOW

PROTECT YOUR ENERGY BY REMOVING NEGATIVE

VIBES FROM YOUR SYSTEM

- Break eye contact to stop the transfer of toxins.
- Use your breath to retrieve your life force. Let it function like a vacuum cleaner. With each inhalation, visualize yourself power-suctioning back every drop of energy she's snatched from you. Keep inhaling until the job is done. Do this in the presence of a vampire or later on.
- Exhale negative vibes out the back of your lower spine. There are spaces between your lumbar vertebrae, natural exit points for energy. Touch the area; get a feel for the anatomy. When toxicity accumulates, expel it through these spaces. Envision dark gunk leaving your body. Then breathe in fresh air and sunlight, a quick revitalizer.

- Jump in a bath or shower to cleanse negative vibes and prevent further drain. Drink plenty of water to flush them from your system too. Burn sage where this vampire has been to purify every nook and cranny. (This works well in hotel rooms when a prior guest's leftover vibes feel smarmy, but use only a little so you don't trigger the smoke alarm!)

Energy Vampire #8: Crowds That Drain

Since crowds intensify energy, they can be uplifting or enervating. Kenny Loggins told me, "A responsive audience is a high. But when we're out of sync I get exhausted—in the music industry we say the room has gone 'gun cold.' " Similarly, you need to be aware of the energy of crowds to comfortably navigate them.

Vampires roam in busy places, a possible cauldron of negative vibes. Being compressed in a mall, sports arena, or airport can leech your energy. Being surrounded by strangers elbowing to get by, jabbering on cell phones, smoking, or nuking you with perfume may deplete you, particularly if there's no fresh air or natural light. I'm pushed to my limit with department store clearance sales. The do-or-die aggression of bargain shoppers rifling through mountains of merchandise looks and feels like a feeding frenzy to me. My impulse is to get out of Dodge fast so I'm not lurched into that vortex of vibes. Whenever there's such close contact, our energy fields merge. Intuitive information is transferred. *Zip. Zip. Zip.* Suddenly, on a subtle level, you may sense a passerby's aggravation, loneliness, or physical pain. Most of us don't realize the energetics of what transpired. We just feel overloaded and drained.

An intuitive-empath patient told me, "I like people, but in crowds I experience every emotion known to man. Recently, my husband and I went to an auto show at a convention center. At first I was okay, but then I started getting anxious. I flipped from happy to sad to angry in minutes. The feelings got so erratic, I had to leave." Like many empaths who seek my help in Energy Psychiatry, she'd previously been diagnosed with panic attacks and prescribed Valium. Now she wanted to learn to cope in other ways.

A crowd-specific solution I offer everyone is to bring an apple or a healthy snack along to keep your blood sugar at optimal levels. Also, never attempt to go among the masses if you're tired, troubled, or ill. You need to be in your finest form. Acclimate to crowds slowly. Avoid taking on too much too fast. Begin with an exposure of ten minutes or less, then build up. Don't hesitate to use deep breathing, shielding, or to physically distance yourself from obnoxious people. In addition, practice the following meditation to offset discomfort.

MAKE CHANGES NOW

PROTECT YOUR ENERGY BY VISUALIZING A SHELTERING OASIS

The moment you feel overwhelmed, find a quiet seating area out of the stream of people. Get a cup of tea; sit down. Take a few deep breaths, close your eyes, and meditate. Imagine a tranquil setting—a crescent of beach at sunset, a pine forest in spring, a rolling meadow. Really be there, centered in your body as the outer hubbub recedes. Immerse yourself in the scene: scents, sounds, textures. Feel replenished by the peaceful beauty. After a short time, you'll be able to continue your activities.

Energy Vampire #9: Unintentional Sappers

People we love can sometimes drain us the most. Our children, mates, or other intimates aren't trying to do us in, but life's demands add up. Somebody has to tend to them; often that somebody is you. After a long day at work you come home to your seven-year-old's out-of-the-ballpark temper tantrum; or your sister-in-law calls with a fever, wants you to fetch her prescriptions; or your husband botched a big business account, needs to vent how terrible he feels. You're pedaling as fast as you can, but there comes a point when you're about to keel over too.

Other unintentional sappers are people in psychic or physical pain. You leave stricken after seeing your brother who's in agony from back surgery. Or a friend's oceanic loneliness about her divorce threatens to tow you under. At nine, I first felt the burden of another's suffering. My superwoman/physician mother suffered a heart attack. It seemed for months she'd just lie inhumanly still in her airless, pitch-black bedroom, moaning with chest pain. I'd sit there in the dark holding her hand. I was scared. I was tired. I felt very alone. When she recovered, those memories and the house's vibes felt so unbearable to me, I pressured my parents to move. Amazingly, they didn't resist; we relocated nearby. Still, I'll never forget the way her weakness overtook me. I had no idea how not to assume it.

With intimates, you need to guard your energy too. Don't feel guilty or restrained about using my strategies for close-to-home drainers, particularly on-the-spot shielding and breathing discomfort from your body. Securing your vital force is the opposite of selfish; it will increase your stamina and capacity to love.

Defining and honoring your personal space is another protective technique, especially relevant to family. Determine the number of inches or feet you prefer to keep during conversations; know how many breaks from loved ones you require so they aren't constantly on top of you. Personal space can vary with situations, upbringing, and culture. (For instance, in China it's considered rude to back up while conversing if the other person moves forward.) My ideal distance to keep in public is at least an arm's length; with friends, about half that. We each have a subtle, invisible energetic border that sets a comfort level; it can be intuitively sensed. When this is persistently violated you're prone to drain or agitation.

My friend Dan, a Navy Special Ops coordinator, learned the primal necessity of personal space when stationed on a five-thousand-person aircraft carrier during Operation Enduring Freedom in Afghanistan. He described living conditions beyond claustrophobic:

> *It's a floating city made of four acres of steel. There's a smell of jet-fuel diesel and the deafening noise of aircraft. The ceilings scrape my head at six foot one. On my first cruise, I was asleep on a two-by-six-foot bed, stacked three beds high—one of the few places with any semblance of solitude. Suddenly I was woken up: someone was messing with the curtain between us. Enraged by the intrusion, I punched through the curtain, which my neighbor had accidentally brushed against. As I glared out of my cave, he stared back surprised, unaware he'd trespassed my personal space. I just mumbled something unintelligible and whipped the curtains shut. From then on, I understood how vital some privacy was. So I found a secret place on the ship where I could meditate and hide every day.*

We must all delineate our personal space. Doing so prevents being overwhelmed by those dear to us and makes intimate relationships achievable for those who've felt suffocated by them before. I know many people, including myself, who've stayed single because living with someone has felt too close for comfort; prospective mates can seem like vampires when we don't know how to express our personal space needs. Once we get this down, creative relationships can be built around that. The next exercise will help you define and assert workable physical limits.

MAKE CHANGES NOW
PROTECT YOUR ENERGY BY STAKING OUT YOUR
PERSONAL SPACE

- *Intuitively map out your physical comfort zone.* Pair off with a friend and start by standing twenty feet apart. Then slowly move closer to each other—nineteen feet, eighteen, seventeen—notice at each increment how it feels. Ask yourself: Is it comfortable or closed in? The point at which you get uneasy is the energy border of your personal space. You may need to enlarge it when out in the world.

- *Negotiate with your family.* Plan regular minibreaks from your children and mate. You must negotiate your personal space needs with loved ones. One patient's husband had a harrowing bumper-to-bumper freeway commute home from work. Every night he'd march in the door tired and irritable, which led to spats. Family contact made him crankier. His solution? Taking twenty minutes to decompress alone in the bedroom where he'd listen to jazz, nap, or meditate. Afterward, he had much more to give to his family.

  We get crazy when we feel trapped. Many of us don't realize that even a brief escape will keep us sane. Spend five minutes in the bathroom with the door shut so the kids can't intrude. Take a stroll around the block. Read in a separate room if your mate's frustrations are weighing too much on you. Of course with babies, there's less flexibility, though taking regular breaks can be done. As children get older, though, help them learn about boundaries through healthy modeling.

- *Experiment with creative living conditions.* The traditional personal space rules for cohabitation must be revamped to make relationships palatable for energy-sensitive people. For instance, I've never liked sitting too close to people in public. At movies, I'm always the one in the back far corner. In doctor's offices I'll pile my purse and folders on the seats beside me to keep others away. Conversations, scents, coughing, movement, and the energy field of another overlapping mine feels intrusive. Even if someone's vibes are pleasant, at times I'd rather not feel them. Personally, this is more than a princess-and-the-pea indulgence; it's about maintaining my well-being in the world, and if I live with someone.

What's worked for me is to have my own bedroom and an isolated office area where I can't hear a peep out of a commingler. I also can see the beauty of separate wings or adjacent houses if that's affordable. I'm inspired by how two of my friends who've had a long, close platonic relationship have divided their living structure. It has a common entryway with independent apartments on either side, a brilliant design decision. If I'm traveling with a companion, romantic or not, I'll always have adjoining rooms with my own bathroom. I'd go mad if I'm stuck with anyone in tight quarters, no matter how much I adore him.

I want to give you permission to explore your personal space requirements. You might need to educate your mate, but get the discussion going. Design a life that makes sense to your energy needs. I've seen a creative approach to square footage save marriages, and make ongoing intimacies feel safe. Honoring your needs can allow more love in.

- *Take special care of yourself, around people in need.* You can be compassionate without maxing-out on empathy. If you're liable to adopting other people's troubles, it's more than okay to fortify your strength in those situations. Be well fed and rested when you arrive. Also, keep a distance that respects your personal-space needs. Sit a few feet away instead of plopping yourself in the middle of an ailing person's energy field. You can hug, but don't hang on her. Walk around the room to deintensify contact. Make the visit short and sweet; don't overdo it. When you leave, remember to recharge yourself rather than jetting to the next stressed-filled event. Take a relaxing walk, gently meditate for a few minutes, or soak in a tub. Such energy restoration will make future visits more do-able since you know you won't be sapped.

THE POSITIVE ENERGY PROGRAM'S Ninth Prescription—protect yourself from energy vampires—will give you the gumption to whomp a whole slew of drainers. It belongs in a Living 101 instruction manual. Practicing this prescription's strategies will preserve your energy, short and long-term.

But also expect to bump into one pesky cosmic certainty: We energetically attract what we haven't worked out in ourselves. So if you keep getting swarmed by a particular vampire, honestly examine why. For instance, if you keep linking up with "fixer-upper" boyfriends who can't commit, don't just blithely dismiss this as "there are no good men out there." Instead, make sure you're not unconsciously playing out, "I'm going to get Daddy to love me" or "I'll make this miserable family better" themes from your childhood. There's a good reason I've chosen to be in psychotherapy most of my adult life. From experience, I've seen that I can guard my energy until lost Atlantis rises, but if I don't strive to heal childhood patterns associated with unhealthy relationships, the same vampires will just keep hovering. Conquering unresolved insecurities strengthens your energy field, reducing a drainer's power.

If you find that vampires evoke intensely judgmental reactions from you, it could be they are mirroring aspects of your personality you don't like or completely understand. I'm always suspicious of my vehemence whenever I point a self-righteous finger at someone and, for instance, intone, "He's so angry and abrupt." Maybe he is, but still the question is, "Why do I have such a charge on that?" One reason: I'm intolerant of, or denying, those traits in myself. If this wasn't true, he, or any vampire, wouldn't have the capacity to get to me so much. Coming clean about your shortcomings stops you from growing as irked (and thus sapped) by others with similar qualities.

What I treasure most about not being at the mercy of drainers is the openness I feel in the world. I'm not always fending off an impending wound. Now, I know exactly how to take care of my energy, a solace better than having money in the bank. This makes the child in me feel safer to come out. I can look deep and long at the details of people. That shaved-headed rapper in his elegant navy cashmere coat getting chicken soup at Nate 'N Al's deli. Or the tattooed biker mama holding tight to her man on a monster Harley. I find it all so beautiful. I don't want to hold back from life anymore. With the prescriptions I teach and use, I don't have to. Nor do you.

Treat Yourself:

Focus on a victory over a vampire. Maybe it was finally excising a mean-spirited "friend" from your life. Or setting limits with a busybody relative who prods at every family dinner, "You're not married yet?" Rejoice in how you held your own. Master of your energy, get used to this triumphant feeling.

INTERVIEW: JAMIE LEE CURTIS ON PROTECTING YOUR ENERGY

JAMIE LEE CURTIS IS A GOLDEN GLOBE AWARD-WINNING
ACTRESS AND BESTSELLING AUTHOR OF CHILDREN'S BOOKS
ON SELF-ESTEEM.

*

People have a certain energy pulse that comes off of them immediately. Energy is communicated through our eyes. When someone really looks at me I can feel we've connected that energy port. Most of the time, it feels positive. But sometimes people can be draining if they're negative or lock in with hostility. It depends on the intention of that connection.

The hardest people for me to be around are "victims" who refuse to be accountable for their actions. It makes me insane to watch them try to get away with blaming others for their misery. They drain off my energy like a battery. With this type I'll be gentle but firm and say, "I'd like to change how we interact. When we finish talking, or rather when YOU finish talking, I don't perceive we've had an exchange. You feel better. I feel worse." I've actually suggested that people find a good doctor to get to the bottom of the problem. After five years in recovery I'm getting better at setting limits. I used to hide my resentments in drugs and alcohol. Now I've had to figure out other ways to handle them. There's still a part of me that goes, "Oh, come on, Jamie. That person needs you. It's not fair." But now I know that to care for myself I must set limits.

Another type who can drain me are narcissists who don't learn from their experiences. Somebody who says the same thing over and over again. The repetition wears you down. They want you to be a sounding board, someone they come to for guidance, but really you're just a repository for their problems. I've realized that's damaging to my energy. So again, I set limits on their behavior.

All my life, I've had an energetic personality and a strong light around me. I'm happy about that. It's a blessing. So, if I'm around a negative person, it's not necessary for me to visualize a protective shield. What really protects me is my intuition. When I'm working on a film I call this my antenna. I intuitively see things. I know what's going on all over the set. I just read the energy of the day. I read people. It's a skill I've now honed over a very long career. Also, I believe that conquering your own issues, whether fear or old wounds, gives you a bit of a protective force field too.

I've never been the type to take on people's negative energy. I'm very grounded. That had a lot to do with my mother, Janet Leigh. She was grounded and transmitted this quality to my sister and me. My mother recognized the ephemeral nature of show business and chose a man who wasn't in the business to raise us. Also, we were brought up around nature. That was a reality we were lucky to have.

In certain situations, though, I sometimes have a hard time with getting my picture taken. It can feel like a freak show to me. It's depleting, like I'm just a "thing." By no means am I complaining about the recognition that comes from being an actor. I enjoy that. But it's a gross feeling when you become a "thing." For instance, I've been in a room with a bunch of drunk people where all they want is a photo with you. That is when I wish I had the power to push the port button to take me away.

As a mother, I know that children get unsettled by negative input too, which can sap their energy. I write books for kids about self-esteem, about liking who you are. I believe that violent images aren't appropriate for young children as they develop mentally. I felt that Spider-Man was too visually stimulating for my six-year-old. There's a reason they rate movies. I can't tell you how many times parents have walked up to me with their three-year-old and said, "We just watched you in *Halloween*. It was so cool!" I think, "Excuse me? Are you out of your mind?" Why on earth would you show such young kids a movie where a babysitter can't protect them? It disturbs a child's sense of safety, scares them. In contrast, a teenager (my daughter included) or adult who understands that this is just a movie can better deal with the sensation of fear and all the things that go along with that.

Motherhood is my most important role. As a mother, I don't look at my two kids as "they drain me." Loving them and caring for them is what I'm here for, but it does take tremendous energy to run around and meet their needs. I wake up at five o'clock in the morning like a jack rabbit. Often, I go all day long. I adore my life. But there is a point where I have to stop, and I honor that.

10

THE TENTH PRESCRIPTION: CREATE ABUNDANCE

ABUNDANCE IS THE BOUNTY that comes from embracing all of your energy. It always begins with opening your heart, then extends outward, not vice versa. In my vision, external achievements alone, no matter how grand, can't penetrate our depths enough to bestow such wholeness. However, as we become wise arbiters of where our energy does and doesn't go, and when all our choices, from what breakfast cereal we choose to whom we marry, are gut-inspired, we will enjoy real abundance. This program will lead you there.

In Energy Psychiatry, part of my work is waking the dead. I don't mean the dearly departed, but the parts of us that become comatose to the abundance right before our eyes. Our society's shameless con is the belief that wealth and fame equal happiness. True, if your heart's in the right place and your ego isn't the size of Godzilla, affluence can be magnificent. Still, that's a big "if." Frequently, my patients who "have it all" are the most miserable. What makes them even worse off than others is feeling, "With all my success, why am I so unhappy?" The reason: They experience an emotional poverty that damns their ability to appreciate what they've got. Until I can help my patients resuscitate their hearts, they cannot grasp their gifts, material and more.

The program's tenth and final prescription has to do with giving and receiving the blessing of abundance. Rest assured, you're worthy of the blessing. We all are. Get used to accepting this. Then poise yourself to welcome joyous prospects, doors opening, and love. Yes, love. Traditionally, abundance implies getting your material wants met, which we'll explore. But a larger view is that abundance is constantly operating, even during times of sadness or seeming lack. It entails grasping the perfection of the moment, arduous or sublime, realizing that what you're giving and being given is good enough. An understanding of abundance helps me stay centered when things are falling apart. Plus it helps me do my darndest not to close my heart, knowing that turmoil isn't all there is. This perspective also lets us see the Big Bang in the minutiae. Our attitudes determine abundance.

Fatigue and despair are never absolutes. They're energies we can shift with the prescriptions I've offered. Quantum physics states that energy is neither created nor destroyed, but can be converted from one form to another. Such magic: photosynthesis turns light into energy for plants; electricity becomes mechanical energy that makes toasters pop. Similarly, living this program can transform negativity into a bouquet.

Abundance also comes from digging what you're doing, and having the moxie to push the envelope for positive change, traits shared by everyone I've interviewed for this book. Take producer Norman Lear, who enthused about how he's brought the Declaration of Independence around the country, "to share the inspiration of the founding fathers who signed it and put their lives, fortunes, and sacred honor on the line." Or my friend the Reverend Michael Beckwith, who shouts, "Yes!" from his seat in the audience if he's excited about a point a speaker is making. The room can be pin-drop silent. Then his uninhibited "Yes!" Wow. Or Jamie Lee Curtis, who suggested that *More* magazine photograph her in her underwear without airbrushing and contrast that with how she looks after time with hair, makeup, and wardrobe pros. Jamie had the guts to show that no one *ever* looks that perfect without hours of hair, makeup, and wardrobe. As a woman, I say a big Amen to that. What all these people ooze is the exuberance that comes from living your own beliefs and passions, in matters large and small.

THE MORE YOU GIVE, THE MORE YOU GET

The formula for increasing abundance is simple: The more you give, the more you get—a paradox to the ordinary mind but a certainty from the standpoint of energy dynamics. Your small self says, "There's not enough. I want to keep it all." Your Large Self says, "There's more than enough. I want to share it." I know the temptation of clinging to what you've got, petrified it'll be snatched from you. (The curse of being an only child is that sharing is often a real feat for me.) But I also know that if I keep inhabiting this mindset, I'll be trapped in a teensy fear-filled box, not a pretty prospect. To liberate our vitality, we must learn to switch from the small to the Large Self, a technique I'll share.

Let me explain how my formula for abundance relates to finances in the Tenth Prescription. I'm defining financial abundance as being able to live comfortably and enjoy what you have, with or without a humongous bank account. Though money typically symbolizes Earth-plane power, in my scheme it can't masquerade for self-worth. Nor does it justify becoming a bitch-on-wheels or pumping up your ego—that kind of "power" is worthless to me. How can money catalyze positive energy? Wondrously, these flimsy pieces of paper with pictures can pay our bills, make life easier, more fun; they can be bartered for a home, a college education, a doctor's care, an escape to Shangri-la. But money can also instigate wars; its loss has prompted people to throw themselves out of high windows. Contrary to many civilizations' warped notions, this program *never* lets it dictate our value as a human being or makes any person "better" than another. In the end, one thing's certain: when you leave this body, you can't bring the fool's gold of possessions along. What you can take, however, is your loving heart. It alone provides the momentum for where you need to go.

I tell this to my patient Bob, who nods a lot, but thinks my advice is impractical. "Sure, Judith, but I'm living in this world now." Bob makes plenty of money, but he always wants more. True, he's got expenses, from a mortgage to his children's middle-school tuition. But overall his life is abundant—though, pity, he's the last to know. Bob gets caught in, "If only I made _____ I could _____." And, "My colleague, who makes _____, has more leverage and respect than I do." Some nights these thoughts keep him awake; every day they siphon his energy. The problem is that Bob equates his paycheck with who he is, a crippling yet pervasive assumption. My continuing work with Bob is to help him find a sense of self that defies outer circumstances, the sure path to emotional freedom. I always point him back to his heart, to the good he's done, which is hugely impressive. Also, to access his Large Self, I have Bob practice the exercise in this section.

I appreciate the seductive undertow of our society's make-more-money push. And how the money = power tic is conditioned. I'm not saying these mass-mind maladies are easy to get past. But I am certain that if we don't try, we'll sacrifice a huge chunk of our energy and self-esteem. First, we must identify forces that blind us to the abundance we already have: feelings of envy and competition; greed; lack of faith in the integrity of our soul's path; fear that we're "not enough" in comparison to others. Getting thrown by these serenity-wreckers doesn't mean you're "not spiritual." But, for heaven's sake, put up your dukes and fight. As my patients and I do, use the following exercise to free yourself from painful thinking.

MAKE CHANGES NOW
SHIFT FROM YOUR SMALL SELF TO
YOUR LARGE SELF

1. *Be candid about what stops you from appreciating abundance now.*
   Whether you feel you can't achieve abundance without $_____
   in the bank, or envy every *schmo* on the street, take a
   compassionate look at what's inside. Know exactly what you're
   dealing with. No editing. This is your small self. Get to know it.
   Let yourself feel the constriction, anxiety, and low energy of
   residing there.

2. *Next, shift to your Large Self.* Begin by taking a few slow, deep
   breaths. With each inhalation, feel yourself growing more
   spacious, more merciful. Gently touch your heart center in the
   midchest; sense the warmth, the comfort. Reconnect with how
   much you're loved by Spirit, whatever your conception. From
   this large-hearted place, know there's enough room for all our
   successes; there's enough love to go around. Then center your
   attention on what's beautiful about your life, *not* on what you
   perceive is lacking. Let your mind meander. Remember the
   money you do have in the bank, your health, the angel on your
   shoulder who's always been there. In these quiet moments, take
   your eyes off other people. Concentrate on your gifts and the
   enormous well of love that's available to tap into, a powerful
   redirection of energy.

INNER OBSTACLES TO ABUNDANCE

Since inner obstacles to abundance can cling, I've also found psychotherapy invaluable. What drives our insecurities is often surpris-

ing. Take my nemesis, envy. For years, I'd turn acidic when a peer, "deserving" or not, got on the *New York Times* bestseller list—a goal I haven't achieved. I felt less-than, overlooked, invisible. I wanted to salute their success, but just couldn't. This might not be Bangladesh, but it ate at me. I never envied those writers personally—I like the package I was born with, quirks and all—nor was the seduction monetary. What I envied was the recognition accorded their work. I'm smart enough to realize that the "public" path is fraught with land mines, that my challenge was to keep believing in the goodness of my work, no comparisons.

But in therapy I also discovered an unsuspected root of my envy: I didn't want to be alone. I was single. An only child. My parents had passed on. While writing, I lived like a hermit. In my mind, larger recognition represented a built-in community, people and opportunities. What an "Ah-ha!" to suddenly grasp the madness of depending on book sales to fulfill such a need. Instead, my task was to create my own extended family, an insight and practice that has much soothed envy's sting. Even so, the Capricorn scrappy-mountain-goat in me (my astrological rising sign) is still up for climbing more of this mountain.

GENEROSITY

Along with removing blocks, another part of the Tenth Prescription for creating abundance includes generosity. It accelerates the free flow of money and everything positive in your life. Of course, when it comes to finances, a good job, smart investments, and saving wisely are important. But beyond these essentials, the secret is to be generous, whatever your net worth.

As Norman Lear told me, "You receive as you give. But you have to expend energy to get energy. Electricity happens from rubbing two wires together. That's what giving does for me." Generosity is an expansive energy. Stinginess is constipated. If you're on the cheap side, don't worry. But wake up! Realize it's a *huge* drawback; take contrary action. How? If someone gives you a nickel, give them a dime. Gradually, resolve to let go of the tit-for-tat mentality, a small-mind approach antithetical to abundance. Be the bigger person: that's generosity. Also, help people out. Charities, tithing, donations. Give what you can; it doesn't have to be a lot. Feel the growing sense of abundance it produces, an energy that circulates far and wide. It'll find its way back to you. Maybe you'll win a jackpot, or perhaps you'll just feel better about yourself. However generosity plays out, you can't lose.

Dare to be unconventional in your giving. Rise to the opportunities presented. For instance, the other day, while I was waiting at a restaurant to pick up my Chinese take-out, a woman had ordered dinner, but had forgotten her wallet. I felt the impulse to pay for her. Should I? Shouldn't I? Thank God my mouth opened before getting mired in that mental debate: "Please let me get the bill," I offered. She lit up, "Oh my God, you're Judith!" Surprised, I said, "Yes." She went on, "Years ago, I saw you for one session. You helped me leave an abusive husband!" Though I truly hadn't recognized her, I'm a lover of synchronicities. "Amazing," I thought. She was smiling. I was smiling. The cashier was smiling. All around, good karma. And it took so little to get it going. Later that week, I received a check for the twenty dollars she'd accepted along with a lovely thank-you note.

My point isn't to be self-congratulatory: it's to encourage you to push past social norms. Jump on all chances to be generous, large and small. If you're shy, try to do it anyway. Personally, I get a charge out of anonymously leaving cash in public places. I first got the idea when eating breakfast at a diner in Manhattan. In a flash, it occurred to me, "Why don't you leave five dollars in the bathroom? Someone will find it and feel lucky. Then they'll believe anything's possible." Now, whenever I get the hankering, I leave a dollar here, five dollars there. Not much, but just enough to get people thinking. Being a self-anointed money gnome brings me great satisfaction.

In this spirit, here's a exercise to stretch your limits of generosity.

MAKE CHANGES NOW
CREATE ABUNDANCE BY ANONYMOUSLY LEAVING
MONEY FOR OTHERS TO FIND

Leave some money—any amount that feels comfortable—at
the location of your choosing, but don't get found out. It can
be anywhere. A hallway in your dermatologist's building, on
the sidewalk, in a potted plant. I want you to experience the
high of this. I consider it delightfully subversive and mischief-
making. I bet you'll feel happy leaving money too. Repeat this
exercise as much as you like.

Let's make it our business to keep reinventing the meaning of generosity. In the area of money, we must be mavericks in what can
seem like a spiritless wasteland. Money is what you make of it.
Whether you have barrels or not, you don't need to be extravagant
to have fun. I promise: those control-freak misers with twenty million bucks stashed away aren't having a good time or prospering. No
reason to envy a scrooge. Much better is to adopt this Buddhist saying as a motto: "Your happiness is my happiness. There is no greater
happiness in the world." Abundance begets abundance, an energetic
principle that'll attract prosperity of many kinds to you.

SERVICE

Wedded to generosity is the concept of service—a giving of yourself
to better the lives of others, your community, the world. It's an attitude and an energy that perpetuates abundance. Good deeds, volunteering, sending e-mail petitions to friends about preserving the
environment are ways to get out of your small self and spread posi-

tive energy around. Plus, it can return you to your heart again and reverse negative thinking. I'm not prescribing service as simply something you're "supposed" to do, nor is it drudgery. Rather, it's about intuiting what you're moved toward; then giving feels good. Also understand that we're energetically connected to all humankind; service is a bow we take to each other. Abundance can never be just about *you*. For better or worse, we're in this time-space adventure together. Abundance necessitates acknowledging that we are inextricably bound to one another.

Experiencing such high-level abundance may require redefining who you are and why you're here. Our world is in crisis. No one is exempt from feeling the social, economic, and environmental repercussions. For the sake of raising your personal energy and the planet's, it's vital to envision how you can help. Ordinary folk like us have the power to change the future. We are not without influence. Day in, day out, we must wage a revolution of love, whether in the nitty-gritty of the mundane or globally. If the concept of service is new to you, don't force your involvement. Explore opportunities that feel natural.

MAKE CHANGES NOW

FIND A FORM OF SERVICE THAT MOVES YOU

The basis of service is opening your heart to lighten someone's load or improve a situation. There are thousands of ways to serve. To determine what appeals, listen to your intuition, try new things. Don't think you have to be a Mother Teresa. In your life, start with random acts of kindness, a springboard to other outlets. Do at least one good deed a day. It could be carrying groceries for a neighbor, picking up trash on the street, or putting coins in someone's expired parking meter. Feel the energy rush from that.

Then consider expanding your repertoire. For example, investigate charities for adults or children, animal rescue, or groups that support peace. All service is valuable. See where your interests lie. Feel what moves you, even a little. Then follow it. Try donating an hour a month to this cause, either from home or in person, whatever's convenient. Any gift of time is a treasure.

For some of us, service is a choice. But it can be thrust upon others, as it was for my friend Hafsat Abiola. At twenty-seven, she's a Harvard graduate and Nigerian human rights activist whose ongoing work is empowering women. Hafsat's father, one of Nigeria's first democratic presidents, was imprisoned by the ruling elite, and "suspiciously" died on the eve of his release. Soon after, Hafsat's mother, also an activist, was assassinated. Despite unfathomable sorrow, Hafsat tells of her life's abundance:

Suddenly my parents were gone. They were prepared for whatever sacrifice democracy required, but the loss was overwhelming. I'll always feel the abundance of love they'd given me. I believe abundance is staying in close contact with gratitude, appreciating each day's fullness. Our country is financially poor, but in terms of our people's wisdom, grace, and decency we're wealthy. Emerging from thirty years of dictatorship, more than ever I see how abundance requires giving back. Service is the rent we pay for being in the world, a generosity that honors all people on this planet. To be grand means to give. Spiritually, I feel small and ugly if I'm not generous. Also, abundance involves forgiving, allowing our hearts to get bro-

ken, then open again. Forgiveness means letting go of baggage, your grudges, and fears. If you don't leave these bags behind, you'll miss the bus. Abundance feels like beautiful, clear water flowing through my soul. It sweeps the dirt away, makes me deeply thankful for all my blessings.

FORGIVENESS

Like Hafsat, I support an abundance that flows from love. The more we succumb to bitterness, the more dangerous our world becomes. To increase positive energy, there can be no new narrative without forgiveness. Otherwise, the narcotic of hatred makes us into war machines, whether in the Middle East or in our own kitchen—a dissociated fugue where we're numb to our pain or another's. In contrast, forgiveness is a striving to release resentments; the basic guidelines for this are presented in the Fourth Prescription. Of course, if you've been wronged, it's natural to feel enraged or hurt, or want to call an abusive relationship quits. However, if anger is all you have, it will crowd out any emotional abundance.

Forgiveness comes from your Large Self, a necessary heightening of perspective. Ultimately, it's more for you than anyone else. While forgiveness might not make all rancor vanish, you'll gain the freedom of seeing beyond it. To facilitate this energizing process, I reiterate: forgiveness refers to the actor, not the act. Not to the offense, but to the woundedness of the offender. The real soul-stretcher, though, is to attempt to empathize with the depths of these wounds. Also to recognize the sanctity of your "enemy," which resonates beyond any war zone. This human-to-human connection helps to obliviate an "Us Versus Them" mentality. Our desire to transcend hatred is a summoning of peace, well worth the dedicated stretching of the soul.

RECOGNIZING OUR COLLECTIVE UNITY

On a global scale, abundance grows when we realize our collective unity. From an energetic perspective, there's no arbitrary division between Us and Them. That's only our small self's hallucination, but one powerful enough to kill off civilization. Every human being is of one family, a truth I'd bet my life on. Alas we no longer have the luxury to keep debating this. Our Earth, our home, is being plundered. No survival without Her. The fate of our species, of all species, depends on caring for nature's ecosystems. At a subtle energy level, when wilderness is raped, so are we. When oceans are poisoned, our bodies wail. Causes of physical and emotional suffering are not as clear-cut as they seem. It's no coincidence that depression is epidemic and cancer is ravaging so many people dear to us. In our own way, we energetically process the violence surrounding us. There's a metabolism between the exchange of nations, communities, the Earth, and our bodies. My final prescription involves doing our part to fight for the abundance of a healthy Earth and its people.

I hold Krishnamurti's words close: "The heart of man is in his own keeping. To end violence, we must relentlessly keep freeing ourselves from the violence within. Inner strife projected externally becomes world chaos." Recognizing that the path to peace is not outside us, we must be cognizant of the energies we project, the thesis of this program. Remaining naive to this is irresponsible; so is lip service. Though talk alone can uplift, its power pales next to embodying the change we long for. Practicing what we preach is the imperative of our millennium. It may be hard, we may falter, but so what? There's no escaping that our energy fields collectively mingle. "Evildoers" never do it alone. Apathy to healing makes us their accomplices.

The Positive Energy Program's Tenth Prescription—create abundance—relies on the premise that love is a sustainable energy. So do all my other prescriptions. Always remember the importance of love. The mandate is simple. If you're tired, love. If you're happy, love. At your final breath, love some more. When it feels utterly impossible—

such moments arrive—try to love again later. I promise: you'll never leave empty-handed when the heart is true. There comes a point when we must decide what our endgame is going to be, personally and for the planet. To me, the only one that makes any sense is love. It's how we have to define ourselves beyond all other criteria. This will ensure abundance.

My hope is that you got more than you bargained for from this book. I wish you energy that keeps renewing throughout your life. But I also want you to bask in the brilliance of the energy emanating from all things. In just the right light, with just the right attitude, you'll be able to see the soles of your shoes sparkle. They do. They will. Let that wonder in. Be dazzled by the energies interwoven throughout the day-to-day. If you can appreciate this, even for brief moments, I've succeeded. The present informs the future. So use my prescriptions to make your present bright. A belief in love is unstoppable. You'll have the courage to do anything.

A Last Treat for Yourself:

As one family, hearts joined, let's keep saying a prayer for the world: "May our people and planet be healthy. May our people and planet be happy. May suffering be lifted. May we know enduring peace."

INTERVIEW: ROSA PARKS ON
THE POWER OF LOVE

ROSA PARKS IS THE MOTHER OF THE CIVIL RIGHTS MOVEMENT. HER
REFUSAL TO GIVE UP HER SEAT TO A WHITE PASSENGER BEGAN A
MOVEMENT ENDING LEGAL SEGREGATION IN AMERICA. SHE IS THE
RECIPIENT OF THE MARTIN LUTHER KING JR. NONVIOLENT PEACE PRIZE.

On December 1, 1955, in Montgomery, Alabama, my decision not to give up my seat on a bus to a white passenger was intuitive and spontaneous. Like usual, I was just headed home from work at the department store. I was forty-two then, had always thought about freedom. My grandfather and mother taught me that all human beings were equal. But on that bus I just knew that we, as a people, had suffered too long. Even though I was afraid to make a protest—I risked being beaten or killed—I set my mind not to give in to fear. I couldn't continue to be mistreated for no reason. Then things would never get better. After my arrest, the bus boycott began. We were fortunate that Dr. Martin Luther King, at twenty-six, was willing to take the lead. After 381 days of the boycott, the Supreme Court overturned the old laws and made segregation illegal on public transportation in Alabama. This became the model for other southern states to change. I don't feel angry or victimized about the past, just grateful that the conditions we were under came to an end. If you stay angry at other people, you might miss finding friends among those you were angry with.

My energy and strength come from faith in God. Intuition is also important because it helps you know you can still go on. I advise others to find a strong faith and intuition too; they'll give you courage and lead to an abundance of heart. At ninety, to increase my energy, I regularly exercise using light weights, stretching, and massage. For over forty years, I've been vegetarian. Growing up, my family had little money—I had health problems early in life because of poor nutrition. Eating healthy is a priority for me. I also love children. Working with them at the Rosa Parks Learning Center keeps me energized. I designed a program where the youth teach seniors basic computer skills. I was in the first graduating class!

I believe that the most positive quality in the human spirit is love. The most negative quality is hatred that has no reason. We can create a more loving world by learning to respect our differences, not judging them. Hatred, like other negative emotions, is a choice. If you choose kindness and humanity, you will have peace and prosperity. It also comes from being generous to others when there is no benefit to yourself. My friend, Dr. King, set a profound example for me and many others. He was an extremely kind person. He understood the soul of man.

I know that we can achieve Dr. King's dream of a world where we come together and live as one. Love, not fear must be our guide. I see a world where children do not learn hatred in their homes. Where people don't call each other names on the basis of skin color. I can see a world free of violence, where people from every race and religion work together to improve life for everyone.

Referrals, Training, and Information

AMERICAN HOLISTIC MEDICAL ASSOCIATION
6728 Old McLean Village Drive
McLean, VA, 22101
703-556-9728
www.holisticmedicine.org

AMERICAN HOLISTIC NURSES ASSOCIATION
2733 Lakin Drive
Flagstaff, AZ 86004
800-278-AHNA
www.ahna.org

ASSOCIATION FOR COMPREHENSIVE ENERGY PSYCHOLOGY
P.O. Box 910244
San Diego, CA 92191
www.energypsych.org

BARBARA BRENNAN SCHOOL OF HEALING
P.O. Box 2005
East Hampton, NY 11937
800-924-2564
www.barbarabrennan.com

CENTER FOR PSYCHOLOGICAL AND SPIRITUAL HEALTH
www.cpsh.org

COLORADO CENTER FOR HEALING TOUCH
12477 W. Cedar Drive, Suite 206
Lakewood, CO 80228
303-989-0581
www.healingtouch.net

NURSE HEALERS–PROFESSIONALS ASSOCIATES, INC.
11250 Roger Bacon Road, Suite 8
Reston, VA 20190
703-234-4149
www.therapeutic-touch.org

Educational Centers

ESALEN INSTITUTE
Big Sur, CA 93920
408-667-3000
www.esalen.org

INSTITUTE OF NOETIC SCIENCES
101 San Antonio Road
Petaluma, CA 94952-9524
707-775-3500
www.noetic.org

INSTITUTE OF TRANSPERSONAL PSYCHOLOGY
744 San Antonio Road
Palo Alto, CA 94303
650-493-4430
www.itp.edu

INTERNATIONAL SOCIETY FOR THE STUDY OF SUBTLE
ENERGIES AND ENERGY MEDICINE (ISSSEEM)
11005 Ralston Road
Arvada, CO 80004
303-425-4625

KRIPALU CENTER FOR YOGA AND HEALTH
P.O. Box 793
Lenox, MA 01240
413-448-3400
www.kripalu.org

OMEGA INSTITUTE FOR HOLISTIC STUDIES
260 Lake Drive
Rhinebeck, NY 12572
800-944-1001
www.omega-inst.org

Beattie, Melody. *Codependent No More: How to Stop Controlling Others and Start Caring for Yourself.* Hazelton, 1997.
 Groundbreaking rules for living that will keep you from giving your energy away.

Brockway, Laurie Sue. *A Goddess Is a Girl's Best Friend.* Perigee Books, 2002.
 A smart, fun look at the energy of the archetypal goddesses.

Dossey, Larry, M.D. *Reinventing Medicine: Beyond Mind-Body to a New Era of Healing.* San Francisco: HarperCollins, 1999.
 A scientifically documented examination of intuition and nonlocal (distant) energy healing.

Eden, Donna. *Energy Medicine.* Tarcher, 1999.
 A helpful text on how to boost your body's subtle energies and increase stamina.

Emery, Marcia. *The Intuitive Healer: Accessing Your Inner Physician.* St. Martin's Press, 1999.
 A psychologist's practical handbook on developing intuition; filled with easy-to-understand exercises.

Gallo, Fred. *Energy Psychology.* CRC Press, 1998.
 A guide to how subtle energy systems such as acupuncture are used to diagnose and treat psychological problems.

Gerber, Richard. *Vibrational Medicine: The #1 Handbook on Subtle-Energy Therapies.* Bear, 2001.
A scientific explanation of how subtle energy is related to health.

Ingram, Catherine. *Passionate Presence: Experiencing the Seven Qualities of Awakened Awareness.* Gotham Books, 2003.
A spiritual teacher's powerful instructions on awakening the intelligence of the heart.

Joy, W. Brugh, M.D. *Joy's Way: A Map for the Transformational Journey.* Tarcher, 1979.
A classic text by a physician and healer on energy healing and the chakra system. Best illustrations of the chakras that I've seen.

Keieger, Dolores. *The Therapeutic Touch.* Fireside, 1992.
A clear discussion about how we can use subtle energy to heal.

Myss, Caroline. *Anatomy of the Spirit: The Seven Stages of Power and Healing.* Random House, 1997.
Written by a gifted medical intuitive, this guide presents a clear overview of the chakra system and energy medicine.

———. *Why People Don't Heal and How They Can.* Three Rivers Press, 1998.
An excellent resource for understanding and overcoming obstacles to healing.

Naparstek, Belleruth. *Your Sixth Sense: Activating Your Psychic Potential.* HarperCollins, 1997.
A straightforward, loving guide to developing intuition plus a penetrating study of different intuitives.

Ram Dass. *Be Here Now.* Crown Publishing, 1971.
A luminary's handbook on energy and living in the Now.

Salzberg, Sharon. *Lovingkindness: The Revolutionary Art of Happiness.* Shambhala, 2002.
A Buddhist teacher describes meditations to embrace energy-liberating lovingkindness in our lives.

Schulz, Mona Lisa, M.D. *Awakening Intuition: Using Your Mind-Body Network for Insight and Healing.* Harmony Books, 1998.
    The autobiography of a neuroscientist and medical intuitive that emphasizes how intuition relates to the body's energy and physiology.

Targ, Russell, and Jane Katra. *Miracles of Mind: Exploring Nonlocal Consciousness and Spiritual Healing.* New World Library, 1998.
    A fascinating look at remote viewing and nonlocal healing from the unique perspectives of Targ, a pioneering psychic researcher, and Katra, a healer.

Tolle, Eckhart, *The Power of Now.* New World Library, 1999.
    A simple, powerful book on how to achieve more happiness and energy in the Now.

releasing resentments and making
    amends, 150–154
removing from system, 309
ridding oneself of, 267
self-loathing as, 142–144
shame as, 148–149
signs of, 25
from sound, 71
taking breaks from, 155
techniques for sensing, 23–27
worry as, 147–148
Negative people/spaces, meditation
    approach to, 69
Negative sexual energy
    interventions for repelling, 170–175
    respecting intuition about, 172
    signs of, 169
Neighbors, constant talkers as, 302
Neurotransmitters, 135
New Thought churches, 61
Ni (Native American energy), 7
Ninth Prescription, protecting oneself
    from energy vampires, 288–317
Noise pollution, self-nurturing with
    silence and, 70–73
"Now"
    enemies of, 43–52
    exercise as moving meditation in, 109
    living in, 39–43
    making changes in, 40
    techniques for tuning into, 40–43
    technodespair and, 48–52
    workaholism as enemy of, 43–48
Nowlan, Alden, 184
Num (African energy), 7
Nurturing spiritual path, 83

O: The Oprah Magazine, 6, 85–86
Obesity, 11, 88–93
Oliver, Mary, xi, 57, 154
Opportunity, energy change and, 83
Organic foods, 95
Ornish, Dean, 94
Overload, 31
Oz, Mehmet, 118

Pacing
    easing into, 39
    intuiting, 36–38
    speed of, 38
    to support energy, 35
    techniques for, 32–39

Packaged foods, 97–98
Pain, meditation and, 65
Painting, energy from, 212
Pampering, 236–242
    beauty services as, 240–241
    body work (massages) as, 238–240
    non-mind-stressing activities as, 241
    splurging on treats as, 241–242
    taking baths as, 236–238
    vegging out as, 241
Panic disorders, 140
Parks, Rosa, on power of love, 334–335
Partner, sleeping with, 117–118
Passion
    igniting, 175–186
    inspiration inventory for finding,
        201–208
    locating, 160
Past
    healing energetic scars from, 139–140
    lingering aspects of, 186
People, attracting positive people and
    situations, 259–284
Personal space
    activities to create, 314–316
    protection through, 312–313
Perspective, shifting of, 47
Physical energy, from prayer, 74
Physical limits
    mapping out physical comfort zone,
        314
    personal space as, 312–33
Physical space, emotional energy in,
    130–131
Play, 227–235
Positive attraction, energy laws
    governing, 260, 262–267
Positive energy
    countering negativity with, 129–158
    Quincy Jones on, 54
    Larry King on, 285–287
    love as, 157
    power of, 5
    proactivity toward, 26–27
    shrinking fear with, 134–135
    signs of, 25
    techniques for sensing, 23–27
Positive Energy Program, 12–15
    intuition and, 22
Positive persons
    becoming, 265–267
    characteristics of, 263–264

ABOUT THE AUTHOR

Judith Orloff, M.D., is a board-certified psychiatrist and assistant clinical professor of psychiatry at UCLA. She is also author of the bestsellers *Guide to Intuitive Healing* and *Second Sight*. Dr. Orloff is an international lecturer and workshop leader on the interrelationship between medicine, intuition, and energy. Her work has been featured on CNN, PBS, and NPR and has appeared in *USA Today, O, The Oprah Magazine*, and *Self*. She lives by the ocean in Los Angeles, California.

For information on Dr. Judith Orloff's books and workshop schedule, visit www.drjudithorloff.com or send inquiries to:

Judith Orloff, M.D.
2080 Century Park East, Suite 1811
Los Angeles, CA 90067